THE

CORDON BLEU
COOK BOOK

• DRAWINGS BY PHOEBE NICOL •

THE

CORDON BLEU

COOK BOOK

by Dione Lucas

LITTLE, BROWN AND COMPANY • BOSTON

Library of Congress Catalog Card No.
81-81639

*Published simultaneously in Canada
by Little, Brown & Company (Canada) Limited*

MV

PRINTED IN THE UNITED STATES OF AMERICA

TO ROSEMARY HUME

INTRODUCTION

To most of us, the Blue Ribbon connotes outstanding achievement in many fields. We associate it, perhaps, with a beautiful painting in an exhibition, a prize-winning novel, or as reward to an individual for unusual merit in his sphere of work. The Blue Ribbon, or Cordon Bleu, is of special significance to those who know and enjoy good food. This diploma, highest award in Europe for fine cooking, is desired and cherished by all who work to earn it.

Originally, the term Cordon Bleu was used in France to designate noblemen who entertained their guests with supreme munificence. These noblemen became members of the Ordre du Saint Esprit, founded in 1518 by King Henry III. The white cross of their knighthood was worn on a ribbon of blue. Later, the name Cordon Bleu became associated with cooks who demonstrated their ability with feasts of vast proportion.

In 1880, l'École du Cordon Bleu was founded in Paris by Mlle. Marthe Distel, not, primarily, for professional chefs, but for the daughters of upper- and middle-class French families. As the years passed, however, the school acquired a reputation that made it the Mecca of aspiring gastronomes, and men and women from all over the world came to learn the art of good cooking. It was to this school that I came as a young girl to take my first lessons from professional chefs. My path to l'École du Cordon Bleu had been a devious one. Having forsaken my first interest, that of making jewelry, my early years in Paris were spent at the Conservatoire learning to play the cello. The preparation of good food is merely another expression of art, one of the joys of civilized living. I still remember one of my early teachers who initiated me into some of the intricacies of the kitchen; before becoming a chef he had been a sculptor with the Prix de Rome to his credit.

Until this time, cooking for me had been only an avocation, with a love of good food instilled into me by my English mother, who was herself supreme in the kitchen. As my training at the school progressed, I became more and more convinced that here was my niche. Whatever talents I had were best expressed in the alchemy of the kitchen. Transforming raw ingredients into a finished product, knowing that my fingers and my skill were responsible for this creation, gave me a tremendous sense of satisfaction. I always imagine this is much the same feeling the leader of an orchestra experiences when he succeeds in drawing exquisite music from each instrument he directs, translating all these sounds into one harmonious composition.

Having decided that food was, from now on, my vocation as well as my hobby, I planned to open a cooking school in London with another young English student at l'École du Cordon Bleu, Rosemary Hume. In order to give our school its authentic name, Au Petit Cordon Bleu, we had to take additional examinations, by permission of M. Henri Pellaprat, distinguished codirector of the Paris school. Passing these examinations also entitled us to award the coveted Cordon Bleu diploma to those of our students who should complete the course satisfactorily.

At last we were ready to open our school in London. Our first students were taught in a little one-room school in Chelsea. Within a year, we had prospered sufficiently to be able to move to bigger quarters in Sloane Street. Both Miss Hume and I were sure that now was the time to enlarge our facilities; so, in addition to our cooking school, we opened the restaurant known as Au Petit Cordon Bleu. We divided our work so that my partner ran the restaurant while I continued with the teaching. Three years later we were the sole, and very proud, owners of our restaurant at 11 Sloane Street. During the eight years we worked together, more than four thousand students attended our school, though we awarded an average of only twenty-five Cordon Bleu diplomas annually. In 1942 I came to New York with my two young sons, by way of Canada, and in October of that year opened the Cordon Bleu restaurant at 117 East Sixtieth Street. Miss Hume continued with the London branch, even during the worst days of the blitz.

My day in New York begins early, for planning and marketing to have fresh fish, meats and vegetables assembled for my morning class takes time. Students arrive early, for my classes start promptly, and at ten o'clock I am ready to give my morning lesson. I have found from experience that students absorb more if recipes are first dictated to them; then if any question arises, information can be given promptly. Following dictation, each student chooses the dish he or she would most like to prepare. Within two hours, everything is completed, and dishes cooked in the day classes are all ready to take home if the student wishes to do so. Afternoon classes run from 3:30 P.M. to 5:30 P.M. and in the evening from 7:00 P.M. to 9:00 P.M. The evening students prepare a complete dinner from soup to dessert, and most of them stay to eat it in the restaurant. Pupils often ask me to teach them the preparation of some favorite dish; some come for a few lessons while others complete the Cordon Bleu course of fifty lessons. The length of time a student spends in my classes, however, does not automatically ensure the diploma, for real ability is necessary to pass both the written and practical examinations.

Saturday mornings I devote to classes for young children, for I feel very keenly that a love and appreciation of good food should develop early. These youngsters are a joy to work with; their enthusiasm and excitement are particularly stimulating to any teacher. There are no restrictions on the age of my young pupils. If they can walk and hold a spoon, I will teach them to cook — simple dishes, to be sure, but a real step forward in the child's education toward better living.

Lunch is the only meal served to the public in the Cordon Bleu restaurant. My *spécialité* is the omelet, with many variations, of course, from *fines herbes* to *Bonne Femme*. All these omelets I make in my special pan, which has not been used for anything else in the sixteen years I have owned it. Neither has it ever been washed, for water would cause the omelets to stick to the pan. In my spare time I take special orders for dishes to carry out, catering to those who have neither the time nor the inclination to cook dinner.

Many of my students ask me how I manage to accomplish the amount of work involved in running this combined restaurant and cooking school. I think the answer is abundant energy, together with a very real love of my work. I look on the finished product as something to be judged critically, but a dish, I hope, to delight the eye and warm the heart of those who eat it.

This book is an attempt to help others who love good food, to inspire them to the level of the creative artist, so that they too will know the real satisfaction that comes from dishes well prepared. Every recipe here has been set up so that the cook should be able to prepare each dish without outside help. Those recipes calling for "a little" of this or that ingredient are not meant to baffle the reader; rather are they an invitation to express individuality and imagination. For the kitchen is the heart of the Home and should not be regarded as a scientific laboratory where each ingredient is accurately measured, much as the druggist compounds a formula. Seasoning must be carried out through the entire cooking process, with frequent testing. Similarly, a chicken cooked in butter might require only three or four tablespoons of that ingredient, while a neighbor's chicken might well require much more. Good cooks therefore cannot be too rigid or dogmatic about certain ingredients called for in a recipe. Foods vary as to size, color and freshness, for nature does not produce uniform quality, and the cook must proceed accordingly, with the instinctive feeling of the artist for the dish she is creating.

In the United States, with an abundance of good food never known in Europe, and with all the native talent and ability available, it is unfortunate that more emphasis is not placed on the importance of cooking as an art. There is a tendency to whisk in and out of the kitchen, to be lured by dishes that can be made most quickly. Cooking cannot be relegated to the same category as dishwashing or making beds. Preparation of good food requires time, skill and patience, and results mean the difference between mere eating to exist and the satisfaction derived from one of the major pleasures of life. Surely there is nothing more uplifting to the soul or more joyful to the spirit than well-flavored, well-prepared food.

ALL RECIPES ARE FOR FOUR PERSONS

CONTENTS

CONTENTS

THE

CORDON BLEU
COOK BOOK

CHAPTER 1

MENUS

First comes the building of your meal. It is a good idea to plan menus well ahead so that there is no last-minute rushing to the store for missing ingredients. Try to visualize your meal beforehand, for the good cook always plans with an eye to contrasting color, shape, and texture of foods. For example, the monotony of plain boiled potatoes, chicken à la king and creamed onions would detract from any appetite, no matter how keen. But garnish those potatoes with the vivid green of freshly chopped herbs, place them alongside crisp, golden corn on the cob, and serve with well-browned chicken leg from a *poulet en casserole*, and you have contrasting colors, shapes and texture, with all the makings of an attractive dinner plate.

Connoisseurs of good food recognize that the fairly formal patterns of our luncheons and dinners have evolved because they have been found most agreeable to the majority. Luncheon is a smaller meal than dinner, since it is gastronomically sound to eat lightly in the middle of the day (this does not apply to those engaged in heavy manual work, of course). So we have for luncheon menus, the cold *hors d'oeuvre* or perhaps a consommé, followed by a fairly simple main dish, a light dessert and coffee. At dinner, however, the day's work is done, there is a feeling of relaxation, and appetites are keener. So we serve for our average dinner menu a soup, hot or iced depending on the season, to whet the appetite further, a small serving of fish perhaps, followed by a substantial main dish with vegetables. The keen tang of crisp, chilled salad serves as a stimulant to the palate after the main course. *Entremets* should be light, and if occasionally a rich *gâteau* is served, small portions are the rule. We know from experience that ending the meal with a sweet food gives it greater "staying" value. The French habit of a *corbeille de fruits* is a sound custom, the natural sugars supplying the necessary sweetness.

Many of the dishes in this book can be prepared beforehand to eliminate much of the rush so often associated with mealtimes. Organization is just as important in the kitchen as in any business office. The cook who plans her work carefully and leaves herself only a few last-minute preparations will have the leisure for fuller enjoyment of her meals.

When entertaining, it is better not to experiment with new recipes. Practice beforehand the dishes you are going to serve and do not attempt too elaborate a menu. There is nothing that detracts from the poise of a hostess quite so much as anxiety about her meal.

The following menus are set up as a guide to help you in planning meals both for everyday and for entertaining.

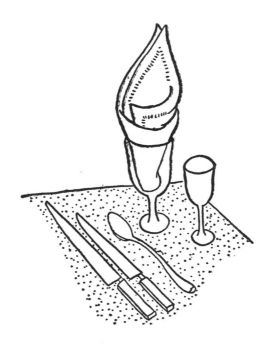

SIMPLE LUNCHES

QUICHES LARAINE

A TOSSED SALAD

MOUSSES AU CHOCOLAT

COFFEE

A glass of red wine would be excellent with this menu.

POTAGES FONTAGES

OEUFS POCHES AU BEURRE NOIR

FRUITS RAFRAÎCHIS

COFFEE

HOT KIPPER SOUFFLÉ

PETIT POIS À LA FRANÇAISE

PEARS IN PORT WINE

A FEW DINNER MENUS

OYSTERS ROCKEFELLER

CLEAR BORTSCH

POULET EN CASSEROLE

POMMES DE TERRE SAUTÉS

SALADE DE SAISON

CRÈME CARAMEL

POTAGE CRÈME OLGA

FILET DE SOLE MEUNIÈRE

PAUPIETTE DE VEAU À LA GREQUE

ÉPINARDES EN BRANCHES

CHOCOLATE ROLL

HOT CHEESE SOUFFLÉ

BOEUF BOURGUIGNON

EGGPLANT AUVERNAISE   POMMES DE TERRE À LA BONNE FEMME

DENTS DE LION

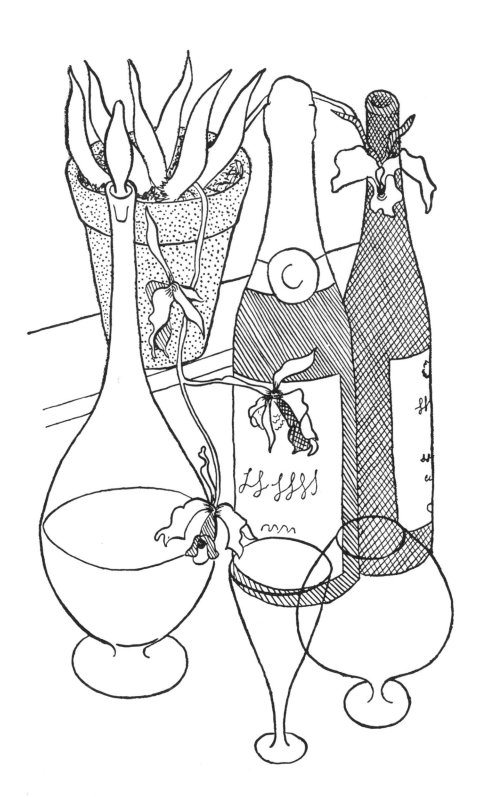

CHAPTER II

WINES

This is not intended as a dissertation on expensive imported wines; we leave that to the connoisseurs. Any cook book, however, using wine in its recipes, would fail in its purpose if some space were not devoted to the use of wine on the table and in cooking. Every good chef will admit that wine is a necessity, both as an ingredient in cooking and as a beverage with meals. But wine, whether it is used to enhance the flavor of a fish sauce or served with it, must be good. A poor wine will give poor results. If a bottle of wine seems to be deteriorating, let it turn to vinegar to be used later in French dressing. Never think it will be disguised in a delicate sauce or *bourguignon*. It will only spoil the dish in which it is used.

Americans have every reason for serving the best meals in the world, with an abundance and variety of food never known in Europe, a heritage of cooking skills from almost every country, and a great variety of fine wines. California makes more than eighty-four per cent of the wine consumed in the United States today. Because of the wide variety of soil and climate in that state, almost every important type of European grape can be grown successfully, producing wines that compare not unfavorably with their European namesakes. Viticulturally speaking, the northern and central coastal counties, including the San Francisco Bay region with Alameda and its famous Livermore and Napa Valleys, produce California's best light wines. Here is an equable climate, ideally suited for grape production. The Livermore Valley, between the arid hills east of San Francisco, has a gravel soil very similar to that of the Graves district in France. The old established growers here cultivate the vine by methods very similar to the French cultivation. The wine is aged according to its worth rather than by set commercial standards. The red wines of the Livermore Valley mature early and are soft in flavor, while the white wines also are very superior.

Wines produced east of the Rocky Mountains, especially in New York, Ohio, New Jersey, Michigan and Missouri are known as "American Wines." They are from grapes native to this country that cannot be crossbred successfully with European types. The Finger Lakes district of northern New York state is especially noted for its fine wine grapes. All types of wines are made there, both red and white, but the sparkling wines predominate, and some of the New York state champagnes are really excellent. The soil, drainage and climate of the Finger Lakes district greatly resemble the Champagne region of France.

It is not necessary to be an expert to use wine at the table and in cooking, but it is necessary to buy it intelligently. The large number of wine names is often confusing to a neophyte. There are those wines named after the European prototype, such as American Chablis, Burgundy and sauterne. Then there are the wines named after the grapes from which they are made, such as cabernet, zinfandel and barbera. Wines are either dry or sweet, with varying gradations between, but dry does not necessarily mean sour. The majority of wines served are called "still" wines to differentiate them from the sparkling, effervescent types such as sparkling Burgundy, Asti spumante and champagne. Wine is not a standardized product like bread, coffee or milk, and a little practice in buying may be necessary until favorite brands and types are finally selected. In choosing wines, the dealer is often able to give helpful advice. It might be more economical also, at this stage, to try out new types in the small "split" bottle which holds enough for two people. For everyday use, an inexpensive red or white wine will serve admirably, much as the Frenchman's *vin ordinaire.*

If planning a moderate "cellar," store wine in a cool, dark spot, and place the bottles on their sides. This is to keep the cork moist and prevent shrinkage, which in turn would allow air into the bottle. After a bottle has been opened, both red and white wine should be stored in the refrigerator and kept tightly corked or even poured into a smaller bottle. This is assuming, of course, that the wine is not going to stand for an indefinite length of time, for once opened, it will not remain good for long periods.

The French have been using wine with food and wine in food for centuries. From their experience, no rigid rules are necessary in serving. It has been found, however, that a glass with a stem is preferred by many so that heat from the hand does not warm the wine. But many a French gourmet has been seen drinking his *vin ordinaire* from a water glass. Never is that glass tinted; it is always clear to reveal the full natural color of the wine. White wines are slightly chilled, while red wines are usually served at room temperature or two or three degrees below. It is a general rule, of course, to serve white wines with fish or chicken, and red wines with red meats, but let individual taste decide.

Wine in cooking will enhance and glorify foods and add a zest which nothing else can give. Since heat drives off the alcoholic content, it is only the flavor which is imparted. The dry white wines have their place in good fish cookery, while the more robust red wines add flavor to many meat dishes. Sherry, in addition to its service as an accompaniment to soup, imparts a delightful flavor when cooked with chicken. Let wine add its savor to soups, fish sauces, meat, game, and desserts; there is a subtlety about it that is indescribable.

WINE	COLOR AND FLAVOR	SERVICE	TEMPERATURE
Sherry	Pale amber to brown. Dry or sweet. Nutty flavor.	Dry sherry with clear soups. Sweet sherry with desserts.	Room temperature.
Madeira and Marsala	Pale to dark amber. Sweet.	With desserts.	Room temperature.
Sauterne	Pale with a golden cast. Dry sauterne is fairly tart. Haut sauterne is sweeter.	Fish or oysters or all through the meal.	Chilled to about 40° F.
Chablis	Delicate straw color. Fruity flavor.	Fish or oysters or all through meal.	Chilled.
Riesling	Greenish, amber cast. Dry, tart wine.	Fish or oysters or all through meal.	Chilled.
Graves and White Bordeaux	Pale golden. Tart flavor.	Fish or oysters or all through the meal.	Chilled.
Rhine and Moselle	Very pale yellow. Slightly sweet.	Fish, chicken or all through the meal.	Chilled.
Claret	Rich, red color. Light, tart flavor.	Red meat, chicken, game, cold meats or all through the meal.	Room temperature.

Wine	Description	Serve with	Temperature
Zinfandel	Deep red. Dry.	Red meat, chicken, game, cold meats or all through the meal.	Room temperature.
Burgundy	Rich, dark ruby red. Distinctive bouquet.	Red meat, dark fleshed game.	Room temperature.
Chianti	Ruby red. Dry. Strongly flavored.	Red meat, chicken, spaghetti, or all through the meal.	Room temperature.
Barbera	Deep red. Distinctive flavor and aroma.	Red meat, chicken, spaghetti, or all through the meal.	Room temperature.
Champagne	Pale amber color. Dry. Slightly sweet.	Dry throughout the meal. Sweeter type with dessert.	Thoroughly chilled.
Port	Deep red to tawny or white. Rich, heavy and sweet.	With cheese.	Room temperature.
Angelica	Straw color to amber. Sweet and fruity.	With dessert.	Room temperature.
Muscatel	Golden to dark amber. Sweet.	With dessert.	Room temperature.
Tokay	Amber. Sweet.	With dessert.	Room temperature.
Liqueurs and Brandies.	Colors vary. Liqueurs very sweet.	With coffee after dessert.	Room temperature.

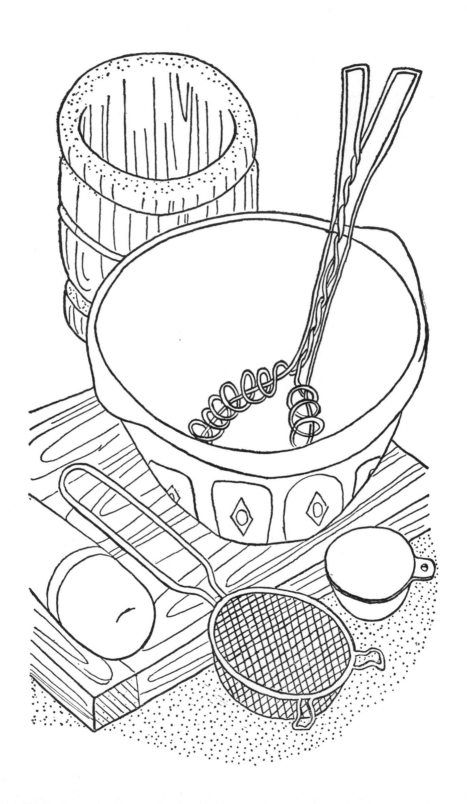

CHAPTER III

UTENSILS

"The young housekeeper should not be led into untoward expend-
itures by the talebearing of itinerant salesmen of newfangled kitchen
helps. For such contraptions husbands do not work at their tasks
to supply the wherewithal."
— *From an old cook book offered to the bride of fifty years ago.*

The average French kitchen does not necessarily contain a
large and expensive array of equipment. Utensils may be as simple
or as elaborate as the cook chooses, and a limited supply need not
preclude the use of the recipes in this book. The most frugal
French housewife is often able to turn out superb meals with a
minimum of equipment. This minimum, however, includes
utensils which are often lacking in the American kitchen. Most
important is a good set of sharp knives which are sharpened at
regular intervals. Always, of course, the continental cook will
have a heavy chopping board, a wire whisk for beating sauces,
and a row of pans in assorted sizes.

Probably the most outstanding feature of the average bour-
geoise French kitchen is the shiny row of copper pans burnished
to the mellow gleam of old topaz. In this same French kitchen
will also be found the less glamorous but equally important soup
pot or marmite of earthenware, together with the cast iron Dutch
oven and frying pan. The French long ago discovered that copper
is an excellent metal for cooking utensils since it is one of the best
conductors of heat. But copper is expensive, and it is not necessary
to insist that every pan in the kitchen be of copper, for cast
aluminum and cast iron have their place too.

Following are listed utensils which will help in the preparation
of each type of recipe in this book. Do not take this list as essential

to good cooking. It is only set up as a guide to help you in planning your equipment. Use discretion and be guided by the state of your purse.

SOUPS

The brown earthenware marmite is essential for every kitchen. For the average family the three-quart size is most practical. Treat your marmite with care and it will give good service. Never expose it to direct heat. Always place it on an asbestos mat when heating on the top of the stove. Extremes of heat are not recommended. If the marmite has been taken directly off the stove to be washed, remember that sudden cold causes such items to crack and you should first immerse it gently in warm water. Glazed earthenware has many advantages. It holds the heat well so that it requires only a gentle flame to keep its contents hot. It is easy to clean and has no cracks or corners to hold food particles.

Stewpans are another essential for soups, but you can manage very well with only two of them. If copper is out of the question insist on cast iron or heavy cast aluminum in a two- or three-pint size. Use one for cream soups and the other for stronger flavored game and onion soups. Of course, these stewpans can be used for other dishes but reserve the pan for strong soups for other highly flavored dishes.

Most kitchens have at least one ordinary sieve. This is highly recommended when making the cream soups and potages. For the really smooth soups such as *Vichyssoise* or *crème Olga,* a hair sieve for a finer textured purée is also recommended. A wooden roller is useful for rubbing mixtures through the sieve.

Two or three wooden spatulas to take the place of wooden spoons are very helpful. Since there is no bowl to collect food there is nothing to spoil the velvety texture of a creamy soup.

FISH

Fish cooking requires very few utensils. Essential are a heat-proof dish for poaching and two sharp knives, one thin and flexible for skinning and filleting, and the other thicker and stronger for cutting lobsters and crabs. A scaling knife for removing the thick scales from fish such as carp and salmon is helpful.

Good sauces for these fish dishes require a fine cone strainer, a small wire whisk for smooth beating, and at least one tin-lined copper pan. Because sauces are such an integral part of French cooking these utensils are necessary. Good sauces require either beating or stirring with a wire whisk, and if this is done in a pan of the same metal, the result is a gray, unappetizing sauce. Always use a tin-lined copper pan.

One or two wooden spoons are necessary and can be picked up for a few cents from any hardware or dime store.

Attractive serving dishes are a nicety which many good cooks insist on using. Oval copper, tin or silver-lined dishes are a delight to the eye but they are not essential. Your fish will taste just as good in flat fireproof or pyrex dishes.

POULTRY

Sharp knives are important in poultry and game cooking. Among these a boning knife is necessary if you plan to make a *galantine* of chicken. A pair of kitchen scissors for disjointing birds and a small cleaver for more efficient dismemberment are necessary. The game press is often used in continental kitchens, though it is not easily found in the United States. This is a piece of equipment for extracting all the red juices from the carcass of a bird, especially domestic and wild duck. These juices with their goodness and flavor are then used in the sauces or gravies to accompany the bird.

MEATS

The earthenware casserole is also useful in meat cookery. The thick metal *cocotte* is much used in French kitchens for braising whole cuts of meat since it retains the slow, even heat of the oven. A heavy aluminum casserole will take its place very well if the *cocotte* is unobtainable. Earthenware which holds the heat well is better for the ragout where the meat is first cut in squares and either braised or simmered on the fire or in the oven. Again, the importance of sharp knives in meat cookery for carving and slicing cannot be too strongly emphasized. The small cleaver used in fowl cookery is useful in meat preparation. A few larding needles are very important indeed as many cuts of meat are much improved by larding. A heavy wooden mallet is a valuable piece of equipment to own when making veal *scallopini*, and it is very useful in pounding out strips of veal or beef for the *paupiettes*. The heavy thick chopping board will do double duty as a carving board. A few inexpensive iron skewers are a good investment if you plan on making *shaslik*.

EGGS AND VEGETABLES

Not much equipment is needed for egg and vegetable dishes, but the few essential utensils are vastly important. Apart from earthenware and metal casseroles, one or two fireproof dishes, some sharp knives, and a fine wire sieve and strainer are invaluable. The omelet pan should be reserved for omelets, and water must never be allowed to touch its surface for then the omelet will stick to the pan. The omelet pan should be of heavy cast iron or cast aluminum, with a rounded base. Always wipe the pan out carefully with a clean dry cloth after each use.

DESSERTS

A marble slab is the best surface to use in pastry making, although a pastry board will take its place satisfactorily. If you have a marble slab, never allow vinegar or any acid to roughen its polished surface.

Spatulas, both long and short, will help considerably in removing cakes from tins and pans. Rely on them too for lifting a cake to the serving plate.

Pastry bags and tubes are needed for piping whipped cream and assorted icings and frostings.

Cookie sheets and flans are used instead of the pie dish occasionally. The flan, which is a strip of metal in the form of a circle or square, is placed on a cookie sheet before lining it with the dough. After cooking, the flan is removed and the pastry shell is carefully carried by spatulas to the serving board for filling.

A rolling pin of wood is necessary and preferably one small in diameter for the easier rolling of pastry.

Long narrow and round boards to act as serving bases for cakes or rolls are helpful.

Cake tins are staples among kitchen equipment. Sizes vary with the number of persons eating the cakes.

One unlined copper pan is essential for caramel and spun sugar. Tin-lined and aluminum pans should not be used since very high temperatures melt these metals.

Cutters of assorted shapes and sizes are part of the equipment for cookie baking.

Brushes of small sizes are required for melted butter and beaten egg, while larger brushes will be needed for glazing with melted jelly. They are important for those final professional touches.

Thermometers for the oven and for syrups are recommended. Perhaps you are an expert at gauging temperatures but there will be fewer failures if you invest in thermometers and eliminate guesswork.

GENERAL

Measuring cups in eight-ounce and sixteen-ounce sizes of heat-proof glass are standard utensils.

Scales are not so commonly used in the United States as they are in Europe. However, with cake and pastry making, accurate measurements are important and the scale is more precise than the measuring cup.

Whisks for beating mixtures are essential.

The egg beater with twin sets of revolving blades for greater speed is also recommended.

Kitchen spoons of assorted sizes, tea, dessert, and tablespoon, will meet all requirements for spoon measurements in this book.

With the exception of the copper pan, none of these utensils needs cost more than two dollars, many of them being available for much less. When planning utensils for your kitchen, plan sensibly and according to your budget.

CHAPTER IV

HORS D'OEUVRES

It is unfortunate that many cook books tend to relegate hors d'oeuvres to the role of cocktail accessories. Yet their savor and unique eye appeal lend themselves well as appetite stimulants for luncheon and dinner. Hors d'oeuvres are international in flavor, from the standard French dishes as we know them, to the Russian *zakouska*, Chinese *T'i Wei Ping*, Italian *antipasto*, and the English savory preferred at the end of the meal. The Scandinavian *smörgåsbord* is, of course, the hors d'oeuvres grown to large proportions where it can, on occasions, make the entire meal.

The standard French classic, *Larousse Gastronomique*, uses thirty-one pages for describing and listing hors d'oeuvres, which indicates that they have an important place in the French cuisine. They may be as simple or as intricate as you wish, but never allow them to dominate the rest of the meal. A good general rule to follow is to serve cold hors d'oeuvres at lunch and the hot variety at dinner, before the soup. Simple glass dishes or plates are most appropriate for serving.

Economical cooks will serve the hors d'oeuvres as a good means of utilizing small leftovers. Thin slices of meat, hard-boiled eggs, radishes, all are good for this form of service.

The hors d'oeuvres in this chapter will serve as a guide in helping to round out colorful and gastronomically sound meals for your family and your guests.

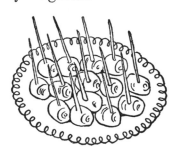

CANAPÉS NORDAISE

(Kipper rolled in bacon and served with a hot, creamed sauce)

2 smoked kippers	2 tablespoons butter
6 slices of thin bacon	1 cup thin cream
few slices of white bread	3 tablespoons grated cheese
3 egg yolks	salt and pepper

Skin and bone the kipper, cut in small fingers and wrap them in the thin slices of bacon. Place on a cookie sheet and bake in the oven for 10 minutes. Remove and arrange on thin slices of white toast the same size as the kippers. Place them on a hot flat dish and pour over the following sauce: —

Sauce: Put in the top of a double boiler the egg yolks, butter, cream, grated cheese, salt and pepper and stir over a slow fire until it becomes thick, but do not allow to get too hot or it will curdle. Add a little cream if it does become too thick. When the sauce has been poured over the kippers brown quickly under the broiler just before serving.

OYSTERS ROCKEFELLER

6 oysters in the half shell	3 tablespoons grated cheese
¾ cup sour cream	few bread crumbs
3 cloves garlic	1 tablespoon butter
salt and pepper	½ cup whipped cream
1 cup raw spinach, put through the meat chopper	

Remove the oysters from their shells, mix ¼ cup sour cream with a little crushed garlic, salt and pepper and put a teaspoon of the mixture in the bottom of each oyster shell. Cover the top with the oyster and cover the oyster with the spinach which has been mixed with the rest of the sour cream, a little garlic, salt and pepper. Sprinkle with a little grated cheese and bread crumbs and dot with butter. Brown under the broiler; remove and put a tablespoon of whipped cream on the top of each oyster and brown under the broiler again.

FINNISH CUCUMBER SALAD

5 small cucumbers	*salt and black pepper*
1 small bunch fresh dill	*a little sugar*
1 cup sour cream	*2 tablespoons fresh tomato pulp*
1 clove garlic	*2 tablespoons tarragon vinegar*

¼ cup oil

Skin the cucumbers, and cut in very thin slices. Place on a flat dish and sprinkle well with salt. Leave for half an hour, then drain off the liquid and mix the cucumbers with the following dressing: —

Dressing: Finely chop the dill and add it to the sour cream with the crushed garlic, salt, pepper and a very little sugar; then mix in the tomato pulp, and add the vinegar and the oil very slowly. Serve very cold.

STUFFED CELERY

2 stalks celery	*tomato paste*
6 tablespoons butter	*6 tablespoons blue cheese*
1 cream cheese (2 ounces)	*rye bread*
salt and black pepper	*1 pimento cap*

Wash the celery; then carefully separate the stalks, and dry them well on a cloth. In one bowl cream 3 tablespoons butter, add the cream cheese with a little salt and pepper and color with a little tomato paste. In another bowl cream the rest of the butter, rub the blue cheese through a strainer and mix it into the butter with a little pepper and no salt. Carefully reshape the celery by stuffing it with the cheese, one stalk to be stuffed with the cream cheese and the other to be stuffed with the blue cheese. Wrap them in waxed paper and put in the icebox to get very cold. Remove and cut into thin slices and place on a round of rye bread. Decorate the top of each with a very small round of pimento and serve.

AUBERGINES CAVIARE
(Eggplant Caviare)

1 large eggplant   *6 cloves garlic*
2 onions   *¾ cup olive oil*
4 skinned tomatoes   *salt and black pepper*

Take a thick piece of waxed paper and brush it well with oil. Wrap up the eggplant in this paper and bake it until soft in a 350° F. oven. While cooking chop the onion and the tomatoes finely, and crush the garlic well with salt. Unwrap the eggplant, carefully remove the skin and chop it up very finely in a wooden bowl. Then add the onion, garlic, and the tomatoes, and continue chopping, slowly adding the olive oil and salt and pepper. When very fine and well mixed, allow to get very cold on ice and serve surrounded by crushed ice with fingers of hot buttered toast.

CROQUES MADAMES
(A mixture of shredded ham and mushrooms put on a toasted slice of brioche and covered with a cheese and egg sauce)

1 brioche loaf   *1 cup milk*
¼ pound mushrooms, sliced   *1 tablespoon reduced white wine*
handful grated cheese   *3 tablespoons cream*
3 tablespoons shredded, cooked ham   *2 tablespoons vinegar*
large lump butter   *1 sliced onion*
1½ tablespoons flour   *4 peppercorns*
salt and pepper   *2 beaten egg yolks*
                    9 tablespoons butter

Cut a brioche loaf in thin slices. Fry slowly in a little butter until light brown on both sides. Sandwich the slices with this mixture: —

Mixture: Cut the mushrooms in slices, and cook them in a little butter and seasoning. Add the ham and bind with a little Bonne Femme Sauce. Arrange the sandwiches on a dish for serving. Sprinkle top with a little melted butter and cheese and pass under the grill.

Bonne Femme Sauce: Melt 2 tablespoons butter in a pan. Add 1½ tablespoons flour. Season and pour in the milk. Thicken and add 1 tablespoon reduced white wine, 3 tablespoons cream and ½ cup Hollandaise Sauce.

Hollandaise Sauce: Reduce the 2 tablespoons vinegar to 1 with the onion and peppercorns. Strain onto 2 beaten egg yolks. Place bowl in *bain-marie* and slowly beat in 9 tablespoons of butter.

HUÎTRES EN ROBE DE CHAMBRE
(Baked Oysters)

2 oysters per person
juice ½ lemon
salt and pepper
2 tablespoons butter
1 level dessertspoon flour
¾ cup white wine
2 tablespoons cream
1 dessertspoon Parmesan cheese
cayenne pepper

Remove the oyster beards. Place 2 oysters in each shell. Sprinkle with lemon juice and season. Pour over each a small quantity of the following sauce and place for about 4 minutes under hot grill.

Sauce: Melt 2 tablespoons butter in a pan; add level dessertspoon flour and season. Pour on the white wine after it has been reduced to half quantity. Add the cream and the grated Parmesan cheese. Bring to a boil and simmer carefully for 3 to 4 minutes. Add a dash of cayenne pepper. Pipe crisscross with very cold shrimp butter. (See p. 88.) Serve.

DANISH PÂTÉ
(Liver Paste)

1 pig's liver	salt and pepper
1 pound fat bacon	cayenne pepper
4 eggs	pinch nutmeg
20 anchovies, well pounded	pinch crushed coriander seed
2 cups cream	4 thin slices bacon

Put the liver and the bacon through the meat grinder twice, then once through a sieve. Mix in the eggs and the anchovies. Mix in the cream carefully. Season well with salt, pepper, cayenne pepper, nutmeg and coriander seed. Line oblong cake tins with thin slices of bacon. Fill with the mixture and cover with waxed paper. Place tins surrounded by water in a pan and bake for 50 to 60 minutes in a moderate oven. Remove and allow to cool. Put a light weight on the top. This keeps very well in the refrigerator and can be used as pâté, or worked smooth with a palette knife and covered with clarified butter for longer keeping.

QUICHES LORRAINE

2 cups flour	1 teaspoon paprika
2 hard-boiled egg yolks	4 tablespoons grated cheese
4 raw egg yolks	5 slices bacon
5 heaping tablespoons fat	2 whole eggs
½ teaspoon dry mustard	¼ cup cream
salt	cayenne pepper

Pastry: Put the flour on a slab, make a well in the center and put in the strained, hard-boiled egg yolks. Add 3 raw egg yolks, fat, mustard, 1 teaspoon salt, paprika and 2 tablespoons grated cheese. Work center ingredients to a smooth paste. Work in the flour and roll out not too thick. Line a flan ring with wax paper. Sprinkle with rice and bake for 20 minutes in a 350° F. oven. Remove and fill with the following: —
Cook finely shredded bacon until crisp in a hot pan; in the

meantime beat 2 eggs and 1 egg yolk in a bowl. Add cream, 2 tablespoons grated cheese, salt, cayenne pepper, crisp bacon and bacon fat. Fill into the tart and put to set for 15 minutes in a slow oven. Remove and eat hot.

CAMEMBERT CHEESE BALLS

½ Camembert cheese	*short cup milk*
1 Philadelphia cream cheese	*salt*
2 tablespoons creamed fat	*cayenne pepper*
2 tablespoons flour	*1 egg, beaten*
1 tablespoon rice flour	*bread crumbs*

Rub the cheese through a strainer and add fat, flour, rice flour, milk, salt and cayenne pepper. Stir over the fire until thick and pour on a plate to cool; form into small balls, roll in flour, brush with beaten egg, roll in crumbs and fry in deep fat until golden brown.

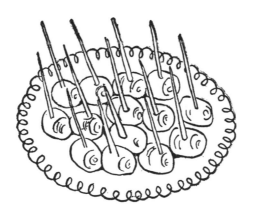

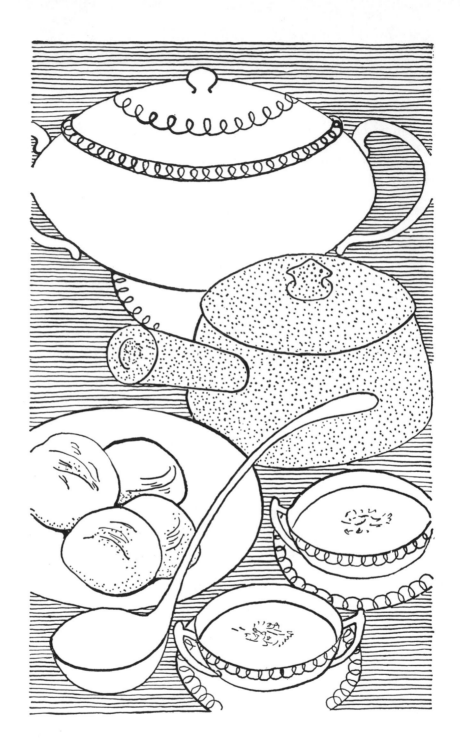

CHAPTER V

SOUPS

Probably no other dishes provoke as much discussion in cookery as soups. Just as one section of France may prefer a thick, creamy *potage* to a clear consommé, as the native of the north of England chooses barley broth rather than the vegetable marrow soup of his neighbor in the south, so do soups vary in different regions of the United States. The New Englander enjoys his clam chowder better than all other versions created by Manhattan and points south. It is an established fact that no two southern gumbos are alike. *Bouillabaisse* also is the source of much discussion. Even a native of Marseilles admits the recipe is flexible enough, but he insists this famous dish cannot truly be called *bouillabaisse* unless made in his city.

With the exception of a few vegetable soups where cream and water may be used liberally, the basis of all good soups is excellent stock. Stock may vary according to the type of soup. For example, delicate cream soups require chicken stock as a base, while beef stock is more often used in soups with a full bodied flavor. When making iced soups, it is important to remove all traces of fat from the stock before using, since it congeals on chilling. Many housewives make their stock from inexpensive and leftover bits of meat and some vegetables. Others prefer to use some of the excellent meat concentrates now on the market. Very good stock from these commercial glazes is made by diluting 1 tablespoon in 1 quart of water or slightly more glaze when the recipe calls for a dark stock.

It is not difficult to prepare an excellent soup. Ingredients in the following recipes are familiar and relatively economical. The ordinary year-round vegetables lend themselves readily to soup dishes, while household staples such as eggs and cream add their unique flavors. Onion soup, for example, may be as economical or expensive as you wish to make it. The story goes in France that the original recipe for onion soup was developed quite by accident by Louis XV. The French king entered his lodge late one night after a day's hunting. He wanted soup, but the only ingredients he could find were butter, onions and champagne. So onion soup was born. However, the soup recipes in this chapter are intended to be within reach of the average purse and champagne is not a prerequisite for good onion soup.

Wines play an important part in soups, but they are not so invaluable as in many other parts of the menu. If you wish to have wine with onion soup, for example, any leftover sparkling white wine which has gone flat may be used. The deep red of still Burgundy lends a jewel-like tone to a bowl of bortsch, while a good dry sherry is excellent in consommé. An extensive "cellar" is not necessary for soup recipes, but red Burgundy, dry sherry and some of the dry white wines should be among the kitchen staples. For this purpose, American wines will serve admirably.

Exercise care and discretion in the seasoning of your soups. Always serve the hot soups piping hot and cold soups with the chill of the ice still on them.

STOCKS

(Pot-au-feu)

Pot-au-feu is not only a dish of beef and vegetables but the foundation of all consommés. Here follows a good, basic recipe: —

1½ pounds flank of beef	*1 leek*
a few chicken giblets	*few mushrooms, peelings and stalks*
1 tablespoon salt	*bouquet of herbs*
2 or 3 veal bones	*2 carrots*
2 pounds top round of beef	*1 stalk celery*
2 onions	*6 peppercorns*
heart of 1 small cabbage	*few tomato skins*

Put the flank together with the giblets, salt and bones in a large, earthenware marmite. Pour on about 4 quarts of cold water and bring slowly to the boil. When boiling, skim frequently. Then add the top round and the remaining ingredients cut in slices. Simmer about 2 hours or until the top round is tender.

Remove the top round and serve it with the vegetables. Put the marmite back on the fire and continue simmering with the lid off for about 1½ hours. Strain and leave until the next day. Skim off the fat and the stock is ready to use. There should be about 2 quarts of stock and if not strong enough, it can be reduced still more. If the color is not a dark clear brown, add 1 sliced, grilled tomato, bring to a boil, and strain again. This stock can be made once a week, kept in the icebox and used for making soups, velouté sauces, casseroles, brown sauces and for aspic jelly. If you do not want to serve the meat separately, use only 1 pound of top round or omit it altogether. This makes a very good light stock. If the stock is drunk as a soup with a few of the vegetables as a garnish, slices of French bread with a spoonful or two of the fat skimmed from the pot-au-feu poured over them and browned in the oven should be served with it. For a chicken consommé, replace the top round of beef with a boiling chicken. The meat of this can be used for a suprême of chicken dish, chicken Tetrazzini, risotto or spaghetti dish, etc.

For plain stock use the following recipe: —

2 veal bones	*salt*
giblets of 1 small chicken or	*little bacon rind*
chicken bones	*mushroom peelings and stalks*
2 carrots	*peelings of tomato and cucumber*
2 onions	*few whole peppercorns*

Put the bones or giblets in a marmite and cover well with water. Bring to the boil, add the remaining ingredients and simmer for about 2 hours. Strain off and remove any fat when cold. This can be used in place of the stronger bouillons for ragouts or for light vegetable soups and light sauces.

GLAZE

Glaze is made by boiling down 1 quart of stock to approximately 3 tablespoons. This concentrated stock is used in béarnaise sauce and in any ragout or braises where strong concentrated beef is used. It is well to have a little bottle in your store closet to be used when necessary.

VEGETABLE STOCKS

The best basic vegetables are celery, onions, carrots, leeks, cucumber, tomato and mushroom skins, and shallots; a very little turnip or parsnip is good but do not overdo it. To make 4 quarts of vegetable stock, use 2 onions, 2 carrots, 1 turnip, 1 parsnip, stalk of celery, 2 leeks, 1 cup of mushroom peelings and stalks, a few tomato peelings and stalks and a little cucumber skin. Heat a little fat in a pan, add 3 sliced shallots and cook briskly until they begin to brown. Add all the other vegetables, cover with the water, bring to the boil and simmer for 2 or 3 hours with 2 or 3 peppercorns and a bouquet of herbs. Strain and use for soups, sauces, etc.

FISH BOUILLON

2 onions	1 leek
1 stalk celery	1 clove garlic
1 carrot	6 fish bones
½ cup dry white wine	few peppercorns
salt	bouquet of herbs

Slice the vegetables and cook them in a little oil for a few minutes. Put the fish bones on top, pour on the wine and cover with 3 quarts of water. Bring slowly to the boil and skim off any scum. Simmer for 1½ hours; then strain. This can be used for fish soups, bouillabaisse, bisques, fish sauces, aspics, etc.

FOR CLARIFYING ASPIC JELLY AND CONSOMMÉ
(Either meat, fish or chicken stock)

To 4 cups of strong stock, cold and free from fat, add 3 stiffly beaten egg whites, 2 tablespoons tomato paste, 1 cut-up tomato, ¼ cup sherry, 3 tablespoons gelatine, 1 tablespoon tarragon vinegar. Put all this into a tin-lined copper pan and beat over the fire until the mixture comes to the boil. Allow to stand for ten minutes, strain through a cold, damp cloth, and use as wanted.

When a meat stock or a chicken stock is used for a consommé or clear soup, clarify as above, but omit the gelatine.

For a consommé madrilène, take 1 quart of strong, cold chicken stock, free from fat, add to it 3 cut-up tomatoes, 4 tablespoons tomato paste, 2 dessertspoons gelatine, 3 stiffly beaten egg whites, ¼ cup Marsala wine, 1 tablespoon tarragon vinegar. Beat over the fire until it comes to the boil, draw aside for 10 minutes, strain through a wet cloth. Chill and when it is just set serve in glasses surrounded by crushed ice. If the chicken stock is very strong and just set before clarifying, it is not necessary to add the gelatine.

TOASTS

There are various kinds of toasted or fried bread which accompany soups, and occasionally salad and game. The toasts must be well prepared as tough or greasy bread would spoil the dish. Here follow a few different toasts that are excellent with soups: —

Mornay Toast: Cut the bread into wafer-thin slices and remove the crusts. Lay on a cookie sheet and sprinkle well with grated Parmesan or other cheese. Dust with paprika and cayenne pepper. Brown in a slow oven.

Plain Grille or Melba Toast: Cut the bread and remove the crusts as in the preceding recipe. Lay on a cookie sheet and bake slowly to a light golden color. This can be stored in a tin box.

Garlic Bread: Cut a long French loaf of bread in slices not quite cut through. Crush 3 large cloves of garlic with some salt until quite smooth. Spread a little on each slice of bread and then spread thickly with butter. Press together again and bake in a hot oven for 5 to 6 minutes. Serve hot.

VEGETABLE SOUP

1 tablespoon butter	handful diced green beans
4 tablespoons oil	4 cups light stock
2 finely sliced onions	small handful elbow macaroni
2 shredded turnips	salt and pepper
2 shredded carrots	2 handfuls coarsely chopped spinach
1 stalk celery, sliced	½ cup frozen peas
2 finely sliced parsnips	3 tomatoes, skinned and sliced

Melt butter and oil in a pan; add onions, turnips, carrots, celery and parsnips. Cook for a few minutes and add the beans. Cook a little longer; then add stock, macaroni, salt and pepper. Cook until vegetables are just tender; then add spinach, peas and tomatoes. Continue cooking a little longer and serve.

APPLE SOUP WITH CAMEMBERT CHEESE BALLS

2 tablespoons fat	salt and pepper
little chopped garlic	little chili pepper
1 level teaspoon tomato paste	¾ cup cream
3 tablespoons flour	1 tablespoon freshly chopped chives
4 cups beef stock	2 apples

Heat fat in a pan and add garlic. Cook for 2 minutes; then add tomato paste and flour. Stir well until smooth; then add beef stock, salt and pepper. Stir until it comes to the boil; then add chili pepper, cream and chopped chives. Garnish with apples, skinned, cored, cut into medium-sized pieces and fried in butter till golden. Reheat and serve with Camembert Cheese Balls (p. 25).

MINESTRA SOUP

4 tablespoons oil	2 tablespoons raw rice
2 tablespoons butter	4 cups chicken stock
1½ cups vegetables shredded: —	bay leaf
6 Brussels sprouts	6 tablespoons peas
6 long string beans	2 tablespoons grated cheese
2 carrots	2 tomatoes, skinned and chopped
1 onion	
1 mushroom	
6 stalks of celery	

Melt oil and butter in pan, add vegetables and cook briskly for 3 minutes; then add rice, stock and bay leaf. Bring to a boil, simmer gently until tender, then add peas, cheese and tomatoes. Serve with a bowl of extra grated cheese.

SQUASH AND CHESTNUT SOUP

2 tablespoons oil	salt and pepper
2 tablespoons butter	¾ pound chestnuts
1 small onion	3 cups stock
1 carrot	2 or 3 acorn squashes, boiled and skinned
1 stalk celery	2 or 3 tablespoons cream
	little chopped parsley

Melt the oil and butter in a pan. Add the onion, carrot and celery cut in slices and season with salt and pepper. Cook for 3 minutes. Cover the chestnuts with cold water in another pan, bring to a boil, and boil for 3 minutes. Remove from the fire and take off both the outer and inner shells of the chestnuts. Add them to the vegetables and cover well with light stock. Simmer gently until quite soft, and if the stock reduces, replace it with more stock. Rub through a fine strainer with the boiled acorn squash. Return to the pan with the cream and the chopped parsley. Do not allow the soup to get too hot before serving. Serve with toasted French bread.

GREEN SOUP

5 cups beef and ham stock
1 cup raw minced spinach
½ cup minced green onion
½ cup raw mixed greens (kale,
    sorrel and beet tops)

bouquet Hamburg parsley, parsley,
    tarragon, chives and rosemary
1 tablespoon flour
5 tablespoons sour cream
4 hard-boiled eggs

Bring the stock slowly to a boil in a pan. Add the spinach, onions, raw mixed greens and herbs and simmer slowly for 1 hour. Remove the pan from the fire. Discard the herbs. Stir in the flour and sour cream mixed to a smooth paste. Return to the fire and stir until it is thick and comes to a boil. Add a little more sour cream and serve it with a hard-boiled egg in each plate.

SOUPE À L'OIGNON
(Onion Soup I)

4 tablespoons fat
2 tablespoons vegetable oil
6 medium-sized onions, finely
    sliced
salt and pepper
½ teaspoon French mustard
1 teaspoon flour

1 cup clear champagne or
    ½ cup dry white wine
2½ cups stock or water
4 tablespoons grated American
    cheese
4 tablespoons grated Parmesan
    cheese

6 slices French bread

Melt the fat with the oil in a casserole. Add the onions, salt, pepper and mustard. Brown slowly to a very dark brown over a low fire for approximately 30 minutes. Then add the flour and stir until smooth. Continue stirring while you add the wine and stock, or water, until you bring it slowly to a boil. Draw aside and leave it to simmer for 25 minutes. Pour into an earthenware casserole or soup bowl. Sprinkle the top with grated American cheese and brown quickly under the broiler. Sprinkle the slices of French bread with a little oil and the Parmesan cheese; brown separately in the oven and serve.

SOUPE À L'OIGNON GRANDE MAISON
(Onion Soup II)

3 large onions	½ sliced French roll
4 tablespoons bacon fat	4 tablespoons pork or beef fat
salt and pepper	grated Parmesan cheese
3 cups boiling water	4 eggs

Blanch the onions, chop or slice finely, and put to brown in the hot fat. When a good color, add seasoning and boiling water. Bring to a boil and simmer for 40 minutes. In the meantime, slice the French roll thinly. Spread with a little beef or pork fat and a little grated cheese and brown slightly in the oven. Pour soup into marmites. Put in 1 or 2 slices of crisp roll. Send to the table with 2 dishes for each person, one containing Parmesan cheese, the other a raw egg. The soup should be really boiling when put into the marmites, and served at once so that when the egg is dropped into it, it will set immediately.

SOUPE AU CHOU
(Cabbage Soup)

3 tablespoons butter	5 cups vegetable stock or water
4 small sliced onions	1½ dozen shredded green beans
1 clove garlic	salt and pepper
¼ pound sliced bacon or salt pork	French bread
½ large cabbage	grated Parmesan cheese

Melt the butter in a casserole. Add the onions, garlic and coarsely cut-up bacon, or salt pork. Sauté over a slow fire for 5 minutes. Add the cabbage, well blanched and cut in pieces. Pour on the stock, or water, and bring slowly to a boil. Season with salt and pepper. Cover and simmer in a slow oven for 50 minutes. Add the beans and continue cooking for another 50 minutes. Take out and serve from the pot with slices of the bread toasted and floating on the top. Serve grated cheese separately.

POLISH BORTSCH

2 tablespoons bacon or other fat
2 bunches beets, finely shredded
2 sliced onions
salt and pepper

2 tablespoons flour
2 cups water or light stock
¾ cup sour cream
4 small boiled potatoes

3 tablespoons chopped fresh dill

Melt the fat in a pan. Add the beets and onions and season with salt and pepper. Cover and cook very slowly until soft. Stir in the flour; pour in the water or light stock. Stir over the fire until the soup comes to a boil and simmer for 10 minutes. Stir in the sour cream carefully. Serve with plain boiled potatoes, one for each person, and dill.

This can be served iced, cooked in the same way except that 4 or 5 tablespoons of water are used instead of the fat in the first cooking.

POTAGE À LA PORTUGAISE

(Portuguese Soup)

3 tablespoons fat
2 tablespoons oil
1 finely chopped, small onion
2 cloves garlic
1 cucumber, skinned and diced
2 diced dill pickles

2 teaspoons potato flour
3 cups water
4 tomatoes
1 tablespoon tomato paste
1 green pepper
salt and pepper

cayenne pepper

Melt the fat in a pan. Add the onion and garlic and cook for 1 or 2 minutes. Blanch, drain and add the cucumber. Add the dill pickle. Season and cook slowly for 10 minutes. Then stir in the potato flour and the water and bring to a boil. Skin the tomatoes, cut in quarters and remove the pith. Rub the pith through the strainer and add to the soup with the tomato paste. Dice tomatoes and add with a finely shredded, blanched green pepper. Season well with salt, pepper and a little cayenne pepper. Reheat and serve with garlic bread.

VEGETABLE BORTSCH

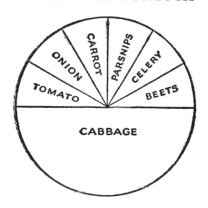

Shred all the vegetables except the tomato. Just cover with light stock. Add salt, black pepper, 4 crushed cloves garlic and simmer until the vegetables are half cooked. Add the shredded cabbage and cook a bit more. Add the skinned, sliced tomato and 2 tablespoons of tomato paste. Add sugar, salt and pepper. Simmer gently for three-quarters of an hour. Before removing from the fire, take one large raw beet, blanch in cold water and strain the liquid into the bortsch for coloring. Serve with sour cream if desired.

For meat bortsch use the same recipe and cook with a piece of ham or corned beef.

NUT SOUP

3 cups veal or chicken bouillon   2 egg yolks
1 tablespoon butter or fat   salt and pepper
2 tablespoons flour   1 cup fresh shelled walnuts
                4 tablespoons sour cream

Bring the stock to a boil in a thick pan and remove from the fire. Mix the fat and flour together and add bit by bit to the stock, stirring all the time. Add yolks and seasoning off the fire. Crush the nuts finely in a wooden bowl and mix with sour cream. Mix this into the soup and serve.

CONSOMMÉ BRUNOISE
(Clear Beef Soup)

5 cups beef stock
2 or 3 egg whites
small glass sherry
¾ pound minced shin of beef
cabbage

knob celery
leeks
carrots
salt and pepper
sugar

To clear the stock, put it in a pan with the egg whites beaten to a froth and the sherry. Whip it all together until it boils, then draw aside and simmer gently for 1 hour. Should you wish the consommé to be richer, add double the amount of minced beef. Strain carefully through a cloth. Just before serving add the following garnish: —

Garnish: Take equal quantities of the vegetables, cut them into very fine squares, put into a pan with a spoonful or two of stock skimmings, dust with salt and sugar, cover with a buttered paper, and cook in oven until tender.

For tomato consommé, add fresh ripe tomatoes with the minced beef, about 1½ pounds, and when in the tureen, add a little port or Madeira. This may be served cold.

For a chicken consommé, take 2 quarts of the stock, a carcass of a fowl and a young chicken weighing about 1¾ pounds and 2 giblets. Add them with the 1 pound of minced beef.

HOT APPLE SOUP

2 tablespoons butter
1 tablespoon oil
2 tablespoons chopped onion
5 apples
salt and pepper

1 tablespoon rice flour
2 cups strong beef stock (or light stock or water to which 1 teaspoon beef extract or maggi has been added)

Melt the butter with the oil in a pan, add the onion and cook for 1 minute. Add apples, cored and sliced but with the skins left on, salt and pepper and cook quite briskly until soft. Remove from the fire, stir in the flour and pour on the stock. Return to the fire and stir until the soup comes to a boil. Then simmer until soft. Be sure the soup is well seasoned. Rub through a fine strainer. Return to the pan and reheat. Garnish with apples, skinned, sliced and fried until golden. Serve with thin, crisp corn bread.

CHESTNUT AND APPLE SOUP

1 pound chestnuts	*salt and pepper*
2 tablespoons fat	*2 cups water*
2 tablespoons oil	*4 large green cooking apples*
little sliced onion, carrot,	*chopped parsley*
celery, leek	*2 teaspoons chopped mixed herbs*

Put the chestnuts in a pan, cover with water, and bring to a boil. Boil for 2 minutes, then remove the outer and inner skins. Melt the fat with the oil in a pan. Add the sliced onion, carrot, celery and leek. Cook for 10 to 12 minutes but do not brown. Add the skinned chestnuts, salt, pepper and 2 cups of water. Bring to a boil and simmer very gently until the chestnuts are quite soft. Rub through a fine strainer. Add a little more water if necessary and reheat. Serve with slices of apple which have been fried in a little hot butter until golden brown on each side and a little chopped parsley sprinkled with the chopped herbs.

BLACK WALNUT SOUP

2 tablespoons fat	*1 bay leaf*
4 tablespoons flour	*½ cup chopped black walnuts*
salt	*¾ cup thin cream*
cayenne pepper	*2 tablespoons sour cream*
4½ cups strong chicken or beef	*1 pinch freshly chopped or dried*
broth	*marjoram*

Melt the fat in a pan. Stir in the flour, salt and pepper. Pour on the stock and stir over the fire until the soup comes to a boil. Add the bay leaf and walnuts and simmer for 15 minutes. Add the cream, sour cream and marjoram and simmer for 2 minutes. Remove the bay leaf and serve.

POTAGE VÉRONIQUE
(Clear Tomato Soup)

4 tablespoons fat
2 small finely chopped onions
1 pound ripe tomatoes
1 pound green tomatoes
1 tablespoon tomato paste
1 bay leaf
1 crushed clove garlic

black peppercorns
salt and pepper
3 cups light stock or water
2 tablespoons cooked rice
2 teaspoons chopped parsley
2 teaspoons chopped mint
1 teaspoon sugar

Melt the fat in a pan and add the onions. Cook for 5 minutes. Add all but 1 of the tomatoes, sliced, with their skins on, and the sliced green tomatoes. Cook briskly for 3 to 4 minutes. Then add the tomato paste, bay leaf, garlic, whole peppercorns, and a little salt. Cover and cook slowly for 10 minutes, stirring occasionally. Rub through a strainer and add to the stock or water. Stir over the fire and bring to a boil. Add the rice and simmer the whole for 15 minutes. Skin the remaining 1 tomato, cut in quarters, remove the pith and cut into fine shreds. Add to the soup with the parsley, mint and sugar. Serve with garlic bread. (See p. 31.)

CONSOMMÉ VERT
(Green Consommé)

3 cups chicken bouillon
1 dessertspoon tomato paste
a sprig of mint
¼ cup white wine
2 teaspoons lemon juice
3 egg whites

salt and black pepper
handful spinach
handful lettuce
1 tablespoon shredded cucumber rind
1 tablespoon peas
1 small glass sherry

Put the bouillon in a pan with the tomato paste, mint, white wine, a squeeze of lemon juice and seasoning, and the whites of eggs beaten to a froth. Whisk over a slow fire until it comes to a boil. Draw aside and let stand for 10 minutes. Pour through a thick cloth wrung out in cold water and return to the pan. Finely shred the spinach and lettuce and blanch these with the rind. Add them to the peas cooked until soft in boiling water and strained. Dry lightly in a cloth and add all to the soup. Add the sherry.

DILL PICKLE SOUP

4 or 5 large dried mushrooms
1 clove garlic
1 skinned and sliced parsnip
1 sliced onion or
  2 sliced scallions

1 sliced carrot
6 sprigs Hamburg parsley
1 bay leaf
3 medium-sized diced potatoes
2 diced dill pickles

Put the mushrooms in a deep pot and cover well with cold water. Bring slowly to a boil and simmer for 50 minutes. Add the flavoring vegetables (garlic, parsnip, onion or scallions, carrot, Hamburg parsley and the bay leaf). Simmer until the vegetables are soft. Rub through a strainer, reserving the mushrooms. Return to the pan with the potatoes, pickles and mushrooms, which have been cut in slices. Simmer until the potatoes are just soft without being mushy.

POTAGE MARGUERITE
(Kidney Bean Soup)

½ pound red kidney beans
4 tablespoons fat
1 sliced carrot
1 sliced onion
1 small sliced turnip

4 tomatoes
2 teaspoons tomato paste
salt and pepper
bouquet of herbs
6 cups vegetable stock or water
pinch grated cheese

Soak the beans for 12 hours; then drain. Melt the fat in a casserole and add the carrot, onion, turnip and beans. Shake over the fire for a few minutes, then add the tomatoes, skinned and quartered, and the tomato paste, seasoning and herbs. Pour on the water or stock and simmer until the beans are soft (approximately 2 hours). Remove the herbs and serve with grated cheese.

BISQUE D'ÉCREVISSE
(Shrimp Bisque)

1 pound flounder bones	*8 tablespoons fat*
¼ cup dry white wine	*4 tablespoons flour*
6 pints water	*1 bay leaf*
salt and pepper	*1 pound raw shrimps*
1 carrot	*1 tablespoon tomato paste*
1 onion	*½ cup thin cream*

1 tablespoon chopped parsley

Put the fish bones, wine, 4 pints of water and seasoning in a pan. Bring to a boil, add the carrot and onion, boil down to 1½ pints, and strain. Melt 2 tablespoons of the fat, stir in the flour, and pour it into the strained fish stock. Stir until the soup comes to a boil. Add the bay leaf and simmer for 15 minutes.

Bring the shrimps to a boil in 2 pints of water, strain and crush fine in a wooden bowl. Then crush in the remaining fat; rub through a hair sieve and add, bit by bit, to the soup the shrimp butter obtained. Mix in the tomato paste. Add a little extra seasoning and the cream and parsley. Remove the bay leaf and serve with small croutons of fried bread. One or two whole shrimps may be reserved and chopped to be added to the soup as a garnish.

(The same recipe may be used for lobster, using the entire crushed lobster shell instead of the whole lobster for the butter, and adding a little chopped lobster meat to the soup as a garnish.)

CLAM AND OYSTER CHOWDER

2 tablespoons butter	*1 dozen raw hard clams*
1 tablespoon oil	*3 cups light cream*
1 tablespoon mixed scallion,	*salt*
onion, garlic	*cayenne pepper*
1 dozen raw oysters	*4 tablespoons butter*

small handful chopped parsley

Heat butter and oil in a pan and add mixed scallion, onion and garlic. Cook for 2 minutes; then add cut-up oysters and clams.

Pour on cream and season with salt and cayenne pepper. Bring very lightly to a boil, then add bit by bit butter and parsley. Simmer a few minutes and serve.

POTAGE CRESSONNIÈRE
(Potato and Water Cress Soup)

5 tablespoons fat	salt and black pepper
2 medium-sized onions	2 bunches water cress
6 potatoes	3 cups milk and water
1 clove garlic	in equal quantities
¾ cup water	¾ cup cream

Melt the fat in a deep kettle. Add the onions, potatoes, garlic, water, salt and pepper. Cook very slowly until mushy. Add 1½ bunches of roughly cut-up water cress. Pour on the milk and water and stir over the fire until the soup comes to a boil. Rub through a coarse strainer. Return to the pan with the rest of the water cress roughly cut up. Add the cream and a little extra seasoning. Serve separately small croutons of bread fried in oil.

APPLE AND CELERY SOUP

2 tablespoons fat	1 carrot
3 tablespoons oil	6 apples
2 sliced stalks celery	2 cups strong beef stock
1 medium-sized sliced onion	1 teaspoon meat glaze
salt and pepper	

Melt the fat with 1 tablespoon of oil. Add the celery, onion, and carrot and cook slowly for a few minutes. Slice 5 apples, leaving the skins on and the core in. Add and cook fairly briskly until soft without browning. Then add the stock and glaze; season and bring to a boil. Rub through a strainer and reheat. Garnish with the remaining apple, sliced, dusted with flour and fried until golden brown in hot oil.

SOUPE AUX MOULES
(Mussel Chowder)

1 pound flounder bones	3 tablespoons flour
¾ cup dry white wine	1 quart mussels
2½ cups water	little sliced onion and carrot
bouquet of herbs	1 egg yolk
1 clove garlic	½ cup cream
2 tablespoons fat	chopped parsley
salt and pepper	2 slices stale white bread

Put the fish bones in a pan with half the wine and all the water. Add the herbs and garlic. Bring to a boil and simmer for about 20 minutes. Dissolve half the fat in another pan and add to it the seasoning and flour. Stir until smooth and strain into the fish stock. Stir over the fire until boiling; leave to simmer for 15 minutes. Wash and scrub the mussel shells with a little dry mustard to help remove the slime. Put the mussels in another pan with the rest of the wine and the onion and carrot. Cover and bring to a boil. Shake over the fire for 2 or 3 minutes and strain the liquid into the soup. Remove the mussels from the shells and take off the small black fringe from the edges. Add the mussels to the soup, whole or chopped according to size, and simmer for 15 minutes. Mix the egg yolk and cream together and pour into the soup off the fire. Garnish with parsley. Serve separately small croutons of fried bread.

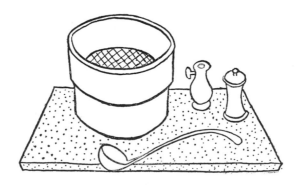

POTAGE BONNE FEMME
(Leek and Potato Soup)

4 tablespoons fat
4 large potatoes, peeled and finely sliced
2 medium-sized bunches shredded leeks
1½ cups water
salt and black pepper

½ teaspoon French mustard
1½ cups milk
2 egg yolks
½ cup cream
chopped parsley

Melt the fat in a pan. Add the potatoes and leeks, reserving one. Add ½ cup water, salt, black pepper and mustard. Cover and cook over a slow fire until the vegetables are soft and mushy. Pour on the milk and remaining water and stir over the fire until the soup comes to a boil. Draw aside for 15 minutes; then rub through a strainer. Add the egg yolks beaten into the cream, and thicken over a slow fire without boiling. Put the remaining leek, finely shredded, in a pan. Cover with cold water and bring to a boil. Drain and dry; stir into the soup. Sprinkle with chopped parsley and serve with croutons of bread.

CRÈME OLGA
(Mushroom and Onion Soup)

4 tablespoons fat
2 bunches scallions
1 clove garlic
salt and pepper

4 tablespoons flour
3 cups light chicken stock
2 cups mushrooms — not too firm
½ cup cream
pinch chopped tarragon

Melt the fat in a pan. Slice the scallions, using the green part, and add them with the garlic. Season. Cook slowly until mushy, and without browning stir in the flour and pour on the stock. Stir over the fire until the soup comes to a boil and simmer a few minutes. Then rub through a strainer with the raw mushrooms, return to the pan and add the cream and tarragon. Reheat and serve.

CRÈME DE CHAMPIGNON

(Cream of Mushroom Soup)

3 tablespoons fat
1 small chopped onion
1 chopped clove garlic
1½ cups mushrooms, put through
    meat grinder

3 tablespoons flour
2½ cups water
salt and pepper
1 bay leaf
½ cup cream

2 teaspoons chopped fresh chives

Melt all but 2 teaspoons of the fat. Add the onion and garlic and cook a few minutes, then add the fresh mushrooms and cook slowly for 7 or 8 minutes. Stir in the flour. Pour on the water and seasoning, and stir over the fire until the soup comes to a boil. Add the bay leaf and simmer slowly for 10 to 15 minutes. Remove the bay leaf. Beat in the remaining 2 teaspoons of fat. Add the cream and the chives. Simmer a few minutes and serve.

CRÈME DE CAROTTES

(Cream of Carrot Soup)

4 tablespoons fat
1 peeled, finely sliced potato
2 finely sliced onions
1½ pounds finely sliced carrots
1 finely sliced clove garlic
½ cup water

salt and black pepper
1 tablespoon flour
3 cups milk and water mixed in
    equal amounts
½ cup cream
1 egg yolk

little chopped chives and parsley

Melt the fat in a pan and add the potato, onions, carrots and garlic. Add ½ cup water, salt and pepper, and cook slowly with the lid on until soft. Stir in the flour. Pour on the milk and water and stir over the fire until the soup comes to a boil. Simmer for 20 minutes. Rub through a fine hair sieve and add the cream mixed into the egg yolk. Add the parsley and chives and stir over the fire until it thickens without boiling. Sprinkle the top with a little more parsley and serve with small squares of fried toast.

FRESH CREAM OF TOMATO SOUP

4 tablespoons butter or fat
1 tablespoon finely chopped onion
1 chopped clove garlic
5 sliced tomatoes with skins on
2 teaspoons tomato paste

2 tablespoons flour
2 cups chicken stock or bouillon
¾ cup cream
2 teaspoons chopped fresh chives
1 skinned and shredded tomato

Melt 3 tablespoons of the butter or fat in a pan. Add the onion and the garlic and cook for 1 minute. Add the sliced tomatoes and cook briskly for 5 minutes. Add the tomato paste and flour. Stir until smooth. Add the chicken stock or bouillon. Stir over the fire until boiling. Rub through a strainer and return to the pan. Simmer for 15 minutes. Add the cream and beat in slowly the remaining butter. Add the chives and the shredded tomato and serve.

CREAM OF LIMA BEAN SOUP

2 tablespoons fat
1 chopped bunch scallions
2 cups shelled Lima beans
2 cups water
1 sprig thyme

1 teaspoon potato flour or
   arrowroot flour
2 teaspoons butter
¾ cup cream
1 egg yolk, if desired

Melt the fat in a pan, add the scallions and cook a few minutes. Add the Lima beans and pour on the water. Bring to a boil and add the thyme. Simmer gently until the beans are quite soft; then rub through a strainer. Mix the flour with the butter to a smooth paste and add it bit by bit to the soup. Bring to a boil and stir in the cream, which, if desired, can be mixed with 1 egg yolk.

CRÈME D'ASPERGE

(Cream of Asparagus Soup)

3 tablespoons fat	*salt and pepper*
2 small bunches asparagus	*4 tablespoons flour*
1 bunch chopped scallions	*2 cups water*
1 small chopped clove garlic	*½ cup cream*
few drops lemon juice	*1 egg yolk, mixed in 2 teaspoons cream*

Melt the fat in a pan. Withhold about 18 asparagus tips and add the remaining asparagus sliced. Add the scallions, garlic, lemon juice, salt and pepper and cook very slowly until mushy. Stir in the flour and pour in the water. Stir over the fire until the soup comes to a boil. Simmer for 10 minutes. Rub through a strainer and return to the pan. Add the 18 asparagus tips, which have been boiled in a little salted water and drained. Add the cream. Reheat and garnish with a little chopped parsley and the egg yolk mixed in cream. Do not boil after adding the yolk.

CRÈME D'ÉPINARD

(Cream of Spinach Soup)

2 tablespoons butter	*1 heaping tablespoon rice flour*
1 tablespoon finely chopped onion	*1½ cups water*
½ pound spinach	*1 bay leaf*
2 or 3 tablespoons cream	

Melt the butter in a pan. Add the onion and cook for 4 minutes. Stir in the spinach, which has been well washed first in cold salted water, then in warm water, and once again in ice cold water, and finely chopped. Cover and cook slowly for 7 to 8 minutes. Remove from the fire and stir in the flour. Pour on the water slowly and stir over the fire until the soup comes to a boil. Simmer until the spinach is soft, then rub through a strainer. Return to the pan with a small bay leaf, a small lump of butter and the cream. Reheat, but do not let it get too hot. Serve with tiny cubes of fried bread.

CRÈME AURORE
(Cream of Tomato and Potato Soup)

4 potatoes	1 pound ripe tomatoes
2 onions	3 tablespoons tomato paste
2 cloves garlic	salt and pepper
6 tablespoons fat	little dried sage
2 cups milk and water mixed in equal amounts	½ cup thin cream
	2 teaspoons chopped parsley

Slice the potatoes and onion and 1 clove of garlic fine. Melt 2 tablespoons fat in a pan, add potatoes, 1 sliced onion and garlic with ½ cup water. Season and cook slowly until soft. Pour on the milk and water and bring to a boil. Draw aside. Then heat the rest of the fat in a pan and add the remaining sliced onion. Cook briskly 2 to 3 minutes. Add the tomatoes, sliced with the skins on, the tomato paste, salt, pepper and sage. Cook slowly for 10 to 12 minutes. Add this to the potato soup and rub through a fine strainer. Return to the pan and add enough thin cream to reduce it to a creamy consistency. Reheat. Sprinkle with parsley and serve.

POTAGE FONTANGE

¾ pound fresh shelled peas	lemon juice
4 tablespoons fat	salt and pepper
1 small sliced carrot	2 teaspoons flour
1 small sliced onion	2 cups water or stock
1 crushed clove garlic	¼ pound sorrel leaves, finely shredded
	½ cup cream

Bring the peas to a boil in a pan of water and drain. Melt the fat in a pan and add the onion and carrot. Cook a few minutes and add the garlic. Then add the peas with a few drops of lemon juice and seasoning. Cover and cook slowly until soft. Stir in the flour and the stock or water. Bring to a boil and simmer for 10 minutes. Rub through a strainer and return to the pan with the raw sorrel. Simmer gently for 5 minutes. Add the cream. Reheat and serve with Melba toast.

POTAGE ST. GERMAIN
(Cream of Pea Soup)

2 cups shelled peas	5 tablespoons fat
½ cup green part of leek	salt and pepper
about 10 spinach leaves	sugar
about 10 lettuce leaves	2½ cups stock or water
little fresh chervil	cream

Put the peas and the green part of the leeks, cut into slices, in a deep thick casserole. Wash thoroughly and dry the spinach and lettuce. Cut into shreds; add to the casserole. Add the chervil, half the fat, the salt, sugar and a little pepper and one cup of cold water. Bring to a boil quickly. Then draw the casserole to the side of the fire, cover and cook very slowly. Rub the mixture through a fine sieve, and return the purée to the casserole. Add the rest of the liquid, stock or water, and a small lump of fat. Stir until the soup comes to a boil and then add a little cream and the rest of the fat, bit by bit. Add 2 or 3 tablespoons cooked peas and be sure the seasoning is correct. Serve.

POTAGE GRAND DUC
(Cauliflower Soup)

2 small cauliflowers	3 tablespoons flour
2 medium-sized onions	2½ cups milk and water mixed
1 tablespoon oil	1 bay leaf
2 tablespoons fat	½ cup cream
little garlic	chopped fresh chives
¾ cup water	croutons of fried bread

Cut cauliflowers in pieces with onions. Heat in a pan with oil, fat and garlic, cook for 2 or 3 minutes, then add water and cook till mushy. Stir in the flour and pour on milk and water. Stir over a slow fire until the soup comes to a boil; then add bay leaf. Simmer for 2 minutes, rub through a strainer and return to the pan. Add cream, reheat and garnish with chives and fried bread. Serve in bowls.

POTAGE BAROQUE

1 tablespoon butter	drop lemon juice
4 tablespoons oil	2 tablespoons flour
2 cups fresh shelled peas	1½ cups turtle stock
½ cup water	½ cup diced green turtle
salt and pepper	1 cup cream

Heat butter and oil in pan, add peas, water, salt, pepper and lemon juice. Cook until mushy; then stir in flour. Pour on turtle stock and stir over fire until boiling; remove, rub through a strainer, return to pan and add diced turtle and cream. Reheat and serve in bowls; top with whipped cream and brown under broiler.

POTAGE SANTÉ

4 or 5 potatoes	salt and pepper
1 bunch scallions	2 handfuls washed sorrel
2 tablespoons hot fat	2½ cups light stock
¾ cup water	1 cup light cream

Slice potatoes and scallions and put in pan with hot fat and water; add salt and pepper and cook slowly until mushy. Add sorrel and cook for 2 minutes; then add stock and stir over fire until the soup boils. Put through a strainer and return to pan with cream. Reheat and serve.

VICHYSSOISE
(Iced Leek and Potato Soup)

4 large potatoes, finely sliced *1 cup water*
1 bunch leeks, finely sliced *1½ cups strong chicken or beef*
1 small stalk celery, finely sliced   *stock*
1 finely sliced onion *1 cup cream*
salt and pepper *finely chopped fresh chives*
finely shredded and cooked carrots

Place the potatoes, leeks, celery and onion in a pan with the water. Season and cook very slowly until mushy. Pour on the stock and bring to a boil. Rub through a coarse strainer and then through a fine strainer. Stir over ice until very cold. Add the cream, garnish with the chives and carrots. It is best served in bowls surrounded by crushed ice.

CRÈME CYRANO I
(Cold Chicken Custard)

1 dozen chicken feet *bouquet of herbs*
2 or 3 chicken carcasses *4 beaten egg yolks*
6 cups water *1 cup cream*
little celery, onion, carrot *salt and pepper*
and leek, sliced *chopped chives*

Put the carcasses and the feet in a pan and cover with the water. Bring slowly to a boil. Skim off the scum and add the celery, onion, carrot, leek and herbs. Boil, reducing slowly until there are 1½ cups left. Strain and add the egg yolks. Add half the cream and a little more seasoning. Stir in a double boiler until it thickens without curdling. Then add the remaining cream and pour into small glasses. Place to jell in the refrigerator and serve ice cold with a little chopped chives on top.

POTAGE SINGHALESE
(Iced Chicken and Curry Soup)

2 tablespoons butter
1 finely chopped onion
1 small apple
2 teaspoons good curry powder
4 tablespoons flour
½ cup fresh pea purée

salt
chili pepper
cayenne pepper
3 cups strong chicken or game stock
1½ cups cream
3 ounces finely diced white chicken
    or game meat

Melt the butter in a pan. Add the onion and sliced apple and cook very slowly until quite soft without browning. Add the curry powder and cook slowly for another 5 to 6 minutes. Stir in the flour and pea purée carefully, add salt, chili pepper and cayenne pepper. Stir in the stock until smooth. Stir over the fire until the soup comes to a boil. Rub through a fine strainer. Stir over ice until very cold. Add the cream and the chicken or game meat. Serve in bowls surrounded by crushed ice.

Note: this can be served hot.

ICED BORTSCH

4 cups strong beef stock
1 bunch grated, raw beets
½ cup red wine
2 tablespoons tomato paste
2 bay leaves

3 stiffly beaten egg whites
grated rind of 1 lemon
salt
cayenne pepper
5 tablespoons sour cream

Put the stock in a tin-lined copper pan. Add the beets, wine, tomato paste, bay leaves and egg whites. Beat over the fire until the bortsch comes to a boil; then draw aside and leave for 10 minutes. Pour through a fine damp cloth and place in refrigerator until cold. Serve with the following: —

Add the grated lemon rind, salt and pepper to the cream and serve separately.

ICED BROCCOLI SOUP

1 finely sliced onion	*salt*
1 finely sliced carrot	*cayenne pepper*
1 small stalk celery, finely sliced	*2 tablespoons rice flour*
1 bunch broccoli, roughly cut up	*1 cup cream*
3 cups chicken stock	*1 tablespoon finely chopped chives*

1 teaspoon finely chopped rosemary

Place the onion, carrot and celery in a pan with a little water; season and simmer until soft and nearly cooked. Bring the broccoli to a boil in cold water, simmer for 5 to 6 minutes and drain. Add the broccoli to the onion, carrot and celery. Pour on the stock. Add a little extra seasoning and simmer until the broccoli is just tender. Add the rice flour, first mixed with a little water. Bring to a boil once more, stirring all the time. Rub through a very fine strainer. Place in refrigerator or stir over ice until very cold. Add the cream with the chives and rosemary and serve in glass bowls surrounded by crushed ice.

CRÈME DE CONCOMBRES GLACÉE
(Iced Cucumber Soup)

3 small cucumbers	*salt*
1 chopped bunch scallions	*cayenne pepper*
3 cups water	*1 tablespoon chopped fresh mint*
3 tablespoons flour	*½ cup cream*

Peel 2 cucumbers and slice all 3. Place in a pan with the scallions and 1 cup water. Season and cook slowly until mushy. Stir in the flour and pour on the rest of the water. Stir over fire until the soup comes to a boil; add salt and cayenne pepper. Rub through a strainer, return to pan, add the mint, and stir over ice until very cold. Then add the cream, and, if desired, a little shredded cucumber, blanched and drained. Serve surrounded by crushed ice and with 1 tablespoon of cream in the center of each portion.

ICED JERUSALEM ARTICHOKE SOUP

1 sliced onion	*2 sliced potatoes*
1 sliced stalk celery	*2 tablespoons flour*
1½ pounds Jerusalem artichokes,	*1 cup cream*
skinned and sliced	*1 small carrot, finely chopped*
2 cups veal stock	*1 teaspoon crushed black*
salt	*peppercorns*
cayenne pepper	*1 tablespoon chopped chives*

Cook the onion and celery in a little water until just soft and add the artichokes. Pour on the stock and season with a little salt and cayenne pepper. Bring to a boil, add the potatoes and simmer gently until soft. Mix the flour with a little of the water in which the vegetables were cooked and add carefully to the soup. Bring to a boil, stirring all the time, and simmer for another 5 to 6 minutes. Rub through a very fine strainer. Stir over ice until cold, then add the cream. Garnish with the carrot, which has been cooked until just soft in a little boiling salted water and drained. Finally add the crushed peppercorns and chives. Serve with fingers of hot buttered toast.

ICED PEA AND CURRY SOUP

¾ pound dried peas	*1 beef bouillon cube*
1 sliced onion	*salt and pepper*
1 sliced carrot	*2 tablespoons curry*
1 sliced clove garlic	*1 cup cream*
1 sliced stalk celery	*½ green pepper, finely shredded*

Soak the peas in water overnight. Strain and put in a pan with the onion, carrot, garlic and celery. Just cover with water in which the bouillon cube has been dissolved. Season and simmer gently until soft, adding a little more water if necessary. Rub through a very fine sieve. Return to the pan and add the curry. Reheat to the boiling point and simmer 10 minutes. Allow to get ice cold. Add the cream and garnish with the blanched green pepper.

ICED ASPARAGUS SOUP

1 bunch asparagus	*2 tablespoons rice flour*
1 bunch sliced scallions	*1 cup cream*
salt and pepper	

Withhold about 4 asparagus tips and place the remaining asparagus sliced, in a pan, with the scallions and 4 or 5 tablespoons water. Cook very slowly until soft. Stir in the rice flour; pour on 2 cups water, salt and pepper. Stir over the fire until boiling. Rub through a fine sieve and allow to get ice cold. Add the cream. Garnish with the remaining asparagus tips, cold boiled.

CREME CYRANO II

(Cold Chicken Custard)

4 or 5 egg yolks	*2 cups hot chicken stock*
salt	*1 good cup cream*
cayenne pepper	*paprika*

Put eggs, salt and cayenne pepper in a bowl, beat well and pour on chicken stock. Stir over the fire until thick; do not boil, and add cream.

Half fill glass dishes and set in ice box till ready to use; remove, sprinkle with paprika and serve with fingers of hot buttered toast.

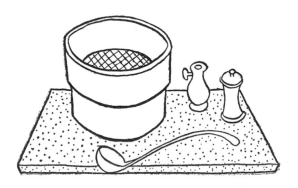

ICED TOMATO SOUP

1 finely chopped onion or
  1 bunch scallions
6 large tomatoes
salt and pepper
¼ cup water
2 tablespoons tomato paste

5 level tablespoons flour
2 cups chicken stock
1 cup cream
2 teaspoons finely chopped dill
2 tomatoes

Put onion or scallions, tomatoes, salt, pepper and water in a pan and cook briskly for 6 minutes. Then add tomato paste and stir in the flour. Pour on chicken stock and stir over the fire till the soup comes to a boil. Put through a strainer, stir over ice till cold, then add cream, dill and tomatoes, skinned, pipped and shredded. Serve in bowls very cold.

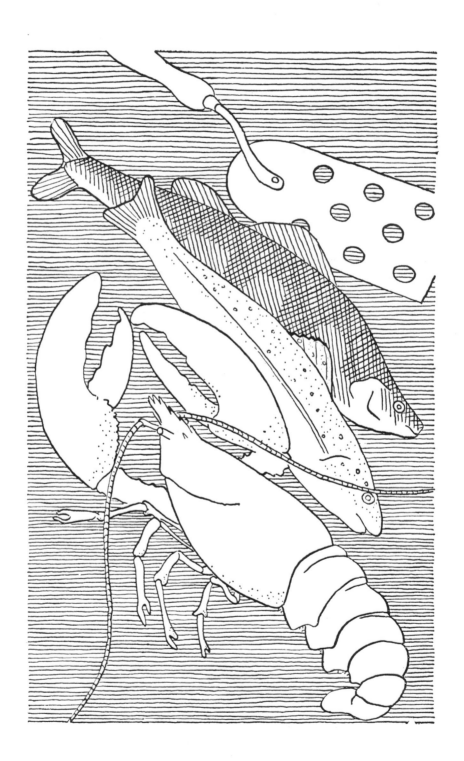

CHAPTER VI

FISH

Fish is an economical food and is very delicious if well prepared. Probably the chief reason fish is not served more often on American tables is the scarcity of good recipes. Broiled, fried, and baked fish rapidly become monotonous, yet there are numerous and exciting methods of preparation and many types of fish on the domestic market.

On Buying Fish: Be sure your fish is perfectly fresh. Indications of a recently caught fish are bright, bulging eyes, firm, elastic flesh, closely adhering scales and an absence of pronounced fishy odor. With flat fish such as sole or flounder, the white skin should be clear and the red parts bright and rosy. Mackerel and herring will pass inspection if their gills are a vivid red.

On Buying Shellfish: It is most important that all shellfish, and this includes shrimps, scallops, and crayfish, be strictly fresh since they deteriorate rapidly. Lobsters should be bought alive and cooked in your own kitchen for better flavor and texture. Mussels and oysters must not be excessively sandy and they should be tightly closed. If any mussel appears to be loosening up before cooking it is probably not fresh and should be discarded.

Preparation and Cooking of Fish: Unless the fish has come directly to your kitchen after being caught, wash it in lemon juice and water before cooking. This whitens the flesh and also helps prevent a fish odor.

Scaled fish should have their scales removed before cooking by rubbing a knife from the tail to the head, traveling against the grain. When a recipe calls for removal of the skin from flat fish, first dip the fingers in salt to prevent slipping. Then take a small sharp knife and loosen the skin at the tail. A sharp, firm pull should be enough to skin the fish swiftly and evenly.

Fish for frying is always skinned, then washed and dried. Dip the fish lightly in flour, then pat it gently to remove the excess flour. Brush with a beaten egg and roll in dry white bread crumbs. Handle fish gently since its flesh is easily torn and nothing is more unappetizing than a dish of broken-up bits of fish.

Fish combines well with both herbs and wines. Indeed, in no other phase of cooking is wine so important, for it accentuates the delicate flavor of the fish. A dry, white wine is most generally used, especially with shellfish. White wine is also used with the coarser fresh-water fish and with cod, haddock, and sole. Red wine is excellent with mackerel.

Herbs too are essential when baking or boiling fish. Thyme, tarragon, and parsley all lend their savor, with a bay leaf for "red" fish such as mackerel. Always use herbs lightly, for over-seasoning ruins the subtle flavor of fish. A mere sprig of each herb is all that is needed.

A tin of bread crumbs is one of the kitchen staples for frying fish. Save all stale pieces of white bread, then rub through a wire sieve and dry thoroughly in the oven without browning. Store in a tin or jar with a tight-fitting cover.

For deep fat frying, an extra deep pan should be used with a wire basket. Have the pan half full of fat, either beef dripping, vegetable shortening, or cooking oil. You will know the fat is the right temperature when you see a slight blue haze. The fat should not smoke heavily, however, or it will "break down," as the chemists say, and develop a rancid flavor. For a perfectly crisp serving of fish, drain well after frying, either in the basket or on a rack.

Preparation and Cooking of Shellfish: If lobster is to be used in a hot dish it is first killed by plunging the point of a sharp knife into the cross marked on its underside. Then cut up for cooking. Remove the small sac at the back of the head; everything else is edible. If the lobster is to be served cold it should be killed by cooking whole in salted water or court bouillon (p. 147) at a simmering temperature. Mussels also are cooked either in salted water or court bouillon and always at a gentle simmer. Too rapid cooking will result in a tough, rubbery texture. Shrimps will retain their flavor better if, after thorough washing, they are cooked with their shells on in slightly salted water. Remove shells and black vein down the center of the back when shrimps have cooled. Scallops improve in flavor if soaked in a little lemon juice and water before cooking.

I have given here some recipes for fish and shellfish, some old, some new, but all of them in fairly simple form with accent on flavor and correct cooking methods.

SOLE AMANDINE

9 fillets	1 tablespoon hot oil
hot butter	1 teaspoon chopped tarragon
5 tomatoes	salt and pepper
2 teaspoons chopped garlic	¾ cup blanched almonds

Dust fillets very lightly in seasoned flour and brown very quickly each side in hot butter. In a different pan skin and chop tomatoes coarsely and add garlic. Cook for 1 minute in hot oil; add tarragon, salt and pepper. Arrange on a serving dish and place sole on top. Add almonds, browned in oven, to the pan the sole was cooked in. Sprinkle with salt, toss for 1 minute, then scatter over fish and serve.

SOLE NEW ORLEANS

8 fillets	1 cup raw spinach
hot butter	¾ cup, or more, thin sour cream
2 tablespoons fat	salt and pepper
garlic	1 tablespoon grated cheese
6 skinned tomatoes	grated cheese
	few drops lemon juice

Dust fillets lightly in seasoned flour and cook until golden on each side.

Melt the fat in a pan, add chopped garlic, cook for 1 minute, then add tomatoes cut in thick slices; cook briskly for 2 minutes, then arrange on the bottom of a serving dish and put fillets on top. Cover with the following sauce: —

Sauce: Take spinach which has been put through the meat chopper; mix in sour cream, salt, pepper, grated cheese and lemon juice. Cover top of sole with this sauce and sprinkle with a very little grated cheese. Brown under the broiler and serve.

FILET DE SOLE À L'ANDALOUSE
(Sole with Tomatoes and Onion Purée)

1 1½-pound sole	4 onions
bouquet of herbs	1½ cups milk
1 slice onion	4 tablespoons butter
1 clove garlic	2 tablespoons flour
juice of ½ lemon	salt and pepper
¼ cup water	1 pound cooking tomatoes
2 large tomatoes	2 dessertspoons tomato paste
2 tablespoons cream	

Sole: Skin, fillet, wash and dry. Fold each fillet in half and place on a well-buttered, fireproof dish, with herbs, 1 slice of onion, and garlic. Add the lemon juice and water. Cover with the bones and poach in a moderate oven for 12 to 15 minutes.

Tomatoes: Cut the 2 tomatoes in half and carefully remove all the pith from the insides. Season and pour a little melted butter into each. Cook gently in the oven; remove and keep warm.

Purée Soubise: Finely slice and blanch the 4 onions. Strain and cook until soft in ¾ cup of milk. Strain again and rub the onions through a sieve. Melt 2 tablespoons of butter in a pan; add, off the fire, 1 tablespoon of flour, salt and pepper, and the milk in which the onions were cooked. Stir over the fire until boiling and add to the paste. Reseason and simmer until of the consistency of thick cream. Cover and keep warm.

Sauce: Cut up the cooking tomatoes and put them in a pan with the tomato paste, a small lump of butter, 1 spoonful of water and salt and pepper. Cook slowly for ten minutes, stirring occasionally, and then strain. Melt in a pan 2 tablespoons of butter. Remove from the fire and add 1 tablespoon of flour. Season, stir until smooth, and pour in ¾ cup of milk. Stir over the fire until the sauce comes to a boil and add the strained tomato pulp. Simmer for 5 minutes; then pour in the cream, with the fish liquor, reduced to 1 tablespoon.

Serving: Arrange the tomatoes on a dish. Fill with the Purée Soubise. Place a fillet of sole on the top of each, and coat the whole dish with the tomato sauce.

Approximate time: 1¼ hours.

FILETS DE SOLE JOINVILLE
(Sole in a Mold, Stuffed with Cod and Shrimps)

¾ pound hake or cod	salt and pepper
⅓ cup butter	4 sole
5 tablespoons flour	¾ cup fish stock
1¾ cups milk	½ pound mushrooms
¼ cup cream	juice ½ lemon
2 eggs	12 shrimps
few drops carmine	

Farce: Skin, bone and mince the hake. Pound in a mortar or beat well with the following panada: Melt some butter in a pan. Add a little flour and when well mixed pour on ¾ cup milk. Stir over the fire until boiling. Season and cool before using. Beat in the eggs and seasoning. Put aside.

Lining and Filling Mold: Skin and fillet the sole. Butter a border mold well, allowing the fillets to overlap slightly so that there is no gap between them. Pour the farce into the mold and fold the tips of the fillets over the top. Stand in a shallow pan on a piece of waxed paper and half fill the pan with cold water. Bring slowly to a boil. Cover mold with waxed paper and poach in a moderate oven for 40 minutes. Remove and keep warm.

Sauce: Melt 2 tablespoons butter in a saucepan. Add, off the fire, the flour and seasoning. Stir until smooth and pour on the stock. Stir over the fire until the sauce thickens. Then add 1 cup milk and bring to a boil; add the cream. Cover the pan and keep warm.

Garnish: Wash and cut the mushrooms in quarters. Cook for 5 minutes with a small lump of butter, a little lemon juice and seasoning. Add 1 level tablespoon flour off the fire. Reboil and put to one side. Shell the shrimps, leaving on the heads. Put to warm between 2 plates with a little melted butter. The shells from the tails should then be pounded with a few drops of carmine and the 2 tablespoons butter which is added at the end to the sauce.

Serving: Turn out the mold onto a dish and with a clean cloth wipe up any juice that may come away from the fish. Pour the sauce over the whole dish. Pile up the mushrooms in the center, and arrange the shrimps on top. Serve the rest of the sauce separately.

FILETS DE SOLE EN PAPIOTTES
(Fillets of Sole Cooked in Paper)

8 fillets
little crushed garlic
2 finely chopped mushrooms
3 tablespoons sour cream
1 tablespoon chopped, mixed herbs
  (including tarragon)
melted butter

9 whole mushrooms
2 tablespoons sherry
salt and pepper
2 apples
2 tablespoons butter
chopped chives
chopped tarragon

Wash fillets well in water and lemon juice and dry. Put 2 of them through the meat chopper and add garlic, chopped mushrooms, cream and herbs; mix well and put a spoonful on each fillet. Fold over and brush each side with melted butter. Place each fillet on a piece of double thickness waxed paper and cover top with thick layer of the following: —

Cut whole mushrooms in thin slices, sauté quickly in hot butter and add sherry, salt and pepper. On top of this place a layer of apples, which have been pared, cored, cut in small pieces and sautéed in butter. At the last minute sprinkle with a little sugar to glaze. Then dot generously with the following: —

Cream butter, mix in garlic, chives, tarragon, salt and pepper. Wrap in paper and bake in a hot oven for 25 minutes. Remove and serve in papers.

FILETS DE SOLE FLORENTINE
(Fillets of Sole with Spinach)

8 fillets of sole
½ cup dry white wine
salt and pepper
1 bay leaf
2 small lobsters
1 tablespoon Marsala wine
3 egg yolks

cayenne pepper
2 tablespoons cream
1 tablespoon tarragon vinegar
3 or 4 tablespoons butter
2 tablespoons cream
½ cup raw spinach
1 tablespoon fish stock

Wash fillets in lemon juice and water; arrange on a greased baking dish and pour over wine, salt, pepper and bay leaf. Cover

with waxed paper and cook for 15 minutes in a moderate oven.
Remove and arrange on a serving dish. Cut the meat of lobsters
in small pieces and toss in foaming butter; season with salt and
pepper. Cook a few minutes; then add Marsala wine. Scatter over
top of fish and pour over the following sauce: —

Sauce: Put egg yolks, salt, cayenne pepper, cream and tarragon
vinegar in a bowl. Place the bowl in a pan of hot water over a
slow fire and beat with a wire whisk until the sauce begins to
thicken; then add, bit by bit, butter, cream, spinach which has
been put through a meat grinder, and fish stock reduced from
liquor in which fish was cooked. Season well, pour over fish and
put under the broiler to brown delicately.

FILET DE SOLE ALPHONSE XIII
(Sole with Eggplant and Green Peppers)

1 1½-pound sole	*4 tablespoons cooking oil*
2 tablespoons flour	*1 pound tomatoes*
salt and pepper	*1 tin shredded sweet peppers*
½ cup butter	*1 dessertspoon tomato paste*
2 eggplants	*1 cup stock*

1 teaspoon finely chopped, mixed herbs

Sole: Skin and fillet; wash and dry. Dust with 1 tablespoon flour
and seasoning and fry in 4 tablespoons butter until golden brown
on each side. Keep warm.

Eggplants: Split the eggplants in half. Make a few incisions
with a sharp knife. Sprinkle well with salt and leave for ¼ hour.
Squeeze dry and fry in hot oil 5 minutes each side.

Tomato Mixture: Skin the tomatoes; cut into quarters and
remove the pips, which can be added to the stock pot. Add 3 tablespoons melted butter, salt and pepper, the sweet peppers and the
herbs. Shake over the fire for 5 minutes.

Sauce: Melt in pan 1 tablespoon butter. Add, off the fire,
1 tablespoon flour. Season. Add the tomato paste and stir until
smooth. Strain on the stock and stir over the fire until boiling.

Serving: Arrange the eggplant on the dish. Cover the tops of
each piece with the tomato mixture. Arrange the fillets on top
and serve the sauce separately.

FILET DE SOLE À LA CRÈME
(Sole with Wine and Cream Sauce)

1 1½-pound sole	*½ bottle dry Graves or Chablis*
juice of ½ lemon	*2 tablespoons butter*
few whole peppercorns	*salt*
1 sprig tarragon	*freshly ground black pepper*
1 crushed clove garlic	*¼ pint well-reduced cream*

1 teaspoon chopped parsley

Skin and fillet the sole. Wash well in lemon juice and water, dry in a cloth and place in a well-buttered, fireproof dish. Flavor with the peppercorns, tarragon and garlic. Cover with the carcass and pour over the wine. Cook in a moderate oven for 12 to 15 minutes. Remove and arrange the fillets in a hot serving dish. Keep warm.

Melt the butter in a pan with salt and the black pepper. Add the cream and slowly beat in the liquid from the sole, which has been reduced to ¾ cup. Bring slowly to a boil and simmer to the consistency of cream. Add the parsley. Pour over the sole and serve very hot.

FILET DE SOLE À LA MORNAY
(Sole with Cheese Sauce)

1 1½-pound sole	*1 clove garlic*
juice ½ lemon	*few whole peppercorns*
2 bay leaves	*½ cup butter or fat*
1 sprig thyme	*1½ tablespoons flour*
1 cup milk	*salt and pepper*
1 slice onion	*2 tablespoons cream*

3 tablespoons grated Parmesan cheese

Sole: Skin and fillet; wash, dry well and fold both ends under. Place on a well-buttered, fireproof dish. Add the lemon juice, bay leaf and little water, and the thyme. Cover with carcass and poach in a moderate oven for 12 to 15 minutes.

Mornay Sauce: Put the milk, onion, garlic, bay leaf and whole peppercorns in a pan. Bring slowly to a boil. Melt in a pan

2 tablespoons butter. Remove from the fire and add the flour and salt and pepper to season. Strain and add the hot milk and stir over the fire until the sauce comes to a boil. Add the cream and simmer for a few minutes.

Serving: Arrange the fillets on a dish for serving. Pour over the sauce. Sprinkle the top with a little grated cheese and brown under the grill.

FILET DE SOLE MACONNAISE
(Sole with Red Wine and Onions)

1 1½-pound sole	*¼ pound mushrooms*
juice ½ lemon	*½ cup butter or fat*
½ cup red wine	*salt and pepper*
¼ cup water	*1½ tablespoons flour*
bouquet of herbs	*18 small pickling onions*
1 clove garlic	*2 tablespoons cream*
1 slice onion	*cayenne pepper*
few whole peppercorns	

Sole: Skin, bone and fillet. Arrange on a well-buttered, fire-proof dish. Add the lemon juice and pour over the wine and water. Add the herbs, garlic, slice of onion and whole peppercorns. Cover with carcass and poach in a moderate oven for 15 minutes.

Mushrooms: Wash and cut in quarters. Add 2 tablespoons melted butter, salt and pepper. Cook for 5 to 6 minutes and keep warm.

Onions: Put in a pan 2 tablespoons butter. Remove from the fire and add the flour, salt and pepper. Stir until smooth. Strain and add ¾ cup of the liquid from the sole. Boil the onions in this, adding, bit by bit, the remaining butter and 1 tablespoon cream.

Sauce: Melt in a pan 2 tablespoons butter, stir in the flour, salt and cayenne pepper. Strain on the stock the fish was cooked in and stir over the fire until the sauce comes to a boil. Add 1 table-spoon cream and a small lump of butter, bit by bit, and simmer for 5 to 6 minutes.

Serving and Glazing: Arrange the fillets on a dish. Scatter the mushrooms and onions on the top. Pour over the sauce. Sprinkle with a few drops melted butter and glaze under the grill.

FILET DE SOLE DUGLÈRE
(Sole with Fresh Tomatoes)

1 1½-pound sole	*¼ cup water*
salt and pepper	*½ cup cream*
3 tablespoons butter	*2 pounds tomatoes*
1 chopped onion	*1 teaspoon chopped mixed herbs*
1½ tablespoons flour	*handful bread crumbs*
½ cup white wine	*little grated cheese*

Sole: Skin and fillet the sole; wash and dry. Lay on a well-buttered, fireproof dish, and dust with salt and pepper.

Sauce: Melt the butter in a saucepan. Add onion and simmer for 1 to 2 minutes without browning. Stir in the flour; pour on the wine and water. Bring to a boil and add the cream slowly. Simmer for 4 to 5 minutes, season, and add the tomatoes, which have been skinned, pipped and cut in shreds, and the herbs.

Serving: Pour this over the sole. Dust over with brown bread crumbs and grated cheese. Put in a moderate oven for 15 to 20 minutes. Remove and serve.

FILET DE SOLE CAPRICE
(Sole with Carrot and Sherry Sauce)

1 1½-pound sole	*1 cup butter*
juice ½ lemon	*2 carrots, finely shredded*
¼ cup white wine	*salt and pepper*
¼ cup water	*¼ cup sherry*
bouquet of herbs	*1½ tablespoons flour*
few whole peppercorns	*¼ cup milk*
1 slice onion	*¼ cup cream*
1 clove garlic	*4 firm tomatoes, skinned*
4 button mushrooms	

Sole: Fillet and skin, wash and dry. Fold over and place on a well-buttered, fireproof dish. Add the lemon juice, wine, water, herbs, peppercorns, onion and garlic. Cover with waxed paper and put in a moderate oven for 15 minutes. Remove the fillets and put under a plate. Keep warm.

Sauce: Melt ½ cup butter in a pan and add the carrots, salt and the sherry. Cover the pan with the lid and cook slowly for 10 minutes, or until carrots are soft, without browning. Remove, add the flour and stir until smooth. Add ¾ cup strained liquid from sole. Thicken over the fire. Add the milk with a little extra seasoning. Stir over the fire until the sauce comes to a boil. Add the cream and, bit by bit, 2 tablespoons butter. Cover the pan with the lid and keep warm.

Tomatoes and Mushrooms: Place the tomatoes on a dish. Season each with salt and pepper and pour over 2 tablespoons melted butter. Place in oven for 5 minutes. Wash the button mushrooms well and, if desired, flute with a small sharp knife. Place in pan and just cover with water. Add a good squeeze of lemon juice, salt and pepper. Cover and cook for 5 to 6 minutes.

Serving: Arrange the fillets on a hot dish and place a tomato on top of each. Pour the sauce over the dish and place a mushroom on each tomato.

FILETS DE SOLE CECILIA
(Sole with Asparagus Tips and Cream Sauce)

6 fillets of sole	*1 tablespoons butter or fat*
little flour	*1 large bunch asparagus tips*
salt and pepper	*little grated Parmesan cheese*
	few slices truffle

Remove the skin of the fillets. Wash, dry, and dust in flour and seasoning. Melt the butter or fat in a pan, and, when foaming, cook the fillets 2 at a time until golden brown on each side. Arrange on a serving dish and add to the pan the fillets were cooked in the asparagus tips, which have been simmered until soft in boiling water and strained. Heat the asparagus tips 3 to 4 minutes in the fish butter. Then arrange around the fish. Sprinkle with grated Parmesan cheese and brown quickly under the grill. Garnish with a few slices of truffle and serve.

MÉDAILLONS DE POISSONS MATELOT
(Halibut Steaks)

5½ tablespoons butter or fat	1 chopped onion
4½ tablespoons flour	¾ cup stock
1 cup milk	¼ cup red wine
1 egg yolk	1 tablespoon cream
salt and pepper	½ pound button onions
1 pound cooked halibut or cod	little chopped parsley
1 well-beaten egg	½ pound small potatoes

few dry white bread crumbs

Médaillons: Melt 2½ tablespoons butter in pan. Add 3½ tablespoons flour. Pour on the milk and stir until boiling. Draw off and add the yolk, seasoning and halibut, free from skin and bone. Beat well with a wooden spatula. Place on a plate and leave for 2 hours. Flour a board; shape the mixture in flat cakes; brush them with egg. Turn, pressing gently, in the bread crumbs. Fry in deep fat until golden.

Sauce: Melt a little butter. Add the chopped onion. Cook for 1 to 2 minutes without browning. Add 1 tablespoon flour, salt, pepper, stock and wine. Bring to a boil and simmer for 5 minutes. Add 1 tablespoon cream.

Garnish: Peel the button onions, blanch, drain and return to the pan with the butter and seasoning. Cover and cook gently until tender. Dust with chopped parsley. Cook the potatoes in hot salted water. Drain and toss in hot butter.

Serving: Arrange the médaillons in one half of the dish and the garnish in the other. Serve the sauce separately.

FILETS DE MERLANS À LA DIEPPOISE
(Fillets of Whiting with Shrimps and Mussels)

6 fillets of whiting	*salt and pepper*
½ cup fish stock	*½ cup water*
¼ cup white wine	*1 cup skinned shrimps*
2 cups large mussels	*6 ounces button mushrooms*
1 sliced onion	*5 tablespoons butter*
1 sliced carrot	*little lemon juice*
1 sliced clove garlic	*4 tablespoons flour*
2 bay leaves	*¾ cup milk*
few peppercorns	*2 or 3 tablespoons cream*

Remove the whiting skins and arrange on a buttered, fireproof dish. Pour over the fish stock and wine. Cover with buttered paper and poach for 12 minutes in a moderate oven.

Scrub the mussels well. Put in a pan with the onion, carrot, garlic, bay leaves, peppercorns, salt and water. Bring slowly to a boil, then simmer for 3 to 4 minutes. Strain the mussels. Remove mussels from shells and cut away and discard the little beard around the outside. Add to them the skinned shrimps, the mushrooms cooked briskly in a little hot butter, lemon juice and seasoning. Scatter this mixture over the top of the whiting.

Melt 3 tablespoons butter and season it. Stir in the 4 tablespoons flour. Strain, add ¾ cup liquid strained from the whiting, and thicken over the fire. Add the milk and bring to a boil. Add, bit by bit, the 1 tablespoon butter and the cream. Pour over the dish, sprinkle top with a little melted butter and brown under the grill.

SMALL FLOUNDER THEODORA
(Whole Flounder with Shrimps)

1 small whole flounder	*2 egg yolks*
1 glass white wine	*4 large potatoes*
1 chopped onion	*2 tablespoons shrimps*
¾ cup butter	*salt and pepper*
1½ tablespoons flour	*1 beaten egg*
1 cup water	*handful white bread crumbs*

Flounder: Wash and trim. Braise the fillets on the dark side. Turn over onto a well-buttered, fireproof dish. Add the wine and onion and cover with waxed paper. Cook in a moderate oven for 25 minutes.

Sauce: Melt in a pan 2 tablespoons butter. Remove from fire and add the flour. Pour on the water; season and bring to a boil, stirring all the time. Add the strained liquid from the flounder, which has been reduced to half quantity. Add 1 egg yolk. Thicken a little over the fire without boiling, and keep warm.

Croquettes: Peel and boil the 4 large potatoes until soft. Strain and return to the pan and dry over the fire. Rub through a fine sieve and beat in 4 tablespoons butter and 1 egg yolk. Add the shrimps and cool. Form into small pear shapes; dust with flour and seasoning and brush with the beaten egg. Roll in the bread crumbs and fry in deep fat until golden brown.

Serving: Arrange flounder on a dish. Pour over the sauce and garnish with the croquettes.

FILET DE SOLE BONNE FEMME
(Sole with Hollandaise and White Wine Sauce)

few fish bones	lemon juice
few whole peppercorns	⅔ cup butter
1 clove garlic	salt and pepper
1 slice onion	1½ tablespoons flour
1 cup water	¼ cup milk
¼ cup white wine	2 tablespoons cream
1 1½-pound sole	2 egg yolks
bouquet of herbs	2 tablespoons tarragon vinegar
½ cup mushrooms	cayenne pepper

Stock: Put the fish bones in a pan with the whole peppercorns, garlic and onion. Add the water and wine and bring slowly to a boil. Simmer for half an hour and strain before using.

Sole: Skin and fillet; wash and dry the sole. Arrange on a well-buttered, fireproof dish and lay the carcass on top. Add bouquet of herbs. Pour over the fish stock and poach in a moderate oven for 15 minutes.

Mushrooms: Wash in cold water and lemon juice. Slice and add to 2 tablespoons melted butter, salt and pepper. Cover the pan with waxed paper and lid. Cook gently for 5 minutes, stirring occasionally.

White Wine Sauce: Melt in pan 2 tablespoons butter. Remove from heat and add the flour. Season and stir until smooth. Pour in ¾ cup of liquid from the sole. Thicken over the fire and add the milk. Stir until the sauce comes to a boil and add 1 tablespoon cream.

Hollandaise Sauce: Put into a bowl the egg yolks, add 1 tablespoon cream, the tarragon vinegar, salt and cayenne pepper. Put the bowl in a small pan surrounded by water and beat well over a slow fire until it just begins to thicken, then add the butter, bit by bit, and a drop of lemon juice.

Serving: Arrange the fillets on the dish. Coat carefully with the white wine sauce. Scatter the mushrooms on top. Cover the mushrooms with the hollandaise sauce and glaze under the grill.

FILETS DE SOLE JACKSON
(Sole with Onions)

6 fillets of sole	*salt and black pepper*
½ cup fish stock	*2 tablespoons heavy cream*
¼ cup white wine	*little tarragon*
2 tablespoons butter or fat	*little parsley*
4 large onions, finely sliced	*3 egg yolks*

Skin and bone the fillets and arrange on a fireproof dish. Pour over the fish stock and the wine. Cover with waxed paper and cook for 15 minutes in a moderate oven. Melt the butter or fat in a pan and add the onions, salt and pepper. Cook slowly until soft without browning. Chop very fine and add the cream and a little tarragon and parsley. Arrange this on the bottom of a hot dish and place the fillets on top.

Strain the stock the fish was cooked in and reduce to 1 cup by boiling. Add the egg yolks, salt and black pepper. Stir over the fire until it thickens without boiling. Pour over the fish and place under the grill to glaze.

PAUPIETTES DE SOLE CLARENCE
(Stuffed Sole with Anchovies)

¼ pound hake	*1 slice onion*
2 egg whites	*bouquet of herbs*
salt and pepper	*juice ½ lemon*
4 tablespoons cream	*1 clove garlic*
5 anchovies	*6 whole peppercorns*
1 1½-pound sole	*⅓ cup butter or fat*
½ cup white wine	*1½ tablespoons flour*
¼ cup water	*¼ cup milk*

Fish Farce: Skin, bone and mince the hake. Put in a bowl and beat in slowly the roughly broken egg whites. Add salt and pepper to season. Beat in slowly 2 tablespoons cream. Add 2 skinned, boned and finely chopped anchovies. (This is best done over a bowl of ice.)

Sole: Skin and fillet; wash and dry the sole. Spread a little farce on the shiny, or skinned, side of the fillet. Roll it up, fasten with thread, and place on a well-buttered, fireproof dish. Pour on the wine and water and add the onion, herbs, squeeze of lemon juice, garlic and peppercorns. Cover with waxed paper and poach for 20 minutes in a moderate oven.

Quenelles: Form the remaining farce in small egg shapes with 2 teaspoons. Drop into a pan of hot salted water. Poach gently without boiling for 10 minutes. Remove carefully and drain on a cloth. Keep warm.

White Wine Sauce: Melt in a pan 2 tablespoons butter. Remove from heat and add the flour. Season and add ¾ cup of the strained liquid from the sole. Add the milk and stir over the fire until boiling. Add 1 tablespoon cream and, bit by bit, 2 tablespoons butter.

Serving: Arrange paupiettes on dish for serving with pile of quenelles in the middle. Cover with sauce. Decorate the top of each paupiette with a small fillet of anchovy and the quenelles with strips of anchovy.

SOLE DORIA
(Sole with Cucumber)

1 small sole	*4 or 5 tablespoons fat*
little flour	*1 small cucumber*
salt and pepper	*⅓ cup butter*
1 egg, beaten	*1 teaspoon fresh chopped mint*
handful dried white bread crumbs	

Sole: Remove the bone from the sole carefully. Fold the fillets on one side, dust lightly with flour and seasoning and brush with beaten egg. Cover all over with the bread crumbs. Fry in boiling fat until golden brown. Remove and place in a hot dish for serving.

Salpicon of Cucumber: Skin the cucumber and cut it in small, even cubes. Melt the butter in a pan; add salt and pepper. Cover with waxed paper and the lid and cook very slowly for 7 to 8 minutes. Remove and add the chopped mint.

Note: this salpicon is excellent with grilled sole, hake or cod.

FILETS DE SOLE NORDAISE
(Sole with Mushroom and Cheese Sauce)

1 1½-pound sole	5 tablespoons butter or fat
juice ½ lemon	salt and pepper
¼ cup water	2 egg yolks
1 slice onion	¾ cup cream
1 clove garlic	3 tablespoons grated cheese
bouquet of herbs	1 cup mushrooms

Sole: Skin and fillet. Wash, dry and place on a well-buttered, fireproof dish. Add the lemon juice, water, onion, garlic and herbs. Cover with the carcass and poach for 15 minutes in a moderate oven.

Mushrooms: Wash and cut in thick slices. Add to 2 tablespoons melted butter, salt and pepper. Sauté with the lid on for 5 to 6 minutes.

Nordaise Sauce: Melt in a pan 3 tablespoons butter. Add the yolks mixed into the cream, the grated cheese, salt and pepper. Stir over the fire until it thickens. Add the mushrooms and the stock in which the sole was cooked, reduced to 1 tablespoon.

Serving: Arrange fillets on a dish. Pour over the sauce. Sprinkle top with melted butter and glaze under the grill.

FILET DE SOLE À LA SUCHET
(Sole with Carrot and Sherry Sauce)

1 1½-pound sole	salt and pepper
juice ½ lemon	½ pound carrots, very finely shredded
¾ cup water	
1 slice onion	¼ cup sherry
1 clove garlic	1½ tablespoons flour
1 bay leaf	¼ cup milk
⅓ cup butter	3 tablespoons cream

Sole: Skin and fillet; wash and dry. Place on a well-buttered, fireproof dish. Pour over the lemon juice and water, and add the onion, garlic and bay leaf. Cover with the carcass and poach for 15 minutes in a moderate oven.

Suchet Sauce: Melt in a pan 3 tablespoons butter. Season with salt and pepper, and add the carrots and sherry. Cover the pan with lid. Cook very slowly until tender, without browning, stirring occasionally (approximately 15 minutes). Then add the flour. Strain and add the liquid from the sole. Stir over the fire until the sauce thickens. Add the milk and stir until boiling. Add, bit by bit, 3 tablespoons butter and cream.

Serving: Arrange fillets on dish and pour over the sauce.

SMALL FLOUNDER À L'ESPAGNOLE
(Flounder with Mussels)

2 cups large mussels	*1 clove garlic*
½ cup white wine	*2 red peppers*
¼ cup water	*1 green pepper*
2 bay leaves	*1 tablespoon flour*
salt and pepper	*1 teaspoon tomato paste*
½ teaspoon paprika	*1 pound shelled peas*
1 small flounder	*4 firm tomatoes, skinned,*
3 tablespoons butter	*pipped and shredded*
1 small sliced onion	*8 pitted olives*
little finely chopped parsley	

Mussels: Wash well in cold water. Place in pan with the wine, ¼ cup water and bay leaves. Season and bring slowly to a boil. Shake over the fire for a few minutes, strain, and reserve the liquid.

Flounder: Remove the head and tail. Cut into 4 pieces crosswise. Place on a well-buttered, fireproof dish.

Sauce: Melt the butter in a pan. Add the onion, garlic and the peppers, which have been shredded and blanched. Cook slowly for 8 to 10 minutes. Add the flour, tomato paste and the peas, boiled until tender. Pour on ¾ cup of the liquid from the mussels. Bring slowly to a boil. Add the tomatoes and olives. Pour this over the flounder. Cover with waxed paper and cook in a moderate oven for 35 minutes.

Serving: Arrange the flounder on a dish. Add the mussels in their shells to the sauce and pile up at one end of the dish. Pour over the remaining sauce. Sprinkle with the parsley and serve.

FILET DE SOLE JUDIC
(Sole with Lettuces)

2 heads lettuce	1 1½-pound sole
salt and pepper	juice ½ lemon
½ cup fish stock	1 clove garlic
¼ cup hake	1 slice onion
2 egg whites	few whole peppercorns
2 tablespoons cream	bouquet of herbs
½ cup butter	½ cup white wine
1½ tablespoons flour	¼ cup water
¼ cup milk	½ cup puff paste
	1 whole egg

Lettuces: Remove outside leaves of the lettuce and cut carefully in half. Cover with cold water in a pan and bring to a boil. Strain and dry on a cloth. Place on a well-buttered, fireproof dish. Sprinkle with salt and pepper and cover with the stock and a piece of waxed paper. Cook in a moderate oven for 35 minutes.

Fish Farce: Skin, bone and mince the hake. Put into a bowl and beat in slowly the roughly broken whites of the eggs. Add ¼ teaspoon each of salt and pepper. Beat again and add the cream slowly. (This is best done over a bowl of ice.)

Sauce: Melt some of the butter in a pan. Remove from fire and add the flour, salt and pepper. Stir until smooth, strain and add the fish stock. Thicken over the fire. Add the milk and stir over the fire until boiling. Add remainder of the butter and the cream.

Sole: Skin and fillet; wash and dry. Spread a dessertspoon of farce on the shiny or skinned side of the fillets. Fold over and place on a well-buttered, fireproof dish. Add lemon juice, garlic, onion, whole peppercorns, herbs, wine and water. Cover with the carcass and poach for 20 minutes in a moderate oven.

Puff Paste: Roll out the scraps of puff paste a good ½ inch thick. Cut into crescents and place on a well-watered baking sheet.

Mark on the top with a knife. Brush with beaten whole egg and bake in a hot oven for 20 minutes.

Serving and Glazing: Remove the lettuces from the dish. Dry lightly on a cloth and arrange on a dish for serving. Place a stuffed fillet on top of each lettuce. Pour over the sauce, sprinkle with a little melted butter and glaze under the grill. Surround with crescents of puff paste.

FILET DE SOLE VIN BLANC AUX ASPERGES
(Sole with Cream Sauce and Asparagus)

1 1½-pound sole	*¼ cup butter*
few whole peppercorns	*1½ tablespoons flour*
1 slice onion	*salt and pepper*
1 crushed clove garlic	*¼ cup milk*
1 bay leaf	*2 tablespoons cream*
¼ cup white wine	*1 small bunch asparagus*
¼ cup water	

Sole: Skin and fillet; wash and dry well. Fold over the narrow end of the fillets and place on a well buttered, fireproof dish. Flavor with the whole peppercorns, onion, garlic and bay leaf. Pour over the wine and water, cover with the carcass and poach in a moderate oven for 12 to 15 minutes. Arrange the fillets on a dish for serving and keep warm.

Sauce: Melt 2 tablespoons butter in a small saucepan. Remove from fire and add the flour, salt and pepper. Stir until smooth, strain and add the liquid from the sole and the milk. Stir well over the fire until boiling. Add, bit by bit, 2 tablespoons butter and the cream. Add the tips of the asparagus after they have been cooked until soft in salt water, strained and split in half lengthwise.

Serving: Carefully pour the sauce over the fillets. Sprinkle the fish with a little melted butter and pass under the grill.

SOLE ALEXANDRE
(Sole with Herb and Tomato Sauce)

1 1½-pound sole	*1 clove garlic*
2 tablespoons flour	*1 onion*
salt and pepper	*4 whole peppercorns*
1 egg	*1 teaspoon mixed fresh herbs*
¾ cup bread crumbs	*2 egg yolks*
1 pound firm tomatoes	*1 tablespoon cream*
¾ cup butter	*1 tablespoon finely chopped*
1 teaspoon finely chopped parsley	*tarragon*
2 tablespoons tarragon vinegar	*1 teaspoon meat glaze*

Sole: Bone carefully, keeping it whole. Dust lightly in flour and season. Brush with the beaten egg and roll in white bread crumbs. Fry in deep fat until golden brown and keep warm.

Tomatoes: Skin and cut in quarters; remove pips. Add to 2 tablespoons melted butter, salt and pepper and the parsley. Shake over a low fire for 3 minutes.

Sauce: Put the vinegar in a pan with the garlic, 1 slice onion, the peppercorns and herbs. Reduce to ½ quantity and strain on the beaten egg yolks. Stand in a *bain-marie* and beat in slowly ½ cup butter. Add the cream with 1 tablespoon finely chopped tarragon, garlic, onion and the meat glaze.

Serving: Arrange the tomatoes in the bottom of the dish and place the sole on top. Serve the sauce separately.

FILET DE SOLE À LA MEUNIÈRE
(Fried Sole with Oranges)

2 large oranges	*1 1½-pound sole*
3 large tomatoes	*4 tablespoons butter or fat*
½ cup butter	*5 thin slices streaky bacon*
little flour	*juice ½ lemon*
salt and pepper	*¼ cup dry white wine*
1 teaspoon chopped mixed herbs	

Remove the pith and rind from oranges and cut in sections. Put between 2 plates and keep warm. Skin, quarter and pip the tomatoes, shake over the fire in a little hot butter for 1 to 2 minutes and keep warm. Lightly flour and season the fillets. Heat a frying pan and drop in ¼ cup butter. When butter is frothing, lay in the fillets and fry until golden brown on each side, turning only once. Arrange on a serving dish with a grilled slice of bacon between each fillet, and garnish with the oranges and tomatoes.

Strain the fat from the frying pan, reheat and drop in the remainder of the butter. When frothing quickly add the lemon juice, ¼ cup white wine, herbs, seasoning and boil 1 minute. Pour over the dish and serve at once.

SOLE DURAND
(Sole with Mixed Vegetables)

2 cups carrots, finely sliced	*1 small whole sole*
2 cups turnips, finely sliced	*6 tomatoes*
1 cup onions, finely sliced	*juice ½ lemon*
2 cups white wine	*⅛ cup cream*
handful chopped mixed herbs	*salt and pepper*
½ cup butter or fat	*handful chopped parsley*

Vegetables: Place in a pan the carrots, turnips, onions, 1 cup wine, part of the herbs and a little melted butter. Cover with a piece of waxed paper and cook until dry, without browning.

Sole: Wash, trim and place on a fireproof dish for serving. Put round the vegetable mixture and the tomatoes, which have been skinned, pipped and cut in shreds. Sprinkle well with more of the herbs. Moisten with the remaining wine and cook for 25 minutes in a moderate oven, basting frequently. Take out and strain the liquor into a saucepan.

Sauce: Reduce the liquid from the sole to half quantity. Add a little lemon juice. Beat in the cream very slowly and season well. Bring slowly to a boil. Draw aside and add, bit by bit, the remaining butter and the parsley.

Serving: Pour sauce over the sole and set in a hot oven for 2 to 3 minutes before serving.

FILET DE SOLE MONTROUGE
(Sole on a Purée of Carrot and Potato)

¾ pound carrots	*1 slice onion*
2 potatoes	*1 bay leaf*
salt and pepper	*juice ½ lemon*
1 cup butter or fat	*few peppercorns*
2 egg yolks	*½ cup water*
1 1½-pound sole	*½ cup white wine*
1 clove garlic	*1½ tablespoons flour*
2 tablespoons cream	

Carrot Purée: Cut up ½ pound carrots roughly. Put in pan with the potatoes, also cut up, and cover with cold water. Add salt, pepper and a small lump of butter. Bring slowly to a boil and simmer until tender. Strain, return to the pan and dry a little on the fire. Rub through a fine sieve and work in 2 tablespoons butter, the egg yolks, salt and pepper. Arrange on bottom of dish and keep warm.

Sole: Skin and fillet; wash and dry. Fold over the tail end of the fillet and place, dull-side-up, on a well-buttered, fireproof dish. Add the garlic, onion, bay leaf, lemon juice, peppercorns, water and wine. Cover with the bones of the fish. Poach for 15 minutes in a moderate oven.

Sauce: Melt 3 tablespoons butter in a pan. Add ¼ pound finely shredded carrots, salt and pepper. Cover the pan and cook slowly until nearly soft. Draw aside and add the flour. Stir in the strained liquid from the sole and bring to a boil. Add, bit by bit, more of the butter and the cream.

Serving: Arrange the fillets on top of the purée. Pour over the sauce and serve.

FILET DE SOLE DIEPPOISE
(Sole with Shrimps and Mussels)

1 2½-pound sole	*1 small carrot*
juice ½ lemon	*few whole peppercorns*
¾ cup white wine	*salt and pepper*
1 slice onion	*¾ cup shrimps*
1 clove garlic	*5 tablespoons butter*
bouquet of herbs	*¼ cup cream*
3 cups mussels	*chopped parsley*
1 bay leaf	*1 tablespoon flour*
1 small onion	*1 tablespoon grated cheese*

Sole: Skin and fillet; wash and dry. Turn over the tail ends of the fillets and place on a well-buttered, fireproof dish, skinned-side-up. Pour over lemon juice, ½ cup wine and water. Add the slice of onion, garlic, herbs and pepper. Cover with waxed paper and poach for 15 minutes in a moderate oven. Put the fillets on a plate and keep warm.

Mussels: Wash well and put in a pan with the bay leaf, garlic and cut-up onion and carrot, a few peppercorns, salt and pepper. Add ¼ cup white wine and a little water. Bring slowly to a boil and shake over the fire for 3 to 4 minutes. Strain, shell and remove the beards from the mussels. Add with the shrimps to 1 tablespoon of melted butter, 2 tablespoons cream and a sprinkling of chopped parsley with salt and pepper. Shake over the fire a few minutes.

Sauce: Strain the liquor into a pan and reduce to 1 cup. Pour on to the following *roux:* Melt 2 tablespoons butter in a pan. Remove from the fire and add the flour. Season and pour on the stock. Stir over the fire until the sauce comes to a boil and add, bit by bit, the rest of the butter and 2 tablespoons cream. Simmer for 3 to 4 minutes.

Serving: Arrange the fillets on a dish. Scatter the mussels and the shrimps on the top and pour over the sauce. Sprinkle with grated cheese and glaze under the grill.

FILETS DE SOLE ALSACIENNE
(Sole with Cabbage)

2 ¾-pound sole	½ cup butter
1 tablespoon lemon juice	salt and pepper
½ cup water	2 tablespoons red wine
1 clove garlic	1 tablespoon flour
few whole peppercorns	1 cup milk
1 slice onion	handful grated cheese
1 small cabbage	2 tablespoons cream

Sole: Fillet and skin; wash and dry. Lay on a well-buttered, fireproof dish. Add the lemon juice, water, garlic, peppercorns and onion. Cover with the bones and poach for 15 minutes in a moderate oven.

Cabbage: Cut in quarters and remove the stalk. Shred very fine and soak in lemon juice and water for half an hour. Blanch, strain and add 4 tablespoons melted butter, salt, pepper and wine. Cover the pan with waxed paper and the lid; simmer until tender without browning.

Sauce: Melt 2 tablespoons butter in a pan. Remove from the fire and add the flour, salt and pepper. Pour on the milk and stir over the fire until it comes to a boil. Add 3 tablespoons grated cheese, a little more butter, the strained liquid from the sole reduced to 2 tablespoons, and the cream.

Serving: Arrange the cabbage on the bottom of the dish. Place the sole on top and cover entirely with the sauce. Sprinkle with remaining grated cheese and brown under the grill.

SOLE COLBERT
(Boned Fried Sole)

4 sole or flounder or gray sole	1 egg
juice ½ lemon	handful white bread crumbs
little flour	3 or 4 tablespoons oil
salt and pepper	handful fresh parsley

Split the sole carefully and remove skin and bones. Wash well in lemon juice and water and dry. Dust with flour and seasoning, brush with the beaten egg and roll in bread crumbs. Fry in hot oil until golden brown. Arrange on a hot serving dish. Garnish with the fresh parsley and serve with Maître d'Hôtel Sauce.

SOLE JULIETTE
(Sole with Eggplant and Tomato)

1 sole	*4 or 5 tomatoes*
salt and pepper	*handful chopped parsley*
¼ cup white wine	*3 tablespoons flour*
¼ pound mushrooms	*cayenne pepper*
1 eggplant	*1 cup milk*
½ cup butter	*2 tablespoons cream*

2 tablespoons finely chopped fried onion

Fillet and skin the sole; wash and dry. Lay the fillet on a long baking dish. Season and pour over the wine. Add the mushrooms and cover with the carcass. Bake for 20 to 30 minutes.

Slice the eggplant diagonally. Sprinkle with salt water, leave 15 minutes and drain. Flour and fry in plenty of butter. Cut some of the tomatoes in half, squeeze out the seeds, cut in small pieces, dust with salt and pepper and saute in butter. Lay the eggplant on a long dish, place the fillets with the mushrooms on top. Pour over the following sauce, garnish round with little heaps of the tomatoes sprinkled with the parsley, and serve.

Sauce: Melt in a pan 2 tablespoons butter, stir in 3 level tablespoons flour, salt, cayenne pepper, pour on 1 cup milk and stir over the fire until the sauce comes to a boil. Add 2 tablespoons finely chopped fried onion, cream, and the stock from the fish reduced to 2 tablespoons.

SOLE AU FOUR MAISON
(Baked Sole)

1 plain sole
3 tablespoons butter or fat
2 small carrots, finely shredded
salt and pepper
¼ cup finely sliced mushrooms
2 tablespoons flour

¾ cup fish stock
½ cup milk
¼ cup cream
1 tablespoon grated cheese
handful brown bread crumbs
handful chopped parsley

Remove both skins and trim off outer scales of sole. Wash and dry. Place on a well-buttered, fireproof dish.

Melt some butter or fat in a pan and add the carrots. Season and cook very slowly until the carrots are soft without browning. Add the mushrooms and cook for another minute. Add the flour and a little more seasoning. Pour on the fish stock and thicken over the fire. Add the milk and bring to a boil. Add the cream and the cheese. Simmer for a few minutes.

Pour over the sauce and sprinkle the top with a little more grated cheese and a few bread crumbs. Put on top a few tiny lumps of butter and bake for 25 minutes in a moderate oven. Sprinkle top with the chopped parsley and serve.

FILETS DE SOLE GEORGETTE
(Sole in Baked Potatoes)

4 or 5 oval potatoes
½ cup shrimps or prawns
3 tablespoons butter or fat
salt and pepper

handful chopped parsley
3 tablespoons cream
béchamel sauce
4 or 5 fillets of sole

white wine

Potatoes: Scrub the potatoes well. Prick and bake in a moderate oven until soft.

Shrimps: Toss the shrimps or prawns in 1 tablespoon hot butter or fat. Season with pepper and chopped parsley and add the cream. Simmer for 2 or 3 minutes.

Sauce Nantua: Pound the shells of the shrimps or prawns with 2 tablespoons butter or fat. Pass through a fine sieve. Add pepper and a light, creamy béchamel sauce. Simmer for 2 or 3 minutes.

Serving: Cut off the top of each potato and scoop out some of the potato meat. Place the shrimp mixture in the bottom of each. Lay a fillet of sole that has been folded and poached in white wine on top of the shrimps. Coat with Sauce Nantua and replace the top of the potato. Serve on a napkin with a bouquet of parsley in the center of the dish.

SOLE AU GRATIN

2 sole or whitings	*1 teaspoon tomato paste*
2 tablespoons oil	*salt and pepper*
2 roughly cut carrots	*1½ cups stock*
2 roughly cut onions	*¼ cup white wine*
1 tablespoon flour	*½ cup finely chopped mushrooms*
1 roughly cut tomato	*2 tablespoons butter*
1 handful mushroom peelings	*1 tablespoon bread crumbs*
and stalks	*1 tablespoon grated cheese*
	1 sliced lemon

Sole: Wash and dry the fish. Score well. Lay on a well-buttered, fireproof dish.

Demi-Glacé Sauce: Heat the oil in a pan; add the carrot and onion and brown slowly. Add the flour and brown also. Add the tomato, mushroom peelings and stalks, tomato paste, salt and pepper. Pour on the stock and bring slowly to a boil. Simmer for 20 minutes. Add the wine, reduced to half quantity. Strain onto the mushrooms, which have been cooked in a little butter.

Cooking and Serving of Sole: Pour sauce over the sole. Sprinkle the bread crumbs and grated cheese over the fish. Cook in a fairly hot oven for 15 minutes. Remove and garnish with a few slices of lemon.

SOLE ALBERT
(Sole with Oysters and Mushrooms)

1 small chicken turbot (or sole)   *2 cups large mussels*
1 cup butter   *2 bay leaves*
handful grated cheese   *1 cup water*
1 finely sliced onion   *8 to 10 oysters*
1 finely sliced carrot   *juice ½ lemon*
1 finely sliced clove garlic   *1 cup small firm white mushrooms*
1 large sprig parsley   *½ cup skinned shrimps*
few peppercorns   *½ cup milk*
salt and pepper   *2 or 3 tablespoons cooking cream*
1 cup good white wine   *paprika*

Turbot or Sole: Place the turbot in a flat, fireproof dish. Pour over a little melted butter, grated cheese, and hold under a hot grill for a few minutes. Scatter the onion, carrot and garlic over the top. Add a large scrap of parsley, a few peppercorns, and salt to season. Pour over the wine. Cover with buttered paper and bake in a moderate oven for 30 minutes.

Mussels: Scrub the mussels well. Put them in a pan with the bay leaves, salt and pepper and 1 cup water. Bring to a boil. Simmer for 3 minutes. Remove mussels from shells, remove beards, and discard. Keep warm in a little hot butter.

Oysters: Remove oysters from shells and cook for 3 minutes in a little lemon juice and water, a small lump of butter and seasoning. Add the mushrooms, sautéed in a little butter and seasoning for 3 minutes. To prepare 6 small bouchée cases, roll out puff paste (see p. 260) ¼ inch thick. Cut in small rounds with a fluted cutter. Place on a wet cooky sheet. Brush with beaten egg. Bake in a hot oven 10 to 15 minutes. Remove and fill with the shrimps mixed with a little of the turbot sauce. Strain turbot and mussel stock through a fine strainer and reduce it by boiling to 1 cup in quantity. Melt 3 tablespoons of butter in a pan and season with salt and pepper. Pour on reduced fish stock and thicken over the fire. Pour on ½ cup milk and bring to a boil. Add 2 or 3 tablespoons cooking cream and, bit by bit, 4 tablespoons of shrimp butter.

Shrimp Butter: Take the head and tail shells of the shrimps and pound in a wooden bowl; then add 5 tablespoons soft butter, salt, pepper and a little paprika. Pound well together and rub through a fine hair sieve.

Serve: Surround top of dish with the filled bouchée cases and in between little heaps of the mussels, oysters and mushrooms.

SOLE MARGUÉRY

1 1½-pound sole	*2 cups large mussels*
½ cup white wine	*½ cup picked, skinned shrimps*
½ cup water	*5 tablespoons butter or fat*
1 bay leaf	*1½ tablespoons flour*
1 slice onion	*salt and pepper*
few whole peppercorns	*2 tablespoons cream*

Sole: Wash and dry. Remove head and trim off outer scales. Skin both sides and place in a well-buttered, fireproof dish. Pour over the wine, water, bay leaf, onion and whole peppercorns. Cover with waxed paper and poach for 20 to 25 minutes in a moderate oven.

Mussels: Wash well in cold water and put in a pan. Strain and pour on the liquid from the sole. Bring slowly to a boil and shake over the fire for a few minutes. Shell the mussels and remove the beards.

Shrimps: Wash well. Warm in a little melted butter and seasoning.

Sauce: Melt 2 tablespoons butter in a pan. Add the flour, seasoning and 1 cup of the mussel stock. Stir over the fire until the sauce comes to a boil. Add the cream and, bit by bit, the remaining butter.

Serving: Arrange the sole on a dish. Scatter the mussels and shrimps over the top. Pour over the sauce. Sprinkle with a little more melted butter and glaze under the grill.

FILETS DE SOLE VERDUETTE
(Sole with Herbs)

8 fillets of sole	1/3 cup dried mushrooms
juice of 2 lemons	3 tablespoons oil
little flour	handful chopped chives
salt and pepper	1 chopped onion
1 egg	handful chopped parsley
handful bread crumbs	little chervil
5 tablespoons butter or fat	little tarragon

Wash the fillets in lemon juice and water and dry in a cloth. Dust with flour and season well. Brush with the beaten egg and roll in the bread crumbs. Heat the butter until it is clear. Cook the fillets in it until they are golden brown on each side. Arrange on a hot serving dish.

Strain the dried mushrooms, which have been soaked for 3 hours, or overnight. Add to the oil, which has been heated in a pan with a bit of chives and chopped onion. Cook slowly until nearly soft. Drain off the oil. Add a small lump of butter, the parsley, chervil and tarragon. Cook for a few minutes. Add a little lemon juice and scatter a little lemon juice over the sole just before serving.

SOLE FLORENTINE
(Sole with Spinach)

4 sole	1/2 cup thick cream
juice 2 lemons	freshly ground black pepper
9 tablespoons butter	3 level tablespoons flour
salt	1 1/2 cups milk
freshly ground white pepper	3 level tablespoons grated Parmesan
1 1/2 pounds spinach	cheese
1/4 cup water	

Remove and discard the heads of the sole. Wash the sole carefully in little lemon juice and water and place with skin and bones intact on a fireproof dish. Pour on the juice of 1 lemon mixed with 3 tablespoons melted butter and salt and freshly ground white pepper to season. Cover with buttered paper and poach in a moderate oven for 20 minutes.

Wash spinach well. Melt 3 tablespoons butter in a pan with seasoning. Turn spinach a few times and simmer for 5 to 6 minutes. Drain and dry very well. Mix spinach with ¼ cup thick cream and a little freshly ground black pepper. Place on the bottom of a flat, fireproof dish and put the sole on top.

Melt 3 tablespoons butter in a pan; season and add the flour. Remove from the fire and add the milk. Bring to a boil, stirring well. Add 3 tablespoons grated cheese, 2 tablespoons cream, and a small lump of butter. Simmer for 5 minutes. Pour over the sole and spinach. Sprinkle with a little more cheese and a few very small lumps of butter and brown under the grill.

FILETS DE SOLE CENTRILLON
(Sole with White Wine Sauce)

4 medium-sized, oval potatoes	*¼ cup white wine*
1 cup butter	*1 bay leaf*
½ cup hot milk	*4 teaspoons tomato paste*
salt and pepper	*1½ tablespoons flour*
4 fillets of sole	*¼ cup fish stock*
¼ cup water	*¼ cup milk*

1 teaspoon cream

Prick the potatoes and bake until soft. Cut the tops off and scoop out the insides. Rub potato through a sieve and beat in a little butter, hot milk, and seasoning. Keep warm.

Remove skin from the fillets. Wash and dry, fold in half, and place on buttered, fireproof dish. Pour over the water and wine. Add seasoning and the bay leaf. Cover with the bones of the fish and a piece of waxed paper and cook for 15 minutes in a moderate oven. Put 1 teaspoon tomato paste in the bottom of each potato skin and a fillet of sole on top. Pour 1 teaspoon White Wine Sauce on top of each fillet and cover with the cap of the potato. Arrange on a hot serving dish and serve at once.

White Wine Sauce: Melt 2 tablespoons butter. Season and stir in the flour. Strain on the fish stock and thicken over the fire. Add ¼ cup milk and bring to a boil. Add the cream and use.

FILET DE SOLE SYLVETTE
(Sole with Mirepoix of Vegetables)

1 1½-pound sole
½ cup white wine
¼ cup water
1 slice onion
1 clove garlic
bouquet of herbs
few whole peppercorns
2 leeks, finely diced
¼ cup French beans, finely diced
2 carrots, finely diced

2 stalks celery, finely diced
2 onions, finely diced
½ cup butter or fat
salt and pepper
2 tablespoons Madeira
¼ pound mushrooms diced
5 small firm tomatoes
¼ pound boiled hake or cod
4 tablespoons cream
1 tablespoon flour

½ cup milk

Sole: Skin, bone, wash and dry the sole. Place on well-buttered, fireproof dish. Pour over wine, water, slice of onion, garlic, herbs and whole peppercorns. Cover with the carcass and poach for 15 minutes in a moderate oven.

Mirepoix: Mix the leeks, beans, carrots, celery and onions and add 3 tablespoons melted butter, salt and pepper. Cover with waxed paper and lid and cook 5 minutes. Place in a moderate oven for 15 minutes. Remove and add the Madeira and the mushrooms, cooked in a little butter for 5 minutes. Keep warm.

Tomatoes: Skin, cut off the tops, and carefully remove the pips without breaking. Pour in each a little melted butter, salt and pepper. Cook in a slow oven for 5 minutes.

Fish: Cook the hake or cod; skin, bone, and mince. Add salt and pepper. Heat in 2 tablespoons cream and a small lump of butter. Fill the tomatoes and set in the oven for 5 minutes.

Sauce: Melt in a pan 1 tablespoon butter. Remove from the fire and add the flour. Season and stir until smooth. Pour on the milk. Stir over the fire until the sauce comes to a boil. Add 2 tablespoons cream, 2 tablespoons butter and the fish stock reduced to 3 tablespoons.

Serving: Arrange the fillets on a dish. Scatter over the mirepoix. Arrange around with the stuffed tomatoes and pour over the sauce.

FILETS DE SOLE NAVAROFF
(Sole with Crab Meat)

2 small turbots (or sole)	salt and pepper
juice ½ lemon	1½ cups water
1 cup butter	½ cup cooking white wine
1 sliced onion	1 small crab
1 sliced carrot	cayenne pepper
1 sliced stick celery	4 or 6 tablespoons cream
1 sprig thyme	3 tablespoons flour
1 sprig parsley	½ cup fish stock
1 bay leaf	½ cup milk
6 mixed peppercorns	2 tablespoons Parmesan cheese

Remove the fillets from the turbots, leaving the skins on, and soak in a little lemon juice and water for 2 hours. Melt a lump of butter in a deep pan. Sauté the onion, carrot and celery a few minutes. Add the fish carcasses, the thyme, parsley, bay leaf, peppercorns, salt, 1½ cups water, and wine. Bring to a boil and simmer down to half quantity. Strain and pour over the fillets, which have been dried and arranged on a flat, fireproof dish. Cover with buttered paper and poach in a moderate oven for 20 minutes.

Remove meat from the crab and add to it a lump of melted butter, salt, black pepper, cayenne and 2 or 3 tablespoons cream. Heat gently. Spread this on the bottom of a hot serving dish. Arrange the fillets of turbot on top.

Melt 2 tablespoons butter in a pan, season with salt and pepper and stir in the flour. Strain and add ½ cup fish stock. Thicken over the fire. Add the milk and bring to a boil. Stir in the cheese, 2 or 3 tablespoons cream and, bit by bit, 2 tablespoons butter. Simmer slowly for 4 or 5 minutes. Pour over the fish. Sprinkle over the top a little more grated cheese and mark crisscross on the top with a red-hot skewer.

FILET DE SOLE VÉRONIQUE
(Sole with White Grapes)

1 1½-pound sole	¼ cup water
2 slices onion	5 tablespoons butter
1 clove garlic	1½ tablespoons flour
juice ½ lemon	salt and pepper
few whole peppercorns	¼ cup milk
bouquet of herbs	2 tablespoons cream
1 bay leaf	½ pound white grapes
1 cup white wine	1 tablespoon chopped parsley

Sole: Fillet after skinning; wash and dry. Fold under the 2 ends and place in a well-buttered, fireproof dish. Add the onions, garlic, lemon juice, whole peppercorns, herbs, bay leaf, white wine and water. Cover with the carcass and poach in a moderate oven for 15 minutes. Place the fillets on a dish for serving and keep warm.

Sauce: Melt in a pan 2 tablespoons butter. Remove from fire and add the flour, salt and pepper. Stir until smooth. Strain and pour on ¾ cup of the liquid from the sole. Thicken over the fire. Add the milk and stir over the fire until the sauce comes to a boil. Add the cream and 2 tablespoons butter.

Grapes: Pour boiling water over the grapes. Then skin and pip. Add 1 tablespoon melted butter, salt, pepper and the parsley. Shake over a slow fire until warm.

Serving: Coat the fillets with the sauce and arrange the grapes at one end. Serve the rest of the sauce in a separate dish.

MOUSSE DE SOLE

1 pound sole	6 tablespoons butter
½ cup white bread crumbs	2 tablespoons flour
2 egg whites	¾ cup fish stock
¾ cup heavy cream	peppercorns
salt and pepper	¼ cup dry white wine
¾ cup water	

Skin and bone the sole and put twice through a fine meat grinder. Add the bread crumbs which have been soaked in a little milk and well dried. Slowly beat in the egg whites. Rub through a sieve and put in a bowl over another bowl of cracked ice. Beat in slowly 8 or 9 tablespoons cream. Season well with salt and pepper. Butter a mold and fill with this mousse. Steam slowly for 25 to 30 minutes; then turn out on a serving dish and pour over a Velouté Sauce.

Velouté Sauce: Melt 3 tablespoons butter and stir in 2 tablespoons flour. Add the fish stock and bring to a boil. Add, bit by bit, 3 tablespoons butter and 2 or 3 tablespoons cream. Pour over the mousse and serve.

Note: it is very good to add 1 teaspoon of finely chopped truffle to the mousse.

Note: the fish stock can be made with the skin and bones of the sole put in a pan with ¼ cup dry white wine, ¾ cup water, salt, peppercorns and a bay leaf. Bring to a boil and simmer down to ¾ cup, strain and use.

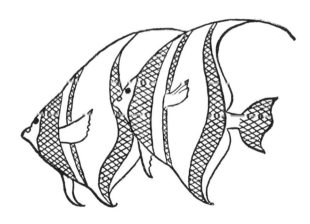

MERLUCHE MAISON
(Cod with Duchess Potatoes and Tomatoes)

2 small fresh haddocks
½ cup red wine
¼ cup water
1 bay leaf
1 clove garlic
salt and pepper
7 tablespoons butter or fat
2 medium onions, finely sliced
1 green pepper

1 red pepper
1 tablespoon flour
½ cup milk
2 tablespoons cream
8 small tomatoes
2 tablespoons grated cheese
1 pound potatoes
pinch French mustard
2 egg yolks

Haddocks: Skin and fillet. Fold in half and place on a well-buttered, fireproof dish. Add the wine, water, bay leaf, garlic and seasoning. Cover with well-buttered paper and poach for 20 minutes in a moderate oven.

Sauce: Melt in a pan 3 tablespoons butter and add the onions. Simmer for 4 minutes without browning; add the peppers, which have been blanched for 3 minutes and finely shredded. Add the flour and seasoning and stir until smooth. Add ¾ cup liquid from the haddocks. Thicken and add ¼ cup milk. Bring to a boil, stirring all the time. Add the cream, 4 tomatoes, pipped and shredded, 1 tablespoon grated cheese and a pinch French mustard. Cover and keep warm.

Pommes Mousselines: Skin and boil the potatoes in salted water until tender. Strain and dry over the fire. Rub through a fine sieve and beat in 2 egg yolks, 2 tablespoons milk and a small lump of butter. Beat for at least 5 minutes.

Tomatoes: Skin and scoop out the pips of remaining tomatoes. Season with salt and pepper and fill with a little of the Pommes Mousselines from a pastry bag with a rose pipe. Sprinkle the tops with a little grated cheese and brown under the grill.

Serving: Pile up with a little of the Pommes Mousselines on a dish. Arrange the fillets on the top. Pour over the sauce and arrange the tomatoes around.

COQUILLES ST. JACQUES EN ESCALOPES
(Baked Scallops)

2 scallops per person
½ cup good dry white wine
salt and pepper
small lump butter

2 tablespoons melted butter
1 cup cream per 4 scallops
handful bread crumbs

Open scallops by putting them in the oven for a few minutes. Remove the black frill. Put the wine in a pan, adding to it salt, pepper and a little water before adding the scallop meat. Drain and cut the scallops in thin slices. Put them in a pan with the melted butter. Cook very gently for about 4 minutes. Season well and add the cream. Mix well. Fill the deep shells, which have been well scrubbed out. Sprinkle thickly with fine bread crumbs. Put a lump of butter on top of each and brown quickly under the grill.

COQUILLES ST. JACQUES PROVENÇAL
(Scallops with Dried Mushrooms)

4 scallops
5 tablespoons butter
salt and pepper
1 tablespoon chopped onion
4 tablespoons cèpes
(dry wood mushrooms)

2 tomatoes
1 tablespoon white wine
1 teaspoon chopped chives
1 clove garlic
handful grated cheese

Wash the scallops well. Add to 3 tablespoons melted butter, salt, pepper and the chopped onion and sauté very gently for 5 to 6 minutes. Remove and arrange on croutons of fried bread on a hot serving dish.

Soak the cèpes overnight. Strain and sauté in 2 tablespoons butter, salt and pepper for 10 minutes. Add the tomatoes, white wine, a little extra seasoning, the chopped chives and garlic. Simmer for another 6 to 7 minutes. Add the liquid from the scallops and pour over the dish. Sprinkle the top with the cheese and butter, brown quickly under the grill and serve.

COQUILLES ST. JACQUES CHAPON FIN
(Scallops with Mushrooms and Tomatoes)

4 scallops	1 sprig parsley
juice ½ lemon	¼ pound sliced mushrooms
½ cup white wine	½ cup butter
¼ cup fish stock or water	3 skinned, pipped, shredded tomatoes
salt and pepper	1½ tablespoons flour
1 bay leaf	2 tablespoons cream
1 sliced onion	handful grated Parmesan cheese
few whole peppercorns	handful bread crumbs

Wash the scallops well in lemon juice and water. Put in a pan and pour over the wine and the water or fish stock. Bring to a boil and simmer for 6 minutes with salt and pepper, the bay leaf, 1 sliced onion, the peppercorns and parsley. Remove the scallops and cut in slices. Mix with the mushrooms, which have been sautéed in a little butter, and the tomatoes.

Melt 2 tablespoons butter and stir in the flour. Strain on fish stock and bring to a boil. Add the cream and mix into the mushrooms, scallops and tomatoes. Fill the shells and sprinkle the top with the grated cheese and bread crumbs. Dot with a few small lumps of butter. Brown under the grill. Surround with a good potato purée applied through a forcing bag with a rose pipe and serve.

COQUILLES ST. JACQUES EN BROCHETTES
(Scallops and Mushrooms on a Skewer)

6 scallops	½ cup grated cheese
salt and pepper	1 cup butter
3 bay leaves	1 dessertspoon salad oil
2 or 3 rashers smoked bacon	½ chopped onion
½ cup flour	½ cup rice
1 beaten egg	1 cup stock
handful white bread crumbs	1 level teaspoon saffron

Poach the scallops for 5 minutes in a little water with seasoning and 1 bay leaf. Strain off the water and wrap the white part of the scallops in very thin rashers of smoked bacon. Lightly flour the coral; brush with beaten egg; roll in white bread crumbs mixed with a little grated cheese. Secure these on little wooden or iron skewers, pour over melted butter and grill.

Melt 2 tablespoons butter in a pan, add the salad oil and the onion. Cook for a few minutes; then add the rice. Cover with stock and bring to a boil, after seasoning well and adding the saffron and 2 bay leaves. Cover with greaseproof paper and a lid and cook for 25 minutes in a moderate oven. Remove and stir in with a fork 3 tablespoons butter and 1 heaping teaspoon grated cheese. Arrange on the bottom of a serving dish, place scallops on top and serve.

COQUILLES ST. JACQUES CARDINAL
(Scallops with Lobster Sauce)

4 large scallops	1/2 cup sliced mushrooms
1/2 cup white wine	2 tablespoons butter or fat
bouquet of herbs	1 1/2 tablespoons flour
salt and pepper	2 tablespoons cream
8 oysters	1 egg yolk
1/2 cup fish stock	2 or 3 skinned, thinly sliced tomatoes
	handful grated cheese

Put the scallops in a pan, pour on the wine and add the herbs, salt and pepper. Bring to a boil and simmer for 5 to 6 minutes. Remove the scallops, slice and keep warm.

Remove the oysters from their shells and put in a pan. Cover with the fish stock and bring to a boil. Strain and add the oysters to the sliced scallops. Add the mushrooms cooked in a little butter and keep warm.

Melt 2 tablespoons butter or fat and stir in the flour. Add the strained stock from the mushrooms and bring to a boil. Reduce the stock the scallops were cooked in to 1 tablespoon and add with the cream mixed into the egg yolk. Simmer a few minutes and mix into scallops, oysters and mushrooms. Fill the scallop shells. Cover tops with overlapping slices of tomatoes. Sprinkle well with the cheese and brown very quickly under the grill.

COQUILLES ST. JACQUES À LA SUCHET
(Scallops with Carrots)

4 scallops
1 small onion, cut up
1 clove garlic, cut up
bouquet of fresh herbs, cut up
salt and pepper
½ cup white wine
½ cup water

3 hard-boiled eggs, cut in quarters
4 tablespoons butter or fat
½ pound finely shredded carrots
2 tablespoons flour
¼ cup cream
3 tablespoons grated cheese
1 tablespoon bread crumbs

If scallops are shut, place in a warm oven for few moments to open. Remove from shells and wash well in salted water. Place in a saucepan with the onion, garlic, herbs, salt and pepper. Add the wine and water and bring slowly to a boil. Simmer for 5 minutes. Remove and cut each scallop in 4 or 5 pieces. Place the eggs and scallops together and keep warm between 2 plates.

Melt 3 tablespoons butter or fat in a saucepan. Remove from the fire and add the carrots, salt and pepper. Cover the pan with waxed paper and the lid and cook very slowly for 10 to 15 minutes, stirring occasionally. Remove from the fire and add the flour; stir until smooth. Strain the stock in which the scallops were cooked and add. Stir over the fire until the mixture comes to a boil and add the cream. Mix with the hard-boiled eggs and the scallops.

Scrape and wash the scallop shells. Fill them with the mixture and sprinkle the top of each with the cheese and bread crumbs. Pour over 1 tablespoon melted butter. Brown under the grill and serve.

COQUILLES ST. JACQUES À LA MORNAY
(Scallops with Cheese)

6 large scallops
juice ½ lemon
salt and pepper
3 tablespoons butter
1 bay leaf

1½ tablespoons flour
¾ cup milk
2 tablespoons cream
4 tablespoons grated cheese
handful freshly chopped parsley

Wash the scallops well in lemon juice and water. Put in a pan and pour over a little water, seasoning, 1 tablespoon butter and the bay leaf. Bring slowly to a boil and simmer for 5 minutes. Remove the coral of the scallop; cut the white part in slices.

Melt 2 tablespoons butter and stir in the flour and seasoning. Pour on the milk and bring to a boil. Reduce the liquor in which the scallops were cooked to 1 tablespoon and add the cream and 3 tablespoons cheese. Simmer for 3 to 4 minutes.

Mix into the sliced scallops and fill the shells. Sprinkle tops well with grated cheese and brown quickly under the grill. Place on top the coral of the scallops, sprinkle with freshly chopped parsley and serve.

COQUILLES ST. JACQUES POULETTE
(Baked Scallops)

4 large scallops	*¼ cup white wine*
juice ½ lemon	*4 tablespoons butter*
1 slice onion	*1½ tablespoons flour*
1 bay leaf	*salt and pepper*
few whole peppercorns	*2 tablespoons cream*
½ cup mushrooms	*1 egg yolk*
1½ cups fish stock	*handful chopped parsley*

Wash the scallops well in lemon juice and water and put them in a pan with the onion, bay leaf, and peppercorns. Add the mushrooms, 1 cup fish stock and wine. Bring to a boil and simmer for 5 minutes. Remove and slice the scallops; keep warm.

Melt 2 tablespoons butter in a pan and stir in the flour. Add ½ cup strained fish stock and bring to a boil, seasoning well. Reduce the stock the scallops have been cooked in to 2 tablespoons and add with the cream mixed into the egg yolk. Stir over the fire until the mixture thickens without boiling. Add a squeeze of lemon juice and, bit by bit, 2 tablespoons butter. Mix this into the sliced scallops. Fill shells, sprinkle with the parsley and serve.

SCALLOPS WITH LOBSTER AND MUSTARD SAUCE

1½ pounds fresh water scallops
1 bay leaf
peppercorns
½ cup dry wine
salt
1 cup mushrooms

1 tablespoon butter
2 tablespoons flour
1 dessertspoon dry mustard
cayenne pepper
strained liquor
¾ cup creamy milk

meat of lobster

Put the scallops in a pan with the bay leaf, peppercorns, wine and salt, and bring slowly to a boil. Drain and, if large. cut in two; then add the mushrooms, sliced and sautéed. Mix into the following: —

Sauce: Melt butter, stir in flour, mustard, salt and cayenne pepper; then pour on strained liquor in which the scallops were cooked, thicken a little over the fire and add milk. Bring to a boil and add the lobster meat, which has been boiled, cut in pieces and tossed in hot butter. Mix with the scallops, fill into shells, sprinkle with crumbs and grated cheese, dot with butter, and brown under the broiler. Garnish with whole, sautéed mushroom.

DEMOISELLES DE CAEN
(Lobster with Cod)

2 live 1-pound lobsters
2 tablespoons oil
large lump butter
2 slip soles
¼ pound hake
2 egg whites
5 tablespoons cream

salt and pepper
onion
mushrooms
1 small shredded tomato
2 tablespoons dry white wine
2 egg yolks
4 tablespoons lobster butter

Split the lobsters and remove the bag from the heads. Remove and crack the claws. Lay the claws together in a pan in which has been heated 2 tablespoons oil and a large lump of butter. Cover and shake over a brisk fire for 2 to 3 minutes. Then put in the oven for 10 to 15 minutes. Take out, remove the meat from the claws and cut into scallops.

Spread the skin side of 2 slip soles, filleted and skinned, with the following Fish Mousse: —

Fish Mousse: Mince the ¼ pound hake and beat in 2 whites of eggs. Add 3 tablespoons cream and season. Roll up the fillets and poach in the usual way. Prepare a salpicon of onion and mushrooms cooked in butter. Add a little shredded tomato after 5 minutes, and a little dry white wine, reduced from 2 tablespoons to 1. Fill this mixture into the body of the lobster shells and lay the poached fillets in the heads. Cover with a Mousseline Sauce and serve at once.

Mousseline Sauce: Put the 2 yolks of eggs in a basin; pour on the reduced fish and lobster stock. Stand in a *bain-marie,* and whisk until thickened with 2 tablespoons cream. Then add 4 tablespoons lobster butter.

HOMARD CHEZ SOI
(Lobsters with Eels)

1 large lobster
6 tablespoons fat
1 small eel
1 large onion, thinly sliced
bouquet of herbs (parsley,
*   thyme, bay leaf)*
2 cloves garlic
salt
cayenne pepper

¾ cup claret
8 firm mushrooms
2 tablespoons oil
lemon juice
little sliced carrot and celery
4 tablespoons flour
1 teaspoon tomato paste
1 tablespoon red currant jelly
handful chopped chives

Cook lobster as in the recipe for Mayonnaise d'Homard I (p. 106). Remove and cut up the meat in large pieces. Cover and keep warm in a little hot fat. Cut the eel in 6 pieces. Heat a little fat in a shallow stewpan, add ¾ of the onion and cook for 1 minute. Put in the eel, bouquet of herbs, garlic, salt and cayenne pepper. Pour on the claret. Cover and cook slowly for 25 minutes. Remove the eel and add it to the lobster with the mushrooms, which have been cooked in a little oil and lemon juice. Cover and keep warm.

Strain the liquid in which the eel was cooked. Add to it ¾ cup of stock the lobster was cooked in. Heat 2 tablespoons fat in a thick pan. Add the remaining onion and the carrot and celery. Brown slowly; then add the flour and brown that to a dark color very slowly. Add a few chopped mushroom stalks and cook for 1 minute. Add the tomato paste and pour on the eel stock. Stir over the fire until it comes to a boil; add a bay leaf, a little crushed garlic and the jelly. Boil this down to a creamy consistency and strain.

Arrange lobster and eel in a shallow serving dish and pour over the sauce. Sprinkle the top with the chives and serve.

HOMARD VILLEROY
(Lobster with Mustard Sauce)

4 tablespoons oil	*¼ cup dry white wine*
1 small sliced onion	*2 large live lobsters*
1 small sliced carrot	*10 tablespoons butter or fat*
1 sliced stalk celery	*2 cups firm white mushrooms*
2 cups water	*lemon juice*
1 bay leaf	*4 large egg yolks*
salt	*1 dessertspoon French or German mustard*
cayenne pepper	*handful grated Parmesan cheese*

Heat the oil, add the onion, carrot and celery and cook for 1 to 2 minutes until golden brown. Pour on 2 cups water, add the bay leaf and seasoning and bring to a boil with the white wine. Boil for 15 to 20 minutes.

Cool lobsters in this liquid for 15 minutes. Remove and cool a little. Split down the center of the back and carefully remove meat from the tails. Cut into scallops and put scalloped meat in a pan. Pour over a little melted butter, season and keep warm. Wash and cut the mushrooms in thick slices without skinning. Add lemon juice. Sauté in a little butter, add the cut-up meat from the claws and the liver of the lobsters, and mix with a little mustard sauce.

Fill the bottom of the lobster shells with this mixture and place on a hot serving dish. Carefully arrange on top the scallops of lobster meat overlapping and pour over the mustard sauce.

Mustard Sauce: Boil down the stock the lobster was cooked in to ½ cup and pour it on the egg yolks. Place in a double boiler and beat well until it begins to thicken and coats the back of a spoon. Add, bit by bit, the remaining butter and the mustard. Strain through a fine strainer and cover the lobsters with this sauce. Sprinkle with grated Parmesan cheese and brown under the broiler.

MAYONNAISE D'HOMARD I
(Cold Lobster with Mayonnaise)

2 live 1-pound lobsters	½ cup sliced French beans
3 tablespoons butter	1 teaspoon sugar
1 sliced onion	½ tablespoon French mustard
3 carrots, 1 sliced	1 teaspoon lemon juice
1 sliced stalk celery	1½ cups salad oil
1 sliced leek	2 egg yolks
salt and pepper	1 tablespoon tomato ketchup
3 cups water	1 tablespoon Lea and Perrin's Sauce
2 tablespoons vinegar	¼ cup cream
5 tablespoons Carolina rice	paprika
½ cucumber, skinned and diced	handful water cress

Wash the lobsters well in cold water. Melt the butter and add the onion, 1 sliced carrot, the celery, leek and seasoning. Cook for 5 minutes without browning. Then pour on the water and 1 tablespoon vinegar. Bring slowly to a boil and when just bubbling put in the lobsters. Cover and simmer gently for 10 to 15 minutes; let cool in the stock. (This stock is excellent and can be used for other things, fish sauce, etc.) Split the lobsters and carefully remove the meat from the tail and claws.

Cook the rice in boiling salted water for 10 minutes. Strain and wash well in cold water. Add the cucumber, 2 carrots and the beans. Simmer until soft without being mushy in boiling salted water; strain and cool.

Put the sugar, ½ teaspoon salt, ½ teaspoon pepper, ½ tablespoon French mustard, 1 teaspoon lemon juice, and 1 tablespoon vinegar in a bowl and beat in slowly 5 tablespoons salad oil. Mix this into the rice and place on a serving dish. Arrange the lobster meat on top.

Put the egg yolks in a bowl with salt, pepper and a pinch of French mustard, the tomato ketchup and the Lea and Perrin's Sauce. Beat in slowly 1 cup of salad oil. Season well and add the cream and 1 tablespoon milk if necessary. (The consistency of the mixture should be that of cream.) Pour over the lobster meat and rice. Sprinkle top with paprika. Garnish with water cress. Serve very cold.

Note: this dish is delicious done with other fish such as fillets of sole, small steaks of cod, salmon, all poached and cooled, etc.

LOBSTER STRUDEL

2¼ cups flour	¼ pound mushrooms
1 egg	4 tablespoons butter
1 tablespoon oil	1 cup milk
salt and pepper	4 tablespoons grated cheese
1 large cooked lobster	pinch French mustard
1 cup shrimps	2 tablespoons cream
¼ pound cod	bread crumbs

Strudel: Put 2 cups flour on a pastry board or marble slab. Make a well in the center. Into the well put the egg, oil and a pinch of salt. Work to a firm paste with warm water. Beat until it becomes a very light and elastic dough. Place on a floured board and brush the top with oil. Cover with a bowl and put in a warm place for 1 hour. Cover a large table with cloth and sprinkle with flour. Roll out the dough into a large square and brush with oil. Roll out to the thinness of tissue paper so that the dough covers the table. Sprinkle with oil again.

Filling: Remove all the meat from the lobster and chop fine. Add the shrimps, the cod (simmered for 10 minutes in a little stock and skinned, boned and flecked), and the mushrooms (sliced and cooked in a little butter and seasoning). Mix all together and arrange on one end of the strudel.

Sauce: Melt the butter and stir in ¼ cup flour. Season and pour on the milk. Bring to a boil. Add the cheese, mustard and cream. Place equally spaced dessertspoons on the filling.

Roll up strudel, breaking off each end of the paste. Roll on a well-buttered baking sheet. Brush with melted butter and sprinkle with grated cheese and bread crumbs. Bake in a moderate oven for 25 minutes until golden brown. Remove and cut off each end. Serve hot with a little seasoning and melted butter separately.

PILAF D'HOMARD
(Lobster Pilaf)

2 tablespoons oil	*1 bay leaf*
4 tablespoons fat	*2 tablespoons grated Parmesan cheese*
1 finely chopped onion	*2 lobsters*
1 finely chopped clove garlic	*4 tablespoons thick cream or sour cream*
2 cups rice	*salt and pepper*
4 cups strong stock	*paprika*

handful chopped chives

Heat 1 tablespoon oil and 1 tablespoon fat in a pan. Add the onion and garlic and cook until soft without browning. Add the rice and cook slowly for 7 minutes, stirring all the time. Cover with the stock, bring to a boil, season and add the bay leaf. Cover with waxed paper and the lid and cook for 25 minutes in a 350° F. to 400° F. oven. Remove. Stir in with a fork the grated cheese and 2 tablespoons fat. Line a well-greased deep round mold with most of this mixture and make a hole in the center.

Wash the lobsters and split in half. Remove the bag from behind the eyes and discard. Heat the remaining oil and 1 table-spoon fat in a pan. Put lobster in pan split-side-down. Cover and cook slowly until a bright red color. Remove meat from shells and cut up roughly. Mix with little grated cheese and the sour, or thick, cream. Season and add a handful of chopped chives if desired.

Fill the hole with the mixture and cover with the remaining rice. Press down gently. Turn out of mold onto a serving dish. Decorate with a few lobster shells.

HOMARD PARISIENNE
(Cold Lobster with Mayonnaise)

2 large live lobsters	*2 tablespoons rich mayonnaise*
2 cups mixed, diced, cooked carrots,	*2 chopped, hard-boiled eggs*
beans and peas	*paprika*

2 skinned, pipped and diced tomatoes

Cook the lobsters for 30 minutes in well-salted water. Remove from the fire and allow to cool in the water. Split the lobsters in half and carefully remove the meat from tails and claws. Fill the shells with a mixture of the cooked vegetables, the tomatoes and the rich mayonnaise. After filling the shells, cut the lobster meat in slices and arrange on top. Pour over a little more mayonnaise. Sprinkle with the chopped eggs and paprika and serve.

HOMARD THERMIDOR
(Lobster Thermidor)

2 1¼-pound live lobsters	salt
4 tablespoons oil	cayenne pepper
3 tablespoons butter or fat	¾ cup milk
1 medium-sized finely chopped	¼ cup cream
onion	pinch dry mustard
½ cup dry white wine	pinch paprika
2 tablespoons flour	handful grated Parmesan cheese

Wash lobsters well in cold water. Split in half, starting from the little cross in the center of the head. Remove the small bag from behind the eyes and cut off the eyes. Place split-side-down in the oil, which has been heated in a pan. Cover and cook slowly for 12 minutes. Remove carefully. Take lobster meat from the shell and cut up roughly. Place shells on hot serving dish and keep warm.

Melt 2 tablespoons butter or fat in a pan. Add the onion and cook until soft without browning. Add the wine and cook slowly until the wine has evaporated.

In another pan heat 1 tablespoon butter or fat. Stir in the flour, salt and cayenne pepper. Stir until smooth and add the milk. Stir over the fire until the mixture comes to a boil. Add this and the cream, mustard, paprika and 2 tablespoons cheese to the onion mixture. Reduce it to a thick, creamy consistency by adding a little of the lobster stock.

Mix lobster meat into this and fill the shells. Sprinkle well with grated cheese and put the rest of the butter or fat in small lumps on the tops. Brown quickly under the broiler and serve.

HOMARD À LA NEWBURGH
(Lobster Newburgh)

1 tablespoon oil	*1 bay leaf*
1 small sliced onion	*2 live lobsters*
1 small sliced carrot	*2 tablespoons fat*
1 small stalk celery, sliced	*3 egg yolks*
4 cups water	*1 cup cream*
salt and pepper	*1 tablespoon grated cheese*
few peppercorns	*pinch dry mustard*
paprika	*3 tablespoons sherry*

Heat the oil in a pan. Add the onion, carrot and celery and cook for 2 minutes. Pour on the water and bring to a boil. Add salt, peppercorns, and paprika to season, and the bay leaf.

Lower the fire. Wash the lobsters and put into this stock. Cover and cook very gently for 15 minutes. (This stock can be strained and kept for use in a chowder.) Carefully remove meat from lobsters; cut in small pieces.

Put in the top of a double boiler the fat, egg yolks, cream, cheese, seasoning, mustard and sherry. Stir over a slow fire until it thickens and coats the back of a spoon; it must not curdle. Add the lobster meat. Serve in a hot chafing dish with a good creamy purée of potato.

HOMARD MARGUERITE
(Lobster with Mushrooms and Tomatoes)

2 live lobsters	*handful chopped parsley*
2 tablespoons oil	*4 small sole or flounders*
¼ pound butter	*½ cup cod*
2 bay leaves	*1 egg white*
2 chopped onions	*5 tablespoons cream*
salt and pepper	*¼ cup sherry*
¾ cup mushrooms	*¼ cup white wine*
juice 1 lemon	*2 beaten egg yolks*

4 skinned, pipped and shredded tomatoes

Pierce and split the lobsters through the heads, removing the little bag from the tops of the heads. Remove and crack the claws.

Put lobsters split-side-down in the oil, heated with a little butter. Shake over a brisk fire for 2 to 3 minutes. Add 1 bay leaf and place in the oven for 10 to 15 minutes. Remove meat from the tail and cut it into neat scallops. Keep in a warm place.

Melt 2 tablespoons butter in another pan. Add the onions, salt and pepper. Cook until nearly soft. Add ½ cup sliced mushrooms and 1 teaspoon lemon juice. Cover and cook for 3 minutes. Add the tomatoes and chopped lobster meat from the head and claws and a little chopped parsley. Cover and keep warm.

Skin, fillet, wash and dry the sole. Spread with a thin layer of the following: Skin, bone and mince the cod. Slowly beat in the egg white. Add salt, pepper and 1 tablespoon cream. Add the rest of the mushrooms finely chopped. Roll up the fillets and fasten with string. Place in a well-buttered, fireproof dish. Add 1 bay leaf and pour over the sherry and white wine. Cover with the bones of the fish and bake in a slow oven for 12 to 15 minutes.

Strain the liquor from the fish and reduce by boiling it down to ¼ cup. Then pour onto the 2 beaten egg yolks, and add 4 tablespoons cream and 2 teaspoons lemon juice. Stir in a double boiler until it thickens, adding, bit by bit, 5 tablespoons of butter and the liquor from the lobsters.

Scrub out the lobster shells and heat slightly in the oven. Place on a hot dish and fill level with the mixture. On the head place 4 stuffed fillets of sole and arrange the lobster scallops overlapping on the tail. Pour over the sauce and serve.

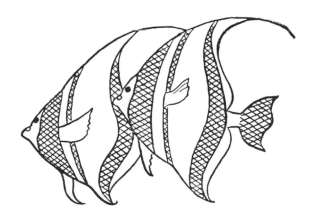

HOMARD À LA TÊTE
(Baked Lobster)

2 large live lobsters
1 cup bread crumbs
½ cup cream
2 tomatoes, skinned and pipped
3 tablespoons chopped shallots
6 anchovies, rubbed through a
   coarse strainer

1 teaspoon anchovy essence
4 tablespoons butter or fat
3 beaten eggs
salt and pepper
juice 1 lemon
handful bread crumbs

Put the lobsters in boiling water for 5 minutes. Remove and cool. Split the backs straight down, remove all the meat and chop the meat fine. Mix 1 cup of bread crumbs with the cream and heat. Mix the chopped lobster meat with the tomatoes, the shallots, the cream-soaked bread crumbs, the anchovies, the anchovy essence, the hot butter or fat, the eggs, salt, pepper and lemon juice. Fill the shells with this mixture and put them over a dish of water. Sprinkle with bread crumbs. Put a well-greased paper over the top and bake in a moderate oven for 20 to 30 minutes. Remove and serve with a velouté sauce.

HOMARD À LA BARANTE
(Lobster au Gratin)

2 1¼-pound live lobsters
2 tablespoons oil
salt and pepper
¼ cup red Burgundy
½ cup diced green beans
½ cup diced carrots
½ cup diced turnips

3 tablespoons fat
1 ounce dried mushrooms
2 tablespoons flour
cayenne pepper
½ cup milk
¼ cup cream
2 teaspoons chopped chives

2 tablespoons grated Swiss cheese

Wash the lobsters. Split in half, starting from the little cross in the center of the head. Take off the heads. Remove the small bag from behind the eyes and cut off the eyes. Cut off small claws and large claws, crack the claws, cut tails in 3 or 4 pieces, according to size. Heat oil in a pan and add the lobsters with a little salt and pepper. Cover and cook to a good red color. Heat the Burgundy, ignite and pour over the lobsters.

Bring the carrots, beans and turnips to a boil in cold water. Drain and add to the pan 1 tablespoon fat, salt and pepper. Dice and add the dried mushrooms, which have been soaked overnight in water. Add the water in which they were soaked, after boiling it down to 2 teaspoons. Cover and cook slowly on top of fire for 15 to 20 minutes. Add to the lobster and pour over the following cream sauce: —

Cream Sauce: In another pan melt 1 tablespoon fat. Stir in the flour, salt and cayenne pepper. Pour on the milk and cream. Beat well over the fire until the sauce comes to a boil and add the chives.

Serving: Remove meat from the lobster shells and mix together with the vegetables and the sauce. Arrange in a shallow, fireproof dish. Put on the top a thin layer of Swiss cheese and brown briskly under the broiler.

HOMARD CORDON BLEU

(Hot Lobster with Sherry and Tomatoes)

1 tablespoon oil	*¼ teaspoon tomato paste*
3 tablespoons fat	*¾ cup cream*
2 1¼-pound live lobsters	*1 pound tomatoes*
¼ cup sherry	*1 tablespoon grated cheese*
1 teaspoon chopped fresh tarragon and chervil	*salt and pepper*

Heat the oil and a little of the fat in a pan. Wash the lobsters well in cold water. Split in half, starting from the little cross in the center of the head. Remove the small bag from behind the eyes; cut off the eyes. Put lobsters into a pan split-side-down. Cover and shake over the fire for 5 minutes; draw aside.

Heat the sherry in a pan; ignite it and pour over the lobsters. Add the tarragon and chervil, the tomato paste and the cream and seasoning. Skin, cut into quarters, seed and shred the tomatoes and add them. Cover and cook in the oven for 15 minutes. Lift out the lobsters, remove all meat and chop it coarsely. Place the shells on a serving dish. Mix chopped lobster meat into the sauce and replace in the shells. Sprinkle with grated cheese and the rest of the melted fat and brown under the broiler. Serve.

MAYONNAISE D'HOMARD II
(Lobster Mayonnaise)

2 cups rice	coarse pepper
3 shredded tomatoes	dry mustard
2 tablespoons chopped parsley	2 tablespoons vinegar or lemon juice
spicy French dressing	1½ cups oil
pieces cold boiled lobster	2 tablespoons cream
2 egg yolks	little tomato pulp

Boil rice, drain and wash in cold water, put in a bowl and add the tomatoes, skinned and pipped, and the parsley. Mix with French dressing and arrange in long shape on a serving dish, covering top with pieces of cold boiled lobster. Then pour over the following mayonnaise: —

Mayonnaise: Put in a bowl egg yolks, pepper, mustard, vinegar or lemon juice. Then carefully beat in the oil. When thoroughly mixed add cream and the tomato pulp. Spread over the top of the lobster and serve.

COQUILLE OF LOBSTER

3 cooked lobsters	cayenne pepper
4 mushrooms	1 cup milk
1 good tablespoon butter	1 teaspoon dry mustard
3 level tablespoons flour	3 tablespoons grated cheese
salt	4 tablespoons cream

1 egg yolk

Remove lobsters from the shell, cut in small pieces and add the mushrooms, which have been lightly sautéed. Mix fish, mushrooms and Mornay Sauce together. Arrange in shells and pipe around with Mousseline Potatoes (see p. 96). Sprinkle with grated cheese, dot with butter and put under the broiler to brown. *Serves 6.*

Mornay Sauce: Melt butter and stir in flour, salt and cayenne pepper. Then pour in the milk. Stir over the fire until the sauce comes to a boil; add mustard, cheese and 3 tablespoons cream. Simmer gently for 5 minutes; then add the egg yolk mixed with 1 tablespoon cream.

LOBSTER AND MUSHROOM PIE

3 boiled lobsters
12 mushrooms
2 tablespoons butter
3 level tablespoons flour
salt
cayenne pepper
1½ cups good beef stock

1 teaspoon fresh chopped chives
2 cups flour
4 egg yolks
4 tablespoons fat
3 tablespoons grated cheese
2 strained, hard-boiled egg yolks
1 level teaspoon paprika

½ teaspoon chili

Remove lobster meat from the shells. Add the mushrooms, halved and sautéed in butter. Add the following sauce: —

Velouté Sauce: Melt butter and stir in 3 level tablespoons flour, salt and cayenne pepper. Then pour on the beef stock and stir over the fire until the sauce comes to a boil. Add chives and pour over the lobster and mushrooms; cover with the following pastry: —

Pastry: Put on a slab 2 cups flour; make a well in the center and put in egg yolks, fat, grated cheese, hard-boiled egg yolks, 1 level teaspoon salt, 1 level teaspoon paprika and the chili and cayenne pepper. Work the center ingredients to a smooth paste with the fingers; then with the heel of the hand quickly work in the flour. Roll out not too thin, cover the top of the pie, brush with beaten egg and bake for half an hour in a hot oven (400° F.). Remove and serve hot.

LOBSTER CROQUETTES

3 medium-sized potatoes
chopped meat of cooked lobster
2 small eggs, beaten

1 tablespoon sour cream
salt and pepper
1 tablespoon chopped chives

Boil potatoes, drain dry and rub through a strainer; add lobster, egg, cream, salt, pepper and chives. Form into pear shapes, dust with flour, paint with beaten egg, roll in crumbs and fry golden in hot fat. Stick a clove in the top of each. Surround the dish and serve.

MORUE À L'ESPAGNOL
(Salt Cod with Onions and Peppers)

1 pound salt cod	*salt and pepper*
3 tablespoons salad oil	*4 large tomatoes, skinned, pipped*
2 finely sliced onions	* and sliced*
2 green peppers	*½ teaspoon saffron*
2 red peppers	*bouquet of fresh herbs*

Soak the cod; dry and remove the skin and bones and cut in slices. Heat the salad oil and add to the cod with the onions. Cook for a few minutes. Add the peppers, cut in shreds and blanched, and the seasoning, tomatoes, saffron and herbs. Simmer for 15 minutes and remove the herbs. This can be served hot or cold.

HOMARD FARCI ST. JACQUES
(Stuffed Lobster St. Jacques)

4 boiled lobsters	*little sour cream*
1 pound sea scallops	*little fresh dill or parsley*
½ cup dry white wine	*butter*
2 tablespoons sherry	*5 tablespoons flour*
½ cup water	*cayenne pepper*
1 bay leaf	*3 tablespoons cream*
salt	*1 egg yolk*
peppercorns	*½ cup raw mushrooms*
grated cheese	

Split lobsters in half, remove bag from the head and carefully take out the meat. Arrange shell on a hot serving dish and fill with the following: —

Put the scallops in a pan with white wine, sherry, water, bay leaf, salt and peppercorns. Bring slowly to a boil and strain; cut lobster and scallops in slices, mix together with sour cream, dill or parsley. Season and fill into shells; then pour over the sauce.

Sauce: Melt 3 tablespoons butter in a pan; stir in flour, salt and cayenne pepper. Strain on the stock the scallops were cooked in, stir over the fire until the sauce comes to a boil and add, bit by bit, 2 teaspoons butter; then add the cream, which has been mixed with the egg yolk. When well blended add mushrooms, finely sliced, using only the white part. (Cut crosswise.) Pour over the lobster, sprinkle with cheese, dot with butter and brown under the broiler.

COLD SALMON MOUSSE

¾ pound salmon	*1 cup milk*
1 onion	*salt and pepper*
1 carrot	*2 tablespoons sherry*
1 bay leaf	*2 tablespoons cream*
¼ cup white wine	*1 cup fish aspic*
1 cup butter	*few sprigs parsley*
3 tablespoons flour	*1 tomato*

Mousse: Place the salmon, onion, carrot, bay leaf, wine and a little water in a pan. Bring slowly to a boil and simmer for 15 to 20 minutes. Cool in the stock. Skin and bone the salmon. Pound well in a mortar with ¾ cup creamed butter and the Béchamel Sauce.

Béchamel Sauce: Melt 3 tablespoons butter in a pan, remove from fire and add the flour. Stir until smooth. Add 1 cup milk and seasoning. Stir over the fire until boiling. Pour on plate to cool. When all is well pounded, add the sherry, cream and a little extra seasoning. Nearly fill a soufflé dish with this mixture. Smooth over and stand in a cool place.

Serving: Put a little of the aspic in a pan and stir over a bowl of ice until thick. Run a thin coating of this jelly on top of the salmon mousse. Dip a few sprigs of pressed parsley into the jelly and stick around at even intervals on the top of the mousse. Peel the tomato and cut the skin into small flowerpot shapes. Dip also into aspic and set at the bottom of each sprig. Put in a cool place. Fill up the rest of the dish with aspic which is on the point of setting. Set again and serve.

This mousse can be made in exactly the same way with ham, chicken, veal, etc. and coated with chicken or game aspic.

Note: for the aspic, see p. 142.

SAUMON À LA MATELOT
(Salmon with Red Wine)

1 pound salmon	*4 tablespoons cream*
½ cup butter	*juice ½ lemon*
¼ cup red wine	*¾ cup button onions*
1 cup water	*¼ pound button mushrooms*
1 slice onion	*salt and pepper*
1 clove garlic	*1 beaten egg*
1 sprig fresh thyme	*½ cup puff paste*
2 egg yolks	*little chopped parsley*

Salmon: Skin, bone, and cut in large squares and place in an earthenware dish. Season and pour over a little melted butter. Put under the grill for a few moments. Pour over the wine and 1 cup water and add the slice of onion, garlic and thyme. Cover with a piece of waxed paper and poach in a moderate oven for 10 to 15 minutes. Keep warm.

Sauce: Strain ¼ cup of liquid from the salmon. Pour onto the egg yolks and add the cream. Whisk over a slow fire in a *bain-marie* until it thickens. Add ¼ cup butter, bit by bit, and, lastly, a little lemon juice. Cover and keep warm.

Mushrooms and Onions: Skin and cook the button onions until soft in boiling salted water. Strain and add the mushrooms, which have been washed, cut in quarters and cooked for 4 minutes in a little butter, lemon juice and seasoning. Add to the salmon and keep warm.

Puff Paste: Roll out the puff paste fairly thick and cut in crescent shapes with a fluted center. Place on a watered baking sheet and brush the tops with the beaten egg. Bake in a hot oven for 15 minutes and keep warm.

Serving: Mix the sauce into the salmon, mushrooms and onions and pour this mixture in the serving dish. Garnish with the puff paste and sprinkle over with the parsley.

SALMON PUDDING

2 pounds raw salmon	dry mustard
1 cup cream sauce	little cream
4 mushrooms	bread crumbs
little cooked lobster meat	grated cheese
3 egg yolks	2 tablespoons fat
3 stiffly beaten egg whites	3 tablespoons flour
salt and pepper	1 cup milk

Skin and bone the salmon and put it through a meat grinder; add a cream sauce. Mix in the mushrooms, sliced and sautéed in butter, lobster meat, egg yolks and whites; season well with salt, pepper and dry mustard and add the cream. Put in a well-greased pyrex dish and sprinkle the top with bread crumbs and grated cheese. Bake in a dish of hot water for 35 minutes in a 350° F. oven. Remove and serve very hot.

Cream Sauce: Melt fat and stir in the flour; pour on 1 cup milk. Stir over a slow fire until the sauce comes to a boil; season with salt and pepper.

SALMON SAUCE VERTE

2½ pounds salmon	salt and pepper
1½ cups rice	1½ cups oil
French dressing	4 tablespoons cooked, strained spinach
3 egg yolks	2 tablespoons cream
1 tablespoon vinegar	cayenne pepper

Skin and bone the salmon; put in a pyrex dish and pour over a little lemon juice and water to cover. Cook for 20 minutes in a moderate oven, cut in sections and arrange on top of a bed of the following:—

Rice Salad: Boil rice in salted water, drain, wash well in cold water and mix with well-seasoned French dressing. Arrange on a serving dish in a loaf shape; place pieces of salmon on top and cover with the following sauce: —

Sauce Verte: Put egg yolks, vinegar, salt and pepper in a bowl and beat well. Add very slowly, beating continuously, the oil, spinach, cream, salt and cayenne pepper.

Garnish the dish with slices of fresh cucumber and serve.

FILETS DE MORUE À L'AIXOISE
(Cod with Capers and Anchovies)

4 small fillets salt cod
1 medium-sized onion, finely chopped
large lump butter
1 tomato

2 tablespoons chopped fresh parsley, capers and fillets of anchovy
¼ cup hot oil
salt and pepper
2 or 3 tablespoons tomato sauce

Soak the cod fillets. Cook the onion in a little butter, add the flesh of a firm tomato finely chopped, and the parsley, capers and fillets of anchovy. Fold cod fillets in half or roll up and fasten firmly with string. Place on a fireproof dish and pour over the oil and seasoning. Cook for 25 to 30 minutes, basting frequently with the oil. Remove the string and place on a hot serving dish. Add the tomato sauce (see p. 226). Pour over the cod just before serving.

BRANDADE DE MORUE
(Mousse of Salt Cod)

1 pound salt cod
fish stock
4 large baked potatoes
½ cup salad oil

2 cloves garlic
salt and pepper
1 cup thick cream
bread

Soak the cod for 1 hour and dry. Cut in large squares. Simmer in the fish stock for 15 to 20 minutes, strain and remove all bones and skin. Pound until smooth in a mortar. Remove baked potatoes from skin and rub through a coarse sieve. Pound this into the fish slowly and well. Add, drop by drop, the salad oil. Add the garlic, which has been crushed in salt, and the cream. Season well and continue to pound for 1 to 2 minutes. Place in a pan and heat over the fire until hot. Arrange on a serving dish and serve with croutons of fried bread. This can be served either hot or cold. In the south of France this is generally served as an hors d'oeuvre.

MORUE À LA LYONNAISE
(Salt Cod)

3/4 to 1 pound salt or fresh cod   4 sliced onions
little flour   4 baked potatoes
large lump butter   juice 1/2 lemon
1 teaspoon chopped parsley

If using salt cod, soak well before cooking. Cut the cod in thick pieces, roll in flour and sauté in butter.

Meanwhile, in another pan, brown the onions in butter. Add the potatoes, which have been sautéed in butter, and mix in the cod. Continue frying for a little longer to insure that all are thoroughly mixed together. Sprinkle in the lemon juice and parsley.

BOUILLABAISSE DE MORUE
(Salt Cod Bouillabaisse)

1/3 cup oil   1/2 teaspoon saffron
3 onions   bouquet of herbs
2 leeks   5 large potatoes
3 cloves garlic   2 pounds salt cod
3 cups water   1 tablespoon chopped parsley
salt and pepper   brown bread

Heat 3 tablespoons of oil and add the onions, leeks and garlic, finely sliced. Cook slowly for 8 to 9 minutes without browning. Add the water, salt, pepper, saffron and the bouquet of herbs. Bring to a boil and boil for 5 minutes. Add the potatoes, peeled and cut in thick rounds, and the cod, previously soaked, skinned and cut in large squares. Add 1/4 cup oil and continue simmering for 20 minutes. Just before it is done add this mixture to the bouillabaisse with a tablespoon of chopped parsley and arrange in a deep casserole. Serve separately slices of brown bread, grilled and rubbed with garlic dipped quickly in the bouillabaisse.

MORUE À L'AMÉRICAINE
(Cod with Carrot and Brandy Sauce)

1 pound cod	*1 glass white wine*
little boiling oil	*½ cup brandy*
3 finely chopped carrots	*1 teaspoon tomato conserve*
1 finely chopped clove garlic	*1 pinch paprika*
1 finely chopped onion	*½ cup water*
2 tablespoons butter or fat	*salt and pepper*

Divide the cod in neat pieces, fry in boiling oil and drain well. Brown the carrots, garlic and onion in the butter. Add the wine, brandy, tomato conserve, paprika, water, salt and pepper. Simmer for 20 minutes, add the fish and continue cooking for 15 minutes.

HOMARD À L'ARMORICAINE
(Lobster with Vegetables)

3 live lobsters	*½ cup dry white wine*
4 tablespoons hot oil	*2 tablespoons flour*
1 cup diced beans and carrots	*1 teaspoon tomato paste*
6 sliced and skinned tomatoes	*2 teaspoons butter*
2½ cups rice	

Take lobsters and split heads in half and backs from behind the eyes; remove big claws and crack; remove small claws and cut tail in pieces. Put into a pan with hot oil. Cook until red, remove and add beans and carrots, tomatoes and white wine; add flour, tomato paste and butter. Add this, bit by bit, to the lobster, season well, cover and simmer gently for 8 minutes. Boil 2½ cups rice for 13½ minutes, drain and wash well in hot water. Fill into a large ring mold, turn out onto a serving dish and fill middle with lobster. Serve hot.

LOTTE À L'ARMORICAINE
(Cod with Carrots and Tomatoes)

1 pound cod
little oil
2 tablespoons butter
3 finely chopped carrots
1 finely chopped clove garlic

1 finely chopped onion
1 glass white wine
½ cup brandy
1 teaspoon tomato conserve
paprika

½ cup water

Cut the cod in neat pieces and fry in boiling oil for 5 minutes. Drain well. Mix and brown in the butter the carrots, garlic and onion. Add the wine, brandy, tomato conserve, a good pinch of paprika and the water. Simmer for 20 minutes. Add the cod, cook for 15 minutes and serve.

CABILLAUD MILANESE
(Cod Steaks with Cheese)

4 small cod steaks
little flour
salt and pepper
1 beaten egg
handful white bread crumbs
little grated cheese

3 or 4 tablespoons fat or butter
1 sliced lemon
4 tomatoes
1 tablespoon butter
clove of garlic
1 small onion

Wash and dry the cod steaks. Dust very lightly in flour, salt and pepper. Brush with the beaten egg and roll in the white bread crumbs and cheese. Cook until golden brown on each side in hot butter or fat. Serve on a good strong Tomato Coulis with lemon.

Tomato Coulis: Skin the tomatoes, cut in thick slices and sprinkle with a little salt and pepper. Heat 1 tablespoon butter in a pan, add a little chopped garlic and onion. Cook until just soft, then add the tomatoes and cook quickly for 3 minutes.

RAIE AU FROMAGE
(Skate with Cheese)

1½ pounds skate	*pinch thyme*
2 tablespoons butter	*2 shallots*
2 tablespoons flour	*salt and pepper*
1 cup milk	*handful grated Gruyère cheese*
1 clove garlic	*12 small white onions*
½ bay leaf	*12 rounds of bread*

Divide the skate in quarters. Melt 1 tablespoon butter in a pan, add 1 tablespoon flour and the milk, bring to a boil and add the garlic, bay leaf, thyme, shallots and a little salt. Simmer the skate in this mixture until cooked. Drain and put the liquid through a sieve. Thicken it with a small lump of butter and 1 tablespoon flour rubbed together and bring again to a boil. Pour half this sauce into a fireproof dish. Shake over it a handful of grated cheese. Lay the skate on this and arrange between the pieces the pickling onions, which have been cooked in the skate stock and well drained. Add 12 rounds of bread, which have been fried until golden in butter. Pour over the rest of the sauce and cover with a thin layer of grated cheese. Brown the top quickly under the grill and serve at once.

MOULES À LA BORDELAISE

2 quarts mussels	*1½ tablespoons butter or fat*
1 cup water	*1 teaspoon tomato paste*
1 sliced onion	*1 clove garlic*
1 stalk celery	*chopped parsley*
bouquet of herbs	*1 slice stale bread*
1 tablespoon flour	*salt and pepper*

Wash and scrub the mussels thoroughly and put them in a pan with the water, onion, celery and herbs. Cover and shake over the fire until the mussels open. Remove the larger shells from the mussels and strain the liquor through a fine cloth. Brown the flour and butter or fat. Add the tomato paste, garlic, parsley and bread, which have been chopped together, and season. Put the mussels in a casserole with this mixture and pour on enough of the mussel liquor to make a sauce of a syrupy consistency. Cook gently for about 15 minutes. Serve in the casserole.

RAIE À L'ORANGE
(Skate with Orange)

1¼ pounds skate	*1 finely chopped clove garlic*
½ cup red wine	*1 dessertspoon flour*
1½ cups water	*1 tomato, skinned and roughly cut up*
juice 1 lemon	*1 handful mushroom peelings and stalks*
½ cup butter	*1 teaspoon tomato paste*
bouquet of herbs	*1 tablespoon sherry*
salt and pepper	*3 oranges*
2 finely chopped onions	*1 pound potatoes*

Skate: Cut the skate in strips and place on a well-buttered dish. Pour over the red wine, water and lemon juice, and a little melted butter. Add the herbs and cover with waxed paper. Cook for 20 minutes in a moderate oven. Keep warm after removing.

Sauce: Melt 3 tablespoons butter in a pan. Add seasoning, onion and garlic. Cook slowly until soft. Stir in the flour and leave to brown a little. Add the tomato, mushroom peelings and stalks, and tomato paste. Pour on the skate stock and stir over the fire until boiling. Simmer for 15 minutes and strain into another pan. Add the sherry and the finely shredded rind of 1 orange, which has been brought to a boil in cold water and strained. Simmer for 5 minutes, adding, bit by bit, 2 tablespoons butter; keep warm.

Potatoes: Peel and pare in neat olive shapes. Cook in hot salted water until soft without becoming mushy. Strain and return to the pan to dry; keep warm.

Serving: Arrange the skate on a dish. Pour over the sauce and place the potatoes at each end. Cut the 2 remaining oranges in sections; heat through in a little butter and place at each side.

HARENGS CALAISIENNES
(Stuffed Herrings)

4 fresh herrings	5 tablespoons butter
2 finely chopped, hard-boiled eggs	1/2 sliced onion
2 finely chopped cloves garlic	few whole peppercorns
1/2 small chopped onion	1 bay leaf
1 dessertspoon chopped herbs	2 tomatoes
salt and pepper	1 tablespoon tomato paste
1 slice white bread	1 tablespoon flour
1 1/2 cups stock	1 thinly sliced lemon

Herrings: Remove the heads, split down the backs with a sharp knife and carefully remove the bone. Wash and dry well in a cloth.

Place the eggs in a bowl with the chopped-up herring roe, garlic, 1/2 chopped onion, herbs, salt and pepper. Bind this with the bread soaked in 1/2 cup of the stock.

Fill the herrings. Place in a fireproof dish and pour over a little melted butter. Cover with a piece of waxed paper and cook in a moderate oven for 25 minutes. Remove and keep warm.

Sauce: Melt 2 tablespoons butter in a pan. Add 1/2 sliced onion, the whole peppercorns, 1 bay leaf, the tomatoes and tomato paste. Cover the pan and cook slowly for 10 minutes. Remove and stir in the flour. Add a little salt and 1/2 cup stock. Stir over the fire until the sauce comes to a boil. Rub through a fine strainer and return to the pan. Stir in 2 tablespoons butter.

Serving: Pour the sauce on the bottom of the dish and arrange the stuffed herrings on top. Garnish round the dish with thin slices of lemon and serve.

MOULES FORESTIÈRES
(Baked Mussels)

3 dozen large mussels	1/2 cup thin cream
salt and black pepper	1 tablespoon grated Parmesan
2 dozen pine cones	cheese
4 tablespoons butter or fat	cayenne pepper

Scrub the mussels thoroughly and put in a pan. Sprinkle with salt and black pepper. Scatter over the top 2 dozen pine cones. Light them and let them burn out. By this time the mussels will have opened. Remove and discard the top shells and arrange the mussels in the bottom shells on a hot, fireproof dish. Melt the butter or fat in a pan and add the cream, cheese, salt, black pepper and a little cayenne pepper. Beat well and pour over the mussels. Sprinkle the top with a little more cheese and brown quickly under the grill. Serve at once.

MACKEREL WITH MUSTARD HOLLANDAISE

8 fillets mackerel	*3 teaspoons dry mustard*
little lemon juice	*1 tablespoon tarragon vinegar*
2 tablespoons oil	*salt*
little chopped garlic	*cayenne pepper*
6 tomatoes	*2 tablespoons cream*
3 egg yolks	*2 or 3 tablespoons butter*

1 or more tablespoons cream

Arrange the mackerel, with skin left on, on a baking dish and pour over the lemon juice and a little melted butter. Cover with waxed paper and bake for 20 minutes in a moderate oven. While cooking, heat in another pan the oil and chopped garlic and add the tomatoes, skinned and cut in thick slices, cook briskly for 2 minutes; arrange on a serving dish. Put fillets on top and pour over the following sauce: —

Mustard Hollandaise Sauce: Put the egg yolks in a bowl and mix with mustard, vinegar, salt, cayenne pepper and cream. Put the bowl in a pan of hot water over a slow fire and heat until the sauce begins to thicken; then add the butter, bit by bit, beating continuously with a whisk and lastly add cream to bring to a pouring consistency. Pour over the fish and brown under the broiler.

MAQUEREAU MOUTARDE
(Mackerel with Mustard Sauce)

2 fresh mackerel	*1 dessertspoon French mustard*
4 tablespoons butter or fat	*salt and pepper*
¼ cup finely diced green beans	*3 cups veal stock*
1 small chopped onion	*2 tablespoons cream*
1 clove garlic	*little chopped parsley*
1 tablespoon flour	*little grated cheese*

Mackerel: Remove the heads; split down the backs with a sharp knife and carefully remove the bone. Place on a fireproof dish. Season and pour on 2 tablespoons melted butter. Cook in a moderate oven for 15 minutes. Remove and keep warm.

Sauce: Melt 2 tablespoons butter in a pan. Add the beans, onion and garlic and cook slowly till tender. Add the flour, mustard, salt and pepper and stir until smooth. Pour on the stock and stir over the fire until the sauce comes to a boil. Add the cream and a little chopped parsley.

Serving: Place mackerel on a dish and pour over the sauce. Sprinkle with a little grated cheese and put to glaze under the grill.

RAIE AU BEURRE NOIRE
(Skate with Black Butter)

2 pounds skate	*2 tablespoons chopped capers*
juice 1 lemon	*salt and pepper*
4 tablespoons butter	*1 pound small potatoes*

Cut the skate in thick strips and wash thoroughly in lemon juice and water. Arrange on a greased dish and pour over it a little lemon juice and water. Cover with waxed paper and cook for 22 to 25 minutes in a 350° F. oven. Arrange on a hot serving dish.

Brown the butter very slowly in a pan. Add a squeeze of lemon juice, the capers, salt and pepper. Pour over the fish. Serve the fish with small steamed potatoes.

PILAU DE MOULES À L'ORIENTALE
(Mussels with Rice Pilaf)

6 tablespoons butter or fat
2 small sliced onions
salt and pepper
¾ cup unhusked or risotto rice
1½ cups stock
2 tablespoons grated Parmesan cheese
1 quart mussels

½ cup white wine
1 cup water
juice ½ lemon
bouquet of fresh herbs
1 tablespoon flour
½ cup milk
2 tablespoons cream

handful chopped parsley

Pilau: Heat a little butter in a pan and add the onions; season with salt and pepper and cook for 2 to 3 minutes. Add the rice and cool for 1 minute longer, pour on the stock and bring to a boil. Cover the pan with waxed paper and the lid and place on the bottom shelf of a moderate oven for 25 minutes. Remove and stir in with a fork a small lump of butter and a little grated cheese. Keep warm.

Mussels: Wash well and put them in a pan with the wine, water, salt, lemon juice and herbs. Bring slowly to a boil, tossing occasionally. Shell and keep the mussels warm, reserving the liquor and removing the beards.

Sauce: Melt 2 tablespoons butter in a pan. Remove from the fire and add the flour and seasoning. Strain the liquor in which the mussels were cooked and add it. Add the milk. Stir over the fire until boiling. Add the cream.

Serving: Moisten the mussels with a little of the sauce. Oil a charlotte mold well and line with the pilau. Fill the center with the mussels and cover level with the rest of the rice pilau, press down well. Turn out of mold quickly onto a hot dish. Pour the rest of the sauce around and decorate the top with one or two mussels and a little chopped parsley.

Note: this can be done with chicken, meat, etc., the sauce to be made accordingly.

MOULES MARINIÈRE I
(Mussels with White Wine)

3 quarts mussels	bouquet of herbs
1 stalk celery, diced	1 crushed clove garlic
2 diced carrots	salt and pepper
1 diced onion	2 egg yolks
¾ cup dry white wine	¼ cup cream
little chopped parsley	

Scrub the mussels thoroughly. Put in a pan and add the celery, carrots and onion, after they have been cooked until nearly done in boiling, salted water. Add the wine, herbs, garlic and salt to season and bring slowly to a boil. Simmer until all the shells are open, but not longer than 5 minutes; discard any unopened mussels. Strain off the liquor and reduce it by one third. Remove from the fire and add the egg yolks mixed in the cream. Stir over the fire until it thickens without boiling, adding the parsley. Arrange the mussels and vegetables on a dish. Pour on the sauce and serve at once.

MOULES MARINIÈRE II

2 quarts mussels	salt and pepper
2 stalks celery	1 bay leaf
2 small carrots	¾ cup dry white wine
2 small onions	3 teaspoons butter
2 small leeks	4 teaspoons flour
3 tablespoons oil	½ cup cream
little crushed garlic	2 small egg yolks

Scrub the mussels very well with a brush. Slice the celery, carrots, onions and leeks very fine and add to the oil, which has been heated in a pan with the garlic. Cook the garlic and oil for 1 minute; then add the sliced vegetables and cook for 2 minutes more; put the mussels on top and season with salt, pepper and bay leaf. Pour over the wine and bring to a boil; cover and simmer until the mussels open. Take out the mussels, remove the top shell, arrange them on a flat dish and pour over the following sauce: —

Sauce: Work butter and flour to a smooth paste. Add, bit by bit, to stock the mussels were cooked in; then add mixed cream and egg yolks. Stir into the sauce, pour over the mussels and serve.

SALADE DE MOULES ET DE POMMES DE TERRE
(Salad of Mussels and Potatoes)

2 quarts mussels	*½ cup red or white wine*
bouquet of herbs	*2 egg yolks*
few peppercorns	*salt and pepper*
1 onion	*½ teaspoon mustard*
1 carrot	*¾ cup oil*
1 stalk celery	*1 teaspoon lemon juice*
1 cup water	*1 teaspoon chopped tarragon and chervil*
4 or 5 potatoes	*2 or 3 gherkins*

Scrub and wash the mussels well. Put them in a pan with a bouquet of herbs, a few peppercorns, the onion, carrot and celery, and a pinch of salt. Add 1 cup water and shake over the fire until the shells open. Shell the mussels and remove the beards.

Steam or boil the potatoes in their skins and peel while still hot. Cut in slices and sprinkle with the wine.

Mayonnaise: Mix the egg yolks, salt, pepper and mustard to season. Add, bit by bit, the oil, lemon juice to sharpen well, and the chopped fresh tarragon and chervil. Add some finely chopped gherkins.

Arrange alternate layers of mussels, potatoes and mayonnaise in a salad bowl. Cover with mayonnaise and decorate with sliced gherkins and mussels.

Note: the potatoes should be firm, not mealy.

MOULES PANÉES
(Baked Mussels)

1 quart mussels
½ cup water
bouquet fresh tarragon, chervil, parsley,
   onion chopped finely together
salt and pepper
1 tablespoon butter or fat
1 tablespoon flour

1 cup cream
1 heaping teaspoon
   chopped herbs
1 drop iodine
bread crumbs
parsley
little chopped parsley

Wash and scrub the mussels thoroughly. Put them in a pan with the water, herbs and seasoning. Shake over the fire a few minutes. Remove from the fire and discard any mussels that have not opened. Strain the liquor through a fine cloth and pour it onto the butter and flour, browned together. Add the cream and, if necessary, a little milk. Bring slowly to a boil and simmer gently with a heaping teaspoon of the herbs. Remove the smaller shells from the mussels. Lay the others in a fireproof dish and cover them with the sauce, to which has been added the drop of iodine. Sprinkle well with browned bread crumbs and chopped parsley. Brown in the oven and serve very hot.

MOULES EN RISOTTO
(Mussels in Risotto)

3 pints mussels
1 sliced onion
bouquet of herbs
2 tablespoons oil
2 chopped onions
1 clove garlic

¼ cup chopped fat bacon
3 tomatoes, skinned and pipped
¾ cup rice
fish stock or water, if necessary
salt and pepper
paprika
little grated cheese

Wash and scrub the mussels thoroughly. Put in a pan with a little water, 1 sliced onion and bouquet of herbs. Shake over the fire until the mussels open. Remove from shells. Heat the oil in a pan and add the chopped onions, garlic, bacon and tomatoes.

Add the mussels and sauté all together again. Add the rice, the liquid from the mussels, and the fish stock or water, if necessary. Season well with salt, pepper and a little paprika. Cover the pan and cook very slowly until the rice is soft and the mixture creamy. If cooking on top of the stove, remove the lid. Serve with the grated cheese.

MOULES À LA POULETTE À LA MODE DE FOYOT

2 quarts mussels
1½ cups diced combined celery,
  carrot, onion and leek
1 bay leaf
salt and pepper
½ cup dry white wine
1 tablespoon sherry

¼ cup water
1 tablespoon flour
1 tablespoon butter
1 clove crushed garlic
2 tablespoons coarse, chopped
  parsley
2 egg yolks

½ cup cream

Soak the mussels in water with quite a lot of mustard, which makes it easier to clean them; then wash in many waters and scrub well. When they are clean put them in a pan with the celery, carrot, onion and leek, bay leaf, salt, pepper, wine, sherry and water. Cover and bring slowly to a boil and shake until the mussels are opened. Remove and take off the top shells; arrange on a platter and scatter diced vegetables on top; pour on the following sauce: —

Sauce: Strain the liquor in which the mussels were cooked, boil down a little, and add, bit by bit, the flour, butter and garlic, which have been worked to a smooth paste. Add the parsley and egg yolks mixed into the cream. Reheat, do not boil, and pour over the fish.

SHAD AND ROE

1 shad	4 tablespoons flour
½ cup white wine	cayenne pepper
½ cup water	1 teaspoon dried basil
salt	¼ cup fresh tomato pulp
peppercorns	3 skinned and chopped tomatoes
2 tablespoons fat	roe, sautéed in butter
sliced tomatoes, sautéed in oil	

Bone the shad, arrange on a greased dish and pour over wine and water. Season with salt and peppercorns. Cover with wax paper and cook for 25 minutes in a 350° F. oven. Remove, arrange on a serving dish and pour over the following: —

Sauce: Melt fat, stir in flour, salt and cayenne pepper. Strain on liquor in which the fish was cooked and add dried basil and tomato pulp. Stir over the fire to boiling point and add chopped tomatoes. Simmer for 10 minutes. If too thick add a little water; then pour over the fish and garnish with roe and tomatoes sautéed very fast in hot oil.

FINNAN HADDIE

1 finnan haddie	cayenne pepper
3 beaten whole eggs	1 cup milk
1 beaten egg white	2 mushrooms
1 cup cream sauce	2 tablespoons butter
2 level tablespoons fat	1 cup stock
4 tablespoons flour	¼ cup cream
salt	1 egg yolk

The finnan haddie should be big and fat; soak in cold water for 5 hours; simmer for 12 minutes in hot water. Remove, skin, bone and flake with a fork; add eggs and egg white and cream sauce as follows: —

Cream Sauce: Melt fat and stir in flour, salt and cayenne pepper; pour on the milk. Stir over the fire until boiling; cool a little and mix in the fish.

Grease a ring mold well and put in the mixture. Cover with waxed paper, set in a pan of water and cook for 40 minutes in a 325°–350° F. oven. Remove, turn out on a serving dish and serve with the following sauce: —

Mushroom Sauce: Chop the mushrooms finely and add to 1 tablespoon butter, which has been melted in a pan; cook briskly for 3 minutes; then add 2 tablespoons flour, salt and cayenne pepper. Pour on the stock and stir over the fire until the sauce comes to a boil; add, bit by bit, 2 tablespoons butter and ¼ cup cream. Simmer for 10 minutes; then add egg yolk mixed with a little cream. Pour over the fish and serve.

HOT KIPPER SOUFFLÉ

1 pair kippers	*salt*
2 sliced, skinned tomatoes	*cayenne pepper*
oil	*¾ cup milk*
onion or garlic	*3 or 4 egg yolks*
2 tablespoons fat	*½ teaspoon dry mustard*
3 tablespoons flour	*1 tablespoon grated Parmesan cheese*

4 or 5 egg whites

Simmer the kippers in water for 5 minutes. Remove, bone, flake with a fork and mix gently into the tomatoes, which have been cooked in a little hot oil with onion or garlic. Put aside; then melt fat in a pan and stir in flour, salt and cayenne pepper. Pour on milk; stir over the fire until the mixture thickens; do *not* boil. Remove and mix in egg yolks, mustard and cheese. Lastly fold in gently the stiffly beaten egg whites and the kipper mixture. Grease a soufflé dish, tie a band of waxed paper around the outside, put in the mixture and bake for half an hour in a 350° F. oven. Remove and serve at once.

FROG LEGS PROVENÇAL

8 frog legs
5 tablespoons butter
2 or 3 teaspoons crushed garlic
salt and pepper

2 tablespoons finely chopped, fresh
  tarragon, chives, parsley
1 tablespoon lighted brandy
2 tablespoons lighted dry white wine

Wash frog legs very well in lemon juice and water, dry and dust lightly with seasoned flour. Put butter in a pan, heat to foaming and add crushed garlic. Cook for 1 minute, put in frog legs and shake until golden on each side; then add salt, pepper, tarragon, chives and parsley. Cook for another minute; then pour over brandy and wine. Serve at once in very hot dish.

BAKED STUFFED FISH

1 large sea bass
2 large mushroom caps
handful spinach
1 large onion
1/2 pound raw cod
1 slice white bread
1 crushed clove garlic
1/4 cup water
3 or 4 large onions

oil
3 carrots
1/4 cup sherry
1 tablespoon butter
1/4 cup red wine
salt and pepper
4 finely chopped, hard-boiled eggs
2 cups finely chopped, green herbs
  (parsley, chives, tarragon)

Bone the bass, leave on the head and stuff with the following: —
Put mushroom caps, spinach, onion and raw cod, skinned and boned, through the meat grinder; then put in a wooden bowl with 1 slice bread, crust removed and soaked in water. Chop garlic very finely, add water gradually, season well, fill into the fish and sew up.

Slice the onions finely and cook until soft without browning in hot oil; arrange on the bottom of a serving dish. Put the fish on top and cover with finely sliced carrots. Blanch and return to pan with sherry, butter, wine, salt and pepper; cook for 2 or 3 minutes until just soft. Cover fish with this mixture and dot with butter; cover with waxed paper and bake in a 375° F. oven for half an hour. Ten minutes before finished remove paper and continue cooking until done. Remove and just before serving sprinkle heavily with chopped, hard-boiled eggs and herbs, mixed thoroughly.

FRIED OYSTERS

3 dozen oysters	1 tablespoon tarragon vinegar
1 egg	2 tablespoons cream
3 egg yolks	salt
1 level teaspoon baking powder	cayenne pepper
1 tablespoon oil	4 tablespoons fat
4 tablespoons milk	2 tablespoons chopped, fresh herbs
	little garlic

Remove oysters from shell and dip in the following mixture: —

Put in a bowl 1 egg and 1 egg yolk, baking powder, oil and milk. Beat until smooth; then add more milk to reduce to the consistency of thick cream. Place in the refrigerator for half an hour; then dip oysters in this batter and fry in hot fat until golden brown. Serve with Béarnaise Sauce.

Béarnaise Sauce: Put in a bowl 2 egg yolks, vinegar, cream, salt and cayenne pepper. Put the bowl in a pan of hot water over a slow fire; beat until the sauce begins to thicken; then add, bit by bit, fat, herbs and garlic. Serve in a separate bowl with the oysters.

CLAM FRITTERS

(Batter)

4 heaping tablespoons flour	salt
1 egg	2 tablespoons milk
1 egg yolk	1 level teaspoon baking powder
1 tablespoon oil	1 stiffly beaten egg white
3 tablespoons milk	12 hard clams

Beat flour, 1 egg, 1 egg yolk, oil, milk, a pinch of salt until quite smooth. Add the extra milk, baking powder and beaten egg white. Place in the refrigerator for half an hour. Dip clams one at a time in the batter, drop in the deep, hot fat and fry until golden brown. Eat immediately.

SEA BASS THEODORA
(Sea Bass with Tomatoes and Shrimps)

1 1½-pound sea bass	*1 dessertspoon tomato paste*
½ cup white wine	*1 pound boiled potatoes*
salt and pepper	*2 small eggs*
1 cup butter	*3 tablespoons grated cheese*
2 tablespoons flour	*2 tablespoons skinned shrimps*
¾ cup milk	*handful white bread crumbs*
¼ cup cooking cream	*little fat*

Fish: Remove dark skin from sea bass. Wash and dry. Place on a well-buttered, fireproof dish and pour on the wine. Season. Cover with buttered paper and poach in a moderate oven for 20 to 25 minutes. Remove and place fish on a serving dish.

Sauce: Melt 3 tablespoons butter. Season and stir in 2 tablespoons flour. Pour on strained liquid from sea bass and thicken over the fire. Pour on the milk and bring to a boil. Add the cream and, bit by bit, 2½ tablespoons butter, simmering all the time. Coat the fish. Take 2 tablespoons sauce, add tomato paste and beat in well. Boil; fill into a paper cornet; cut a very small piece off the bottom of the cornet and pipe in large crisscrosses over the fish. Surround with the following garnish: —

Garnish: Boil the potatoes. Strain and dry. Rub through a sieve. Beat in a lump of butter, 1 small egg, 3 tablespoons cheese and the shrimps. Season and form in small pear shapes. Dust lightly in flour and brush with beaten egg. Roll in white bread crumbs and fry in deep fat until golden brown. Stick a clove on the top of each to form the pear stem and serve.

TRUITE SAUMONÉE REINE MARIE
(Salmon Trout with Eggplant and Mushrooms)

2 pounds salmon trout
1 cup fish stock
2 cups red wine
bouquet of herbs
few whole peppercorns
1 clove garlic
1 sliced onion
1 small sliced carrot
3 egg yolks

¾ cup butter
1 teaspoon tomato paste
½ cup thick cream
1 eggplant
5 or 6 firm tomatoes skinned, pipped and shredded
little chopped mint
salt and pepper
5 or 6 sliced mushrooms
juice ½ lemon

Salmon Trout: Wash and dry the fish and place on a well-buttered, fireproof dish. Season and pour over the fumet, wine, herbs, whole peppercorns, garlic, onion and carrot. Cover with waxed paper and braise slowly in the oven for 45 minutes, basting well.

Sauce: Beat the yolks in a bowl. Pour on ½ cup of the liquid from the fish. Season and stand in a *bain-marie.* Beat in slowly, bit by bit, ½ cup butter, the tomato paste and cream.

Garnish: Cut the eggplant in slanting slices. Sauté a few minutes in hot butter and keep warm. Sauté the tomatoes in hot butter with the mint and season; keep warm. Add the mushrooms and lemon juice to the melted butter. Sauté over the fire for 5 to 6 minutes.

Serving: Place the trout on the dish. Arrange on each side the eggplant, alternating with a tablespoon of mushroom and tomato. Pour over the sauce and glaze under the grill.

SARDINES À LA BASQUE
(Sardines with Peppers and Vegetables)

5 tablespoons butter
2 large, finely diced carrots
1 pound button onions, sliced and divided in rings
1/4 cup finely diced green beans
salt and pepper

4 tomatoes, skinned, pipped and diced
2 tinned sweet peppers, skinned, pipped and diced
1 large tin sardines
1 tablespoon grated cheese

Melt 4 tablespoons butter in a pan. Add carrots, onions and beans. Season and stir well. Cover pan with waxed paper and the lid and cook slowly for 5 to 6 minutes, stirring occasionally. Add the tomatoes and peppers. Place on the bottom of a serving dish. Skin and bone the sardines and arrange slightly overlapping on top. Sprinkle the top with the grated cheese and melted butter. Brown under the grill and serve.

SMELTS À LA BRETONNE

1 carrot
1 onion
salt and pepper
little fat
2 large cloves garlic, chopped
3/4 cup white wine

little chopped parsley
juice 1/2 lemon
1/4 cup water
2 mushrooms
1 stalk celery
8 or 10 smelts

few bread crumbs

Cut the carrot in small matchsticks and the onion in half slices. Mix with a little salt and pepper and put in a pan with a little fat. Cover with waxed paper and bake in the oven for 7 to 8 minutes. Cook the garlic in a pan with a little butter or fat until white. Add the wine and allow to reduce to half. Add salt and pepper, the parsley, lemon juice and 1/4 cup water. Bring to a boil. Add the carrot, onion and mushrooms, sliced and cooked in a little fat with the finely shredded celery. Simmer for 20 minutes. Put a little of this sauce in the bottom of a fireproof serving dish. Place well-washed smelts on top. Sprinkle with salt and pour over the rest of the sauce. Sprinkle with bread crumbs and little dabs of fat. Bake for 15 minutes in a 400° F. oven.

MARSEILLES FISH STEW

½ pound halibut	salt and pepper
½ pound salmon	3 tablespoons flour
1 pound mackerel	1¼ cups stock or water
¼ pound deep sea scallops	pinch dry mustard
1 small lobster	pinch cayenne pepper
¼ pound shrimps	¼ cup red wine
4 tablespoons olive oil	1 medium-sized onion
2 teaspoons tomato paste	4 tomatoes
4 cloves garlic	2 bay leaves
steamed potatoes	

Cut the halibut, salmon, mackerel, scallops and lobster in large squares. Place the shrimps in 2 tablespoons olive oil and brown. Remove from pan. Add to the pan the tomato paste, the cloves of garlic crushed with a little salt, and the flour. Stir until smooth, then add the stock or water, salt, pepper, mustard and cayenne pepper. Stir over the fire until the mixture comes to a boil. Add the wine and the following mixture: —

Heat 2 tablespoons olive oil in a pan. Add the chopped onion and cook until it begins to get golden brown. Then add the tomatoes, skinned and sliced, and cook briskly for 3 minutes. Add this to the other pan with the fish. Add the bay leaves. Cover and cook gently for 15 to 20 minutes, gently shaking the pan once or twice. Serve in a casserole with steamed potatoes on the side.

TRUITE AU BLEU PRINTANIÈRE
(Trout with Spring Vegetables)

lump of butter	2 bay leaves
1 sliced stalk celery	½ cup white wine
little sliced shallot	2 tablespoons tarragon vinegar
1 sliced carrot	2 cups water
salt and pepper	3 live trout
½ dozen fish carcasses	1 cup fresh tomato pulp
few peppercorns	3 tablespoons gelatine
1 teaspoon thyme and parsley	1 sliced lemon

Make a good fish stock. Melt a lump of butter, add to the pan a little sliced celery, shallot and carrot. Season and cook a few minutes without browning. Add the fish carcasses, a few peppercorns, thyme, parsley and the bay leaves. Pour on the wine, tarragon vinegar and 2 cups water.

Quickly remove the guts of the trout by pinching the mouth open and sticking a finger or skewer down the throat. Drop quickly into the stock. Cover with a lid and simmer very gently for 20 minutes. Allow fish to become quite cold in the stock. Take them out and arrange in a flat earthenware dish and pour over the following fish aspic: —

Fish Aspic: Strain the stock the trout were cooked in; add 1 cup fresh tomato pulp and season well. Put in a pan with 3 tablespoons gelatine and stir over the fire until the gelatin melts, without boiling. Then cool over ice. Pour over the trout. Put to set a few minutes. Garnish with thin slices of lemon and serve.

DEVILED CRAB

1 cup crab meat	2 tablespoons cream
½ teaspoon mustard	salt and pepper
1 dessertspoon Worcestershire sauce	cayenne pepper
2 tablespoons dry white bread crumbs	1 tablespoon Parmesan cheese
2 tablespoons fat or olive oil	

Put crab meat in a bowl. Add the mustard, Worcestershire

sauce, bread crumbs, cream, salt, pepper, and cayenne pepper. Mix thoroughly and refill crab shells. Sprinkle top liberally with grated cheese and a little fat or olive oil and bake for 5 to 10 minutes in a hot oven.

SHRIMP CREOLE

2 cups raw shrimps	*1 cup cream*
3 tablespoons foaming butter	*2 tablespoons sour cream*
3 tablespoons oil	*salt*
little more butter	*cayenne pepper*
4 finely sliced mushrooms	*chili pepper*
2 tablespoons Marsala wine	*2 sliced onions*
1 tablespoon finely chopped	*little chopped onion*
red and green peppers	*1 cup raw rice*
¼ teaspoon meat glaze	*light stock*
¼ teaspoon tomato paste	*3 tablespoons almonds*

Toss the shrimps in 1 tablespoon butter and 2 tablespoons oil for 1 to 2 minutes. Remove shrimps and add more butter and mushrooms. Cook briskly for a couple of minutes and add wine and peppers. Cook until the liquid is reduced; add a little more butter if necessary and the meat glaze and tomato paste. Mix in very slowly the cream, sour cream, salt, cayenne pepper and chili pepper. Put back the shrimps with the 2 sliced onions, which have been cooked in butter until brown and crisp. Simmer very slowly until heated through and the shrimps are pink. Serve with the following: —

Rice Pilaf: Heat 2 tablespoons butter and 1 tablespoon oil in a pan. Add chopped onion and rice and season. Cover with light stock and bring to a boil; add blanched and shredded almonds. Cover with waxed paper and the lid and cook in a moderate oven for 25 minutes. Remove, arrange in loaf shape on a serving dish, pour shrimp over and garnish the top with more almonds, which have been blanched, shredded and fried until golden in hot oil.

POIREAUX AUX CREVETTES
(Shrimps with Leeks)

3 large leeks
½ cup cooked, shelled shrimps
2 hard-boiled egg yolks
salt and pepper
handful chopped parsley
2 raw egg yolks

½ teaspoon French mustard
½ teaspoon English mustard
sugar to season
1 cup salad oil
wine, vinegar or lemon juice to
    sharpen

½ cup spinach juice

Remove outside leaves of the leeks; wash and cut in pieces 2 inches long. Bring to a boil in cold water for 5 minutes; drain and dry thoroughly. Pound or mince finely the shrimps and 2 hard-boiled egg yolks with pepper. Bind this with a spoonful of Mayonnaise Sauce. Add a large pinch of chopped parsley. Split the leeks down the middle when cold. Fill with the stuffing. Arrange on a dish, cover with green mayonnaise and serve very cold.

Mayonnaise Sauce: Put the 2 raw egg yolks in a bowl. Mix well with the French and English mustards, salt, pepper and sugar. Add the salad oil drop by drop and from time to time a little wine, vinegar or lemon juice to sharpen. To color green, add the spinach juice.

FISH BUTTERS AND SAUCES AND TWO WAYS OF MAKING STOCK

ANCHOVY AND TOMATO BUTTER
(For Cod, Haddock, Salmon, etc.)

1 level teaspoon tomato paste
½ chopped clove garlic
4 tablespoons creamed butter

4 fillets chopped anchovy
salt and pepper
paprika

½ teaspoon mixed herbs

Mix all the ingredients and let harden.

GARLIC BUTTER

(Excellent with Broiled Cod or Mackerel)

2 cloves garlic   *2 or 3 tablespoons creamed butter*
salt and pepper   *1 teaspoon Worcestershire sauce*
1 teaspoon chopped basil

Crush the garlic with 1 teaspoon salt and beat into it the creamed butter. Add salt and pepper to season, the Worcestershire sauce and the chopped basil.

GREEN BUTTER

handful spinach   *little chopped dill*
handful sorrel   *3 tablespoons creamed butter*
handful beet tops   *salt and pepper*

Blanch the vegetables, drain well and rub through a strainer. Mix this and the dill into the butter and add the seasoning. Chill in the refrigerator.

MAÎTRE D'HÔTEL BUTTER

(For Sole, Mackerel or Salmon)

4 tablespoons butter   *1 dessertspoon lemon juice*
1 teaspoon chopped parsley   *salt and pepper*

Beat the butter to a cream with a wooden spatula and work in the parsley and lemon juice by degrees. Add seasoning. Leave to harden before serving.

ORANGE BUTTER

1 crushed clove garlic   *1 teaspoon shredded, blanched orange*
4 tablespoons butter   *rind*
grated rind 1 orange   *salt and pepper*
1 dessertspoon orange juice   *½ teaspoon paprika*

Rub the bowl with the crushed garlic. Cream the butter in this bowl. Add other ingredients and leave to harden.

MUSTARD BUTTER
(For Herring or Mackerel)

1 crushed clove garlic	few drops each of wine, vinegar and
4 tablespoons butter	tomato ketchup
1 teaspoon French mustard	½ teaspoon English mustard
	salt and pepper

Rub the bowl with the crushed garlic. Cream the butter in this bowl and add other ingredients. Season and leave to harden.

RICH MAYONNAISE SAUCE

2 raw egg yolks	1 tablespoon tarragon vinegar
salt	1 cup oil
cayenne pepper	1 hard-boiled egg yolk
little dry mustard	2 or 3 tablespoons cream

Put the raw egg yolks in a bowl and add salt, cayenne pepper, mustard and tarragon vinegar. Mix well and beat the oil in slowly. Add the hard-boiled egg yolk, which has been rubbed through a sieve, and the cream.

PLAIN MAYONNAISE

1 egg	1 tablespoon vinegar
salt	1 cup oil
cayenne pepper	little milk, if needed

Put the egg in a bowl with the salt, cayenne pepper and vinegar. Beat the oil in quickly. If too thick, dilute with a little milk.

GARLIC MAYONNAISE

2 cloves garlic	½ teaspoon curry powder
½ teaspoon salt	1 or 2 drops lemon juice
	1 teaspoon Worcestershire sauce

Crush the garlic in ½ teaspoon salt. Add, with the above ingredients, to plain mayonnaise.

COLD SAUCE

3 stiffly beaten egg whites
½ cup sour cream

grated rind 1 lemon
paprika

Mix the egg whites into the sour cream. Add to plain mayonnaise. Add the lemon rind and paprika. Serve cold.

COURT BOUILLON
(For boiling fish or shellfish)

2 finely sliced carrots
3 finely sliced onions
lump butter
bouquet of herbs

4 cups water
½ cup white wine
salt and pepper

Cook the carrots and onions in a little butter without browning. Add the water, wine and seasoning and bring to a boil. Cool before putting in the fish. Bring to a boil again slowly and simmer gently, allowing 15 to 20 minutes for every pound of fish.

FISH FUMET OR STOCK
(For braising, sauces, soups, aspics)

few sole bones
few haddock bones or head
3½ cups water
½ cup white wine

6 peppercorns
bouquet of herbs
1 carrot
1 onion

Break up the bones. Put them in a pan with the other ingredients. Simmer until the liquid is reduced by one-third. Then strain and use.

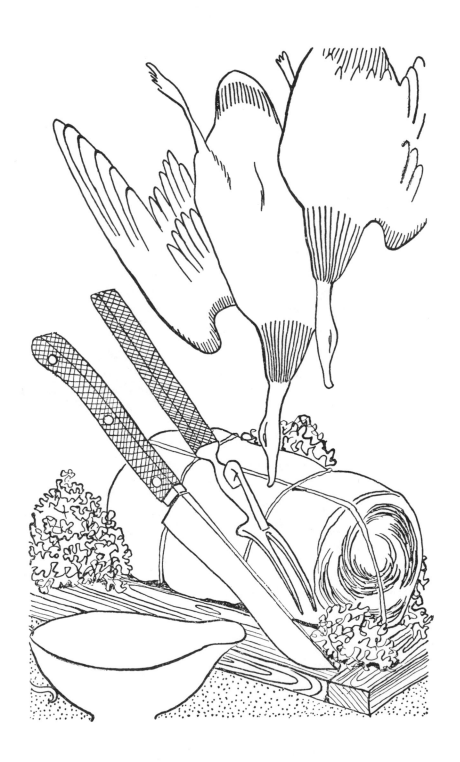

CHAPTER VII

GAME, POULTRY AND MEATS

Game, poultry and meats can be served in many varied and interesting dishes in addition to the usual roasting, broiling and frying. The French have utilized their knowledge of sauces to excellent advantage in the preparation of game and poultry. Meats also when combined with savory wine and herb sauces are delightful and different. Hitherto little used and relatively inexpensive cuts of meat can and should be served more often, for when properly prepared they are equally as delicious as the better known and more costly cuts.

Correct temperatures and proper length of cooking time are important in the preparation of these dishes. Moderate temperatures are the general rule since consistently high heat toughens meat and causes undue shrinkage. There are certain dishes, however, where high heat is desirable in the early stages of preparation, as, for example, when browning chicken livers. Unless liver is browned quickly there is a loss of blood which exudes from the meat on turning. Too prolonged a cooking period also has an adverse effect on game, poultry and meats, resulting in a stringy texture and poor flavor.

On Buying Game, Poultry and Meats: There are several reliable tests for making an intelligent selection of game, poultry and meats when the advice of a good dealer is not available. Game should be examined for shot, since large quantities of pellets are not always visible at first glance. Supple claws are some clue to good quality. Game generally should be hung for six to ten days, depending on the season, for aging takes place more rapidly in warm weather. Correct aging is indicated by pulling the feathers near the tail. If they come away easily the bird is ready for cooking. Many gourmets prefer the female bird, since she is more tender and better flavored, though smaller, than the cock.

When selecting poultry look for the flexible breastbone, since this is a sign of a young and tender chicken. Poultry for braising or boiling should not be too fat, for excess fat is an indication of poor quality meat. The drumstick of any fowl is improved if the sinews are drawn. An accommodating dealer should be able to take care of this minor operation.

Good economical cuts of beef are the topside, top-rump and flank. For braising (cooking with moist heat), the topside is first choice, while the slightly fatter flank or brisket is good for pressed beef or galantines. Roasted, sautéed and grilled meats call for the rolled ribs, sirloin or fillet.

Veal offers a wide range of cuts. The oyster from the shoulder is excellent for a ragout and as a roast when boned and stuffed. Knuckle of veal is also a good cut, although it has slightly more bone. It does, however, make an excellent base for bouillons. The choicest cuts of veal are the loin and fillet. Since it is often difficult to have a fillet cut the way you wish, it may be easier to buy the loin, bone it yourself and cut the meat as thin as you need it.

Since lamb and pork are from smaller animals than beef and veal, they do not offer as great a choice of cuts. Use the leg and shoulder of both for roasting and braising, and the loin and neck for grilling.

Cooking Game, Poultry and Meats: Game and poultry for *en casserole* dishes are first browned by placing the whole bird breast-side-down in hot, foaming butter. When the bird is browned before disjointing, the flesh does not shrink away from the bones as readily. A wooden spoon rather than a metal fork for turning the bird is used by chefs, since this does not so easily break the skin.

Continental cooks use wine extensively in game, poultry and meat cookery. A good general rule is to use red wine with beef and some game, and white wine with the lighter meats such as veal and poultry. When a recipe calls for wine to be flamed before adding to the dish, pour it into a small pan and tilt gently over direct heat until the surface begins to burn.

Wine is not only used as a choice flavoring agent, but it is also used as a tenderizer for the tougher cuts and for older game, rabbits and hares, in the form of a marinade. A marinade is made up of wine, oil and herbs. This mixture is then heated and poured over the raw meat. This is left for twelve hours to three days at room temperature, depending on the meat and the temperature. Frequent basting is the rule when meat is marinading. Always dry the meat well when removed from the marinade. Cutlets are frequently marinaded for thirty minutes in brandy or sherry. The liquid remaining is used in the sauce or gravy afterwards.

Herbs also are an important part of game, poultry and meat cooking. The herb bouquet is frequently used and consists of a sprig of thyme, marjoram, parsley and a bay leaf tied together with string. If attached to one handle of the casserole it may be easily removed before serving. Certain herbs belong with certain dishes. The secret of the famous *Poulet roti à la française* is the delicate flavor of tarragon, which is placed inside the bird together with butter before roasting. As the butter melts, the flavor of the herb permeates the entire chicken. The stronger flavor of bay is used with casseroles of game, especially in red wine sauces and in marinades. An adequate selection of herbs for succulent French dishes need not be elaborate. For example, lemon and black thyme, marjoram, summer and winter savory, bay, tarragon, chervil and chives will meet all the herb requirements in the following poultry recipes, while the last three will be used as salad herbs also. Country people with a garden should have no difficulty growing their own herbs. City dwellers may need to canvas several markets to find a grocer specializing in herbs. Garlic is one of the most readily obtainable of these flavoring agents. It is a valuable addition to French cooking when used with discretion. It may be necessary on occasion to use dried herbs; they should be used much more sparingly than fresh herbs since their flavor is very pronounced.

MARINADE CRUE
(For Meat and Game)

salt and pepper	1 crushed clove garlic
3 finely sliced onions	10 red and black peppercorns, mixed
3 finely sliced carrots	4 sprigs parsley
2 cloves	2 cups white or red wine
1 bay leaf	½ cup oil
	¼ cup wine vinegar

Season the meat to be marinated. Lay in an earthenware dish and cover with the onions, carrots, cloves, bay leaf, garlic, peppercorns and parsley. Mix the liquids together and pour over the dish. Leave for 2 or 3 days, basting and turning frequently.

MARINADE CUITE
(For Meat and Game)

2 tablespoons butter	1 cup water
1 sliced carrot	2 tablespoons oil
1 sliced onion	½ cup white or red wine
bouquet of herbs	4 tablespoons tarragon vinegar
1 clove garlic	salt and pepper
	4 peppercorns

Melt the butter, add the sliced vegetables and herbs. Cook a few minutes, add the liquids and simmer until they are reduced to about one-third. The pan should be covered. Allow to cool before pouring over the meat or game. Marinate for 24 hours.

MARINADE CRUE RAPIDE
(For Small Game, Cutlets, Tournedos, etc.)

salt and pepper	4 chopped sprigs parsley
handful finely chopped shallots	1 bay leaf
1 chopped sprig thyme	½ cup oil
	½ cup lemon juice

Season the game or meat with salt and pepper. Scatter over the shallots, thyme, parsley and the bay leaf. Moisten thoroughly with oil and lemon juice, using the juice of ½ lemon to each tablespoon oil. Soak for 12 to 24 hours.

These marinades can be kept 4 to 5 days after use and if strained can be bottled and used when required if fresh wine and vinegar are added. The marinades, however, should not be kept longer than 7 to 10 days.

POULET AUX DENTS DU CHAT
(Chicken with Cat's Teeth)

1 4-pound chicken	*1 tablespoon tomato paste*
½ cup butter	*3 level tablespoons flour*
2 tablespoons hot sherry	*1½ cups light stock or water*
1 chopped clove garlic	*¼ cup large shredded almonds*
2 tablespoons finely chopped	*salt and pepper*
onion	*1 bay leaf*
5 or 6 skinned tomatoes	*¾ cup thin sour cream*
1 tablespoon grated Gruyère cheese	

Brown the chicken all over in hot butter. Pour over the hot sherry and remove the chicken. Place in the pan the garlic, onion and 3 skinned and sliced tomatoes. Cook for 2 to 3 minutes. Remove from the fire and stir in the tomato paste and the flour until smooth. Pour on the stock or water and stir over the fire until the mixture comes to a boil. Add the almonds, salt, pepper and bay leaf; put back the chicken, breast-side-down. Cover and cook very slowly for 45 to 50 minutes, turning the chicken once or twice during the process of cooking. Remove and cut the chicken in neat joints and arrange in a shallow casserole.

Add to the liquid in which the chicken was cooked the sour cream, two skinned and sliced tomatoes and the cheese. Simmer a few minutes and pour over the chicken. Sprinkle with more grated cheese, dot with butter and brown under the broiler.

POULET À LA RÉGENCE
(Sautéed Chickens with Green Olives)

2 3½-pound chickens	*1½ cups stock*
butter	*salt and pepper*
2 tablespoons brandy	*1 bay leaf*
1 teaspoon meat glaze	*2 or 3 slices cooked bacon, shredded*
1 tablespoon tomato paste	*24 small white mushrooms, sautéed*
3 teaspoons potato flour	*24 stoned green olives*

24 stoned ripe olives

Brown chickens all over in hot butter. Pour over the brandy and remove the chickens. Place in the pan the meat glaze, tomato paste, potato flour, and stock. Stir over the fire until the mixture comes to a boil. Add salt, pepper and the bay leaf. Put chicken back in the pan breast-side-down, cover and cook slowly for 35 to 50 minutes, until just tender, turning occasionally.

Remove skin from 1 chicken. Remove breast from each side; cut in halves lengthwise. Remove remaining meat from this chicken and cut in fine shreds. Add the bacon, mushrooms, green olives and ripe olives. Arrange on a flat platter. Arrange the whole chicken on top. Place the breast of chicken at each side. Pour over the sauce and serve.

POULET EN CASSEROLE
(Chicken in a Casserole)

1 3½-pound chicken	*6 hearts of leek*
large lump butter	*12 small mushroom heads*
2 tablespoons Marsala wine or sherry	*1 teaspoon tomato paste*
18 small white onions	*3 level teaspoons potato flour*
12 small carrots	*1½ cups light stock*
12 baby turnips	*salt and pepper*
6 hearts of celery, cut in halves	*1 bay leaf*

handful chopped parsley

Brown the chicken all over in foaming hot butter; pour over the Marsala wine or sherry. Remove the chicken. Place in the pan the onions, carrots, turnips, hearts of celery and hearts of leek. Sauté for 2 to 3 minutes. Add the mushroom heads and cook for 2 minutes. Remove from the fire and stir in the tomato paste and potato flour. Pour on the stock. Stir over the fire until the mixture comes to a boil. Put back the chicken, turning breast-side-up halfway through cooking time. Remove and cut chicken in neat joints, arrange in casserole and scatter the vegetables over the top. If sauce is too thin, thicken it with a little more potato flour, which has been mixed in a little water. Reboil and pour over the chicken. Sauté the chicken liver and use as garnish. Add a little chopped parsley.

POULET À LA VALLÉE D'AUGE
(Chicken with Celery and Apple)

1 3½-pound chicken	*½ teaspoon meat glaze*
large lump butter	*1½ cups light stock*
2 tablespoons hot sherry	*salt and pepper*
1 sliced onion	*bouquet of herbs*
1 small stalk celery, sliced	*½ cup thin sour cream*
2 sliced apples	*little grated Parmesan cheese*
3 level tablespoons flour	*1 apple, cored and cut in rings*

Brown chicken all over in hot butter; pour over the hot sherry. Remove the chicken. Place in the pan the onion, celery and 2 sliced apples; cook slowly until vegetables are soft and nearly cooked. Remove from the fire and stir in carefully the flour and meat glaze. Pour in the stock. Stir over the fire until the mixture comes to a boil. Put back chicken with salt, pepper and herbs. Cover and cook very slowly until tender (approximately 40 minutes). Remove the chicken. Joint carefully and arrange in casserole.

Strain liquid in which chicken has been cooked and pour over the vegetables in the pan. Bring slowly to a boil. When bubbling, stir in the sour cream and the grated cheese. Simmer for 4 to 5 minutes. Pour over the chicken and garnish top with apple rings, which have been fried until golden in butter, and little bundles of celery, which have been cooked in sherry.

POULET SAUTÉ LOUISETTE
(Chicken with Ham and Tongue)

2 3½-pound chickens
lump bacon fat
1 thinly sliced onion
salt and pepper
2 tablespoons dry white wine

2 firm white mushrooms
2 slices shredded cooked tongue
1 slice shredded cooked ham
½ teaspoon meat glaze
1 teaspoon flour

bread

Brown the chickens in hot bacon fat. Place a few thin slices of the onion on top. Season with salt and pepper. Cover and sauté very slowly for 35 to 40 minutes. Remove the chickens. Stir in the wine and add the mushrooms, which have been cut in thick slices and sautéed a few minutes. Add the tongue and ham. Cook another minute. Stir in the meat glaze and the flour. Bring to a boil and season well. Replace the chickens and shake over the fire for a few minutes. Arrange in casserole and garnish round with the bread, which has been cut in ¾-inch slices and fried until golden in hot butter.

POULET SAUTÉ AU CITRON
(Chicken with Lemon Cream Sauce)

1 4-pound chicken
½ cup butter
1 tablespoon sherry
1 tablespoon white wine
1 large lemon

1 small orange
2 teaspoons lemon juice
salt and pepper
1 cup thin cream
little grated cheese

Cut the chicken up carefully, as for casserole. Cook until brown all over in foaming butter. Cover with the lid and continue sautéing over a slow fire until nearly cooked. Remove the chicken and stir into the pan the sherry and white wine. Add the grated rind of the large lemon, the grated rind of the orange, the lemon juice, and season with salt and pepper. Turn up the fire and stir in the cream slowly. Put back the chicken and toss over the fire for a few minutes. Arrange on a serving dish. Pour over the sauce and sprinkle with the grated cheese. Put a few thin slices of lemon and a few small pieces of butter on top. Brown under the broiler.

POULET AU BLANC À L'ESTRAGON I
(Chicken with Tarragon)

8 chicken breasts	paprika
little sliced onion	5 tablespoons butter
carrot	4 tablespoons flour
celery	cayenne pepper
3 sprigs tarragon	2 cups liquor chicken was cooked in
¼ cup white wine	2 tablespoons cream
1½ cups rice	3 tablespoons tarragon leaves
2 or 3 tablespoons melted butter	1 egg yolk
salt and pepper	1 tablespoon milk

Remove skin from the chicken and trim bone neatly. Put in a pan with sliced onion, carrot, celery, tarragon and white wine. Add just enough water to float the chicken; bring to a boil and simmer for 25 minutes. While this is cooking, boil the rice in salted water; drain, wash well in cold water and mix in melted butter, salt, pepper and paprika. Arrange in the bottom of a serving dish, place chicken on top and pour over the following sauce: —

Sauce: Melt 3 tablespoons butter, stir in flour, salt and cayenne pepper. When blended, strain on the liquor the chicken was cooked in. Stir over the fire until the sauce comes to a boil; then add the remaining butter and cream, bit by bit. Simmer for 5 to 6 minutes; add tarragon leaves and egg yolk mixed into milk. Pour over the chicken, garnish with extra tarragon leaves and paprika.

PETITS POUSSINS À LA HAMBOURG
(Stuffed Squab)

2 small squab chickens
1 finely sliced onion
6 tablespoons butter
salt and pepper
3 large chicken livers
½ cup shredded cooked ham or tongue
6 sliced mushrooms
2 skinned, cored and sliced apples
1 tablespoon blanched pistachio nuts

1 egg yolk
½ cup sherry
bouquet of herbs
1 pound spinach
1 tablespoon fat
½ cup sour cream
¾ cup fried croutons
little grated cheese

Split skin down the back of each squab. Cut meat off the carcass, keeping the thigh bone. Lay meat flat on board.

Place the onion, 1 tablespoon hot butter, salt and pepper in a pan. Cook for 1 to 2 minutes. Add the chicken livers. Cook briskly for 3 minutes with lid on. Remove livers and cut in thin strips. Return to pan with ¼ cup ham or tongue, the mushrooms and apples, which have been sautéed in a little butter, the pistachio nuts, which have been blanched and split in half. Cook for 3 to 4 minutes. Stir in the egg yolk.

Melt 2 tablespoons butter in a casserole and brown the squabs when they have been trussed. Heat 4 tablespoons sherry in a pan. Ignite the sherry and pour over the squabs. Add the herbs, and cook breast-side-down in a slow oven for 35 minutes, basting and turning frequently.

Wash the spinach. Drain well and put in a pan with the fat, salt and pepper. Cook briskly for 5 to 6 minutes. Drain and dry thoroughly. Chop up coarsely in a bowl and mix well with 2 tablespoons sour cream and ¾ cup croutons, which have been fried in butter until golden.

Mold in egg shapes with 2 tablespoons. Arrange on a cookie sheet and pour over a little sour cream. Sprinkle with the grated cheese, dot with butter, broil for a few minutes under the broiler. Remove and keep warm.

To Serve: Remove squabs from casserole. Add a little extra sherry and stock to squab gravy and bring to a boil, reducing it

to the consistency of thin cream. Pour on the bottom of a serving dish, arranging the squabs on top. Arrange the spinach at each
end and serve.

POULET AMANDINE
(Chicken with Almonds)

3½-pound chicken	*1½ cups light stock*
2 tablespoons hot Marsala	*¾ cup light sour cream*
4 or 5 skinned tomatoes	*¾ cup almonds, blanched and shredded*
1 teaspoon tomato paste	*¼ cup almonds, blanched and crushed*
3 tablespoons flour	*1 bay leaf*
	salt and pepper

Brown chicken well in hot butter and pour on the hot Marsala.
Remove chicken and add the skinned tomatoes to the pan. Cook
briskly until pulpy; then stir in tomato paste, stirring this off the
fire, flour, salt and pepper. Add the stock, stirred over the fire
until the mixture comes to a boil. Then pour on sour cream;
add ¼ cup blanched and shredded almonds and ¼ cup blanched
and crushed almonds.

Put back the chicken, breast-side-down. Add bay leaf, salt and
pepper, cover and cook slowly for 35 minutes. Remove the
chicken, cut in portions, arrange on a serving dish, pour the
sauce over and sprinkle with ½ cup shredded almonds. Dot with
butter, put under the broiler until the almonds are golden brown
and serve.

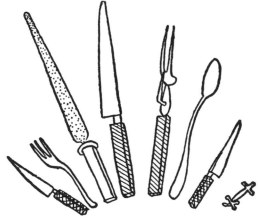

SAUTÉED CHICKEN WITH VEGETABLE GARNISH

2 broilers
2 tablespoons hot brandy
1 teaspoon tomato paste
2 tablespoons flour
1 cup stock
¾ cup sour cream
2 tablespoons grated Parmesan
* cheese*
1 grated lemon rind
salt and pepper
1 cup peas
1 cup beans
2 or 3 tablespoons water
2 tablespoons butter

squeeze of lemon juice
celery
leeks
broccoli
carrots
cauliflower
bread crumbs
1 chopped, hard-boiled egg
2 tablespoons chopped, green herbs
little garlic
1 tablespoon oil
juice ½ lemon
mushrooms
tomatoes

Brown the broilers all over in hot butter, slowly, and pour over hot brandy. Remove chicken from the pan and stir in tomato paste and flour; then pour on stock. Stir over the fire until the mixture comes to a boil; then beat in slowly, with a whisk, sour cream, grated cheese, grated lemon rind, salt and pepper. Cut chicken in pieces for serving, put back into sauce and sauté gently for 40 minutes. Remove, arrange in a pile in the center of a serving dish, pour some sauce over, serve the rest in a bowl and surround with 1 cup peas and 1 cup beans.

Use separate pans, but the method is the same. Blanch, drain and return to the pan with 2 or 3 tablespoons water, 1 tablespoon butter, squeeze of lemon juice and salt. Cook slowly until soft, about 15 minutes, the celery, leeks, broccoli, carrots and cauliflower; cook slowly in salted water and garnish the cauliflower with the following sauce: —

Sauce: Take 1 tablespoon bread crumbs, hard-boiled egg, 1 tablespoon chopped herbs and a little garlic; season, fry gently in butter until golden and pour over the cauliflower.

Garnish the other four vegetables with the following: —

Melt 1 tablespoon each butter and oil; add juice of ½ lemon, herbs, salt and pepper and pour over the vegetables.

Sauté the mushrooms whole in butter.

Cut tomatoes in half, sprinkle with crumbs and grated cheese, dot with butter, season, and brown under the broiler.

Surround the chicken with the vegetables and serve.

SUPRÊME DE VOLAILLE PARISIENNE
(Breast of Chicken Parisienne)

8 half-breasts of chicken	2½ cups chicken stock
salt and pepper	½ cup chopped mushrooms
4 tablespoons hot sherry	3 tablespoons chopped, dried mushrooms
¼ cup mushroom stock	2 egg yolks
2 tablespoons butter	1 tablespoon tarragon vinegar
4 tablespoons flour	2 tablespoons cream
cayenne pepper	3 tablespoons fat
	sautéed mushrooms

Trim the bones off neatly and remove the skin; dust with flour and seasoning and carefully brown each side in hot butter; then pour over hot sherry, salt and pepper. Cover with the lid and cook slowly for 15 to 20 minutes, gradually adding the mushroom stock. (This is made by soaking dried mushrooms in water for several hours.) When tender, remove the chicken, arrange on a serving dish and pour on the following sauces: —

Mushroom Velouté Sauce: Melt butter in a pan, stir in flour, salt and cayenne pepper; pour on chicken stock and add chopped mushrooms. Stir over the fire until the sauce comes to a boil; then add dried mushrooms, which were previously soaked to make the stock, and the liquid from the pan in which the chickens were cooked. Pour over the chicken and just before serving pour over each breast the following sauce: —

Hollandaise Sauce: Put in a bowl 2 egg yolks, salt, cayenne pepper, vinegar and cream. Put the bowl in a pan of hot water over a slow fire, beat until the sauce begins to thicken, and add fat, bit by bit. Pour over breasts and place on top of each a sautéed mushroom. Serve immediately.

SUPRÊME DE VOLAILLE AUVERNAISE

½ chicken breast
flour
hot butter
3 tablespoons hot sherry
1 tablespoon dried mushroom
   stock

salt and pepper
1 medium-sized eggplant
tomatoes
2 tablespoons finely chopped, dried
   mushrooms
2 tablespoons white wine

Use ½ chicken breast for each person. Remove skin and trim off the bone, dust lightly with flour, brown well each side in a little butter, and pour over the hot sherry. Cover and cook slowly for 25 minutes, adding the mushroom stock from time to time. Season with salt and pepper.

Cut the eggplant in slices, sprinkle with salt and let stand for half an hour; fry until golden in hot oil. Arrange on the bottom of a hot serving dish and cover with tomatoes, sliced, skinned and sautéed, using the same pan the eggplant was cooked in. Put a layer of tomatoes over the eggplant and arrange the chicken on top. Add to the pan the chicken was cooked in 2 tablespoons finely chopped, dried mushrooms, which have been soaked in white wine. Boil up, pour over the chicken and serve.

ARROZ CON POLLO
(Rice with Chicken)

2 frying chickens
4 tablespoons butter
2 tablespoons Marsala or sherry
2 teaspoons tomato paste
3 teaspoons potato flour
2 cups chicken stock
1 bay leaf
salt and pepper
2 sautéed mushrooms
1 green pepper

2 canned pimentoes
2 chicken livers
2 tablespoons oil
1 tablespoon fat
2 tablespoons chopped onion
1½ cups raw rice
stock
3 tomatoes
2 tablespoons grated Parmesan
   cheese

Cut up chickens, brown well in foaming butter and pour over sherry or Marsala. Remove chicken. Add to pan the tomato paste and potato flour. Mix well and pour on the stock. Stir over the fire until the mixture is boiling; put back chicken and add bay leaf, salt and pepper. Cook gently; then add mushrooms, pepper and pimentoes, shredded and blanched, and chicken livers, sautéed and sliced.

Rice: Melt oil and fat, add chopped onion and cook until golden brown; then add raw rice. Fry a little; then cover with stock. Season with salt, pepper and bay leaf. Bring slowly to a boil, cover with waxed paper and put in the oven to cook for 25 minutes. Remove and add tomatoes, skinned and sautéed, and grated cheese. Mix with chicken and serve on a platter.

BREAST OF CHICKEN PARISIENNE

4 double breasts of chicken
2 tablespoons hot Marsala wine
½ teaspoon tomato paste
1 tablespoon flour
scant ½ cup stock
1 to 1½ cups sour cream
salt and pepper

1 tablespoon currant jelly
1 tablespoon grated Parmesan
* cheese*
4 tablespoons butter
2 cups mushrooms
cayenne pepper
1 tablespoon sherry

1 tablespoon finely chopped dill

Remove meat from bone, leaving little wing bone at end. Dust lightly with flour, brown quickly in foaming butter, then pour over wine. Remove chicken and add to the pan tomato paste and flour; stir in the stock. Stir over the fire until the mixture thickens; then add very carefully, with a whisk, the sour cream. Season with salt, pepper, jelly and cheese. Put back the breasts, cover and cook gently for 15 to 20 minutes. Remove, arrange on a serving dish, pour over the sauce, sprinkle with grated cheese, dot with butter and brown under the broiler. Serve with the following: —

Mushrooms with Wine and Dill: Slice the mushrooms finely, put into very hot butter and add salt and cayenne pepper. Cook briskly for 3 to 4 minutes; then pour over sherry and finely chopped dill.

POULET SAUTÉ À LA MAINTENON
(Sautéed Chicken with Mushrooms)

3 chicken livers
little fat
6 finely sliced mushrooms
½ cup finely shredded, cooked tongue
salt and pepper

1 teaspoon dry thyme
2 broilers
chopped parsley
3 tablespoons white wine
3 tablespoons water

Sauté livers very quickly in fat; remove and add to pan sliced mushrooms, cooked tongue, salt, pepper and dry thyme. Have prepared rounds of bread fried in hot fat. Arrange on a serving dish, put a pile of this mixture on each and on top of that put a piece of broiled chicken. See following directions: —

Chicken: Split broilers and season with salt and pepper. Pour over a little hot chicken fat and broil slowly on both sides. Cut in quarters and put 1 piece on each garnished round. Garnish top with slices of liver and sprinkle with chopped parsley. Pour over the following gravy: —

Gravy: Add to the pan the chickens were broiled in white wine, water, salt and pepper. Boil up and pour over the chicken.

POULET MARENGO I
(Chicken with Lobster and Fried Eggs)

2 broilers
2 tablespoons hot sherry
1 tablespoon tomato paste
2 tablespoons flour
1½ cups stock

3 finely chopped mushrooms
4 or 5 tomatoes
1 bay leaf
salt and pepper
lobster meat

Cut up chicken and brown well in hot butter; pour on the hot sherry. Remove chicken and add to the pan the tomato paste and flour. Stir until smooth; pour on stock. Stir over the fire until the mixture comes to a boil; add chopped mushrooms. Put back chicken with tomatoes, skinned and sliced, bay leaf, salt and pepper. Cover and cook fairly fast for about 45 minutes. Remove, arrange chickens on serving dish and place on top slices of cooked lobster meat.

Pour over the sauce and garnish with lobster shells, croutons of fried bread and fried eggs.

CHICKEN PIE

2 small chickens	¼ cup cream
1 sliced onion	2 finely chopped, dried mushrooms
1 sliced carrot	3 sliced, hard-boiled eggs
1 stalk celery	2 tablespoons chopped herbs
salt and pepper	1½ cups flour
1 bay leaf	4 tablespoons fat
3 tablespoons butter	3 egg yolks
4 level tablespoons flour	2 tablespoons water
cayenne pepper	3 tablespoons grated cheese
1½ cups stock	½ teaspoon paprika

Put the chickens in a pan with onion, carrot, celery, salt, pepper, bay leaf and water to cover. Bring slowly to a boil and simmer for 25 to 30 minutes until tender. Remove chickens and take meat from the bones. Remove all skin, cut in coarse shreds and add to the following sauce: —

Sauce: Melt 2 tablespoons butter in a pan; add flour, salt and cayenne pepper and pour on the chicken stock. Stir over the fire until the sauce comes to a boil; add the remaining butter, cream, and mushrooms, bit by bit. The mushrooms should be soaked several hours in water. Add a little juice in which the mushrooms were soaked. When well blended, add the chicken with hard-boiled eggs and chopped herbs. Fill a deep dish, brush the edge of the dish with beaten egg and cover with the following crust: —

Crust: Put flour on a slab, make a well in the center and put in the fat, egg yolks, water, grated cheese, paprika and salt. Work the center ingredients to a smooth paste, work in the flour, roll out not too thin and cover the top. Trim neatly, brush with beaten egg and bake for 30 to 35 minutes in a 375° F. oven.

CHICKEN CASSEROLE

1 3½-pound broiler
2 tablespoons sherry
12 small onions
12 baby carrots
12 baby turnips
1 stalk celery

5 mushrooms
1 teaspoon tomato paste
1 level teaspoon potato flour
1½ cups stock
salt and pepper
1 bay leaf

chopped parsley

Brown the chicken well all over in hot butter and pour over the sherry. Remove chicken and add to the pan onions, carrots and turnips (12 pieces of carrot or turnip cut about 1 inch thick), 1 stalk celery cut in quarters. Cook for 5 or 6 minutes and add mushrooms cut in halves. Cook another minute and stir in tomato paste and flour. When well blended pour on stock. Stir over the fire till the mixture comes to a boil.

Cut up the chicken and return to pan with salt, pepper and bay leaf. Cook slowly for 40 minutes covered. When tender, arrange chicken in a casserole, scatter vegetables over the top, sprinkle with chopped parsley, pour the sauce over and serve.

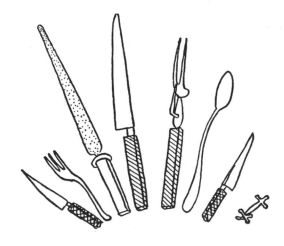

POULET PAYSANNE
(Chicken with Vegetables)

1 4-pound boiling fowl	*1 chopped clove garlic*
6 onions	*2 slices bacon, diced*
6 carrots	*¼ cup red wine*
1 stalk celery	*2 cups stock*
bouquet of herbs	*1 teaspoon tomato paste*
salt and pepper	*handful chopped fresh herbs*
peppercorns	*2 turnips*
6 tablespoons butter	*½ cup light stock*

Simmer fowl gently in water for 1 to 1½ hours with a little sliced onion, 3 carrots, celery, bouquet of herbs, salt and peppercorns to flavor. Remove the fowl and cool slightly. Melt 1 tablespoon butter in a casserole and brown fowl lightly. Remove the fowl. Add a little finely sliced onion, carrot, the chopped garlic and the bacon. Cook for 2 to 3 minutes; then stir in carefully the wine, 2 cups stock, the tomato paste, salt, pepper and herbs. Bring to a boil. Replace the fowl and braise in the oven, basting frequently, for 1 hour, or until the fowl is tender. (This is always shown by shrinking of meat from end of drumsticks.) Remove the fowl. Carve and keep warm. Strain the gravy and reduce it to half the quantity; keep warm.

Melt 3 level tablespoons butter in a pan. Add 3 sliced onions, 3 sliced carrots, 2 sliced turnips, salt, pepper and ½ cup light stock. Cover with waxed paper and the lid. Simmer until vegetables are tender. Arrange vegetables in the middle of a round dish. Place fowl on top. Pour over a little of the gravy. Serve remaining gravy separately. Sprinkle with fresh chopped herbs and serve.

POULET CRÉOLE I
(Chicken Creole)

2 small chickens
1 crushed clove garlic
parsley
salt and pepper
butter
white wine
2 tablespoons oil
2 tablespoons chopped onion
little garlic
1½ cups rice
handful of raisins
¾ cup sautéed mushrooms
shredded raw green pepper
½ cup blanched, split and browned
  almonds
very little Parmesan cheese
½ cup sliced onions

2 bananas
3 tablespoons oil
sliced onion, carrot and celery
3 tablespoons flour
1 sliced tomato
1 teaspoon tomato paste
2 cups strong stock
1 tablespoon apple jelly
2 tablespoons red wine
1 tablespoon sherry
½ teaspoon meat glaze
1 bay leaf
½ tomato per person
oil
thin slices onion
grated cheese
paprika

Put in the center of each chicken crushed garlic, parsley, salt, pepper and a lump of butter. Rub the outside with more butter, cover with waxed paper and pour over a little white wine. Roast very slowly for 1 hour, basting occasionally. Remove carefully, cut off all the breasts and remove entire breast bone; fill with Rice Pilaf.

Rice Pilaf: Heat in pan 2 tablespoons oil, 2 tablespoons chopped onion, a little garlic. Cook for 1 minute; then add rice and raisins. Cook for 2 to 3 minutes, stirring constantly; cover with stock and bring to a boil. Add enough stock to rise ½ inch above rice; cover with waxed paper and lid and put in the oven for 25 minutes. Remove and mix in mushrooms, green pepper and almonds; season well and add a very little Parmesan cheese and ½ cup sliced onions, which have been cooked dark brown. Shape to look like chicken; slice the breasts very thin and arrange on top of rice as follows: 1 slice chicken and 1 slice fried banana. Arrange on a dish and pour over the following sauce: —

Sauce: Put in pan 3 tablespoons oil. Add onion, carrot and celery sliced finely; cook for a few minutes and add flour. Brown dark very slowly, add stalks and peelings of mushrooms, 1 sliced tomato with the skin on, and tomato paste. Pour on strong stock; stir over the fire until the sauce comes to a boil; then add apple jelly and red wine, sherry, meat glaze, bay leaf, salt and pepper. Boil down to a creamy consistency, strain, pour over chicken and garnish with broiled tomatoes.

Broiled Tomatoes: Take ½ tomato per person. Leave skin on; pour over a little oil, put on top a thin slice onion; pour on a little more oil, sprinkle with cheese and brown under the broiler. Arrange around dish, sprinkle with paprika and serve.

POULET CRÉOLE II
(Chicken Creole)

1 4½-to-5-pound roasting chicken	½ chopped red pepper
1 cup butter	½ chopped green pepper
bouquet of herbs	2 skinned, sliced tomatoes
1 sprig tarragon	handful large shredded almonds
1 crushed clove garlic	½ cup raisins
salt and pepper	few chopped fresh herbs
2 small sliced onions	2 bananas
1 sliced carrot	2 pounds spinach
¼ cup white wine	1 tablespoon fat
¾ cup rice	2 or 3 tablespoons sour cream
1 chopped clove garlic	¾ cup sweet cream
5 or 6 sliced mushrooms	little mustard to flavor

Place inside chicken 1 lump butter, bouquet of herbs, the tarragon, crushed clove of garlic, salt and pepper. Place in a roasting tin. Spread a little butter on top; surround with 1 small sliced onion and the sliced carrot; pour over the white wine. Cover with waxed paper. Roast in a moderate oven for 35 to 40 minutes, basting frequently. Each time you baste add a little water if the chicken gets too fat. Remove paper after 30 minutes. Remove chicken from the oven and carefully take off each side of breast and cut in thin slices. Cut out breastbone with scissors.

Boil the rice in boiling salted water for 13 minutes. Drain and wash well in hot water. Shake well until dry. Melt 1 tablespoon butter in a pan. Add the clove of chopped garlic and cook for 1 minute. Add the mushrooms, which have been sautéed, salt and pepper. Cook for 5 to 6 minutes. Add the chopped red and green peppers, sliced tomatoes, almonds, raisins and fresh chopped herbs. Fill the chicken. Cover the rice alternately with a slice of chicken breast and a slice of banana cut lengthwise and fried until golden brown in hot butter; keep warm.

Wash the spinach well. Drain and put in a pan with 1 tablespoon fat, salt and pepper. Cook briskly for 5 to 6 minutes. Drain and chop finely in a bowl. Mix in the sour cream. Arrange on the bottom of a serving dish and place chicken on top. Cover top with thin slices of onion, cooked until crisp in hot butter.

Add water to the pan in which the chicken was roasted. Stir over a brisk fire until well blended with the glaze. Mix the sweet cream in carefully. Flavor with salt, pepper and a little mustard. Pour around the dish and serve.

POULET SAUTÉ À LA VICHY
(Chicken with Carrots)

1 3½-pound chicken	flour
large lump butter	½ cup red wine
1 bunch new carrots	1 cup stock
1 finely sliced onion	1 bay leaf
4 or 5 mushroom stalks	1 sprig fresh tarragon
salt and pepper	lemon juice to flavor
1 teaspoon meat glaze	2 tablespoons white wine
½ teaspoon tomato paste	handful chopped parsley
2 or 3 tablespoons sour cream	

Brown the chicken all over in hot butter, beginning with each side of the breast, and remove. Place in pan 1 finely sliced carrot and the onion and cook slowly until just tender. Add the mushroom stalks, salt and pepper and cook for 2 to 3 minutes. Add the meat glaze, the tomato paste and handful of flour; mix well. Replace the chicken and pour over the red wine and stock. Bring slowly to a boil. Add the bay leaf and tarragon. Cover and cook on top shelf of a moderate oven for 35 to 40 minutes. Remove and strain liquid and boil it down to the consistency of cream. Joint the chicken.

Scrape the remaining carrots and cut in thin slices. Bring to a boil in cold water. Drain and add 1 tablespoon butter, salt, pepper, and a little lemon juice. Add the white wine. Cover and cook until just soft. Add the parsley and sour cream. Arrange on the bottom of a serving dish. Place the cut-up chicken on top. Pour over the sauce and serve.

POULET À LA STANLEY
(Chicken with Mushrooms and Paprika)

large lump butter
2 large, finely chopped onions
1 cut-up chicken
salt and pepper
1 cup thin cream
3 level tablespoons flour

1 cup milk
1 tablespoon tomato paste
½ teaspoon curry powder
½ teaspoon paprika
2 teaspoons lemon juice
3 sliced mushrooms

bread

Melt a little butter in a pan. Add the onions and cook slowly without browning for 6 to 8 minutes. Add a little more butter, the cut-up chicken, salt, pepper and cream. Cover and cook slowly for 30 minutes. Remove chicken and keep warm.

Melt 1 tablespoon butter in a small pan, stir in the flour and add the milk. Stir over the fire and bring to a boil. Stir carefully into onion mixture. Add the tomato paste and rub through a strainer. Add the curry powder and paprika, lemon juice and mushrooms, which have been sautéed in a little butter. Bring slowly to a boil. Replace the chicken and simmer for 10 minutes. Arrange on a flat dish and pour over the sauce. Surround the dish with crescents of bread, fried until golden in butter.

POULET À LA KIEV
(Fried Chicken Breast Stuffed with Butter)

2 small chickens
lump butter
chopped garlic
finely chopped, mixed fresh herbs
salt and pepper

flour
1 beaten egg
few bread crumbs
fat
water cress

Remove breast of chickens from bone and carefully take off skin. Carefully cut in half and place between 2 pieces of waxed paper. Beat with a wooden mallet until very thin. Remove paper. In the center of each place a small finger of firm butter and the garlic. Sprinkle with the herbs and season with salt and pepper.

Roll up and tuck in each end. Roll in flour, brush with beaten egg, roll in bread crumbs, and fry in hot fat until golden brown (approximately 3 minutes). Remove and drain well on paper. Stick with a cocktail stick and arrange on a hot serving dish. Garnish with water cress and serve at once.

GALANTINE DE VOLAILLE
(Galantine of Chicken)

1 4-pound roasting chicken
½ cup sausage meat
1 egg white
3 tablespoons sour cream
2 teaspoons chopped, mixed
  fresh herbs

salt and pepper
few slices cooked ham or tongue
2 or 3 slices liverwurst sausage
1 hard-boiled egg
3 or 4 chicken livers

Cut off the neck, the big joint of wings and the tops of the leg joints of the chicken. Turn over and slit skin down the center of the back. Remove all meat from the carcass and avoid splitting any of the skin. Remove leg bones and the little wing bone. Spread out on a board.

Mix smoothly in a bowl the sausage meat, egg white, sour cream, herbs, salt and pepper. Spread on the chicken. Cover with slices of ham or tongue and slices of liverwurst sausage. Remove yolk from hard-boiled egg and insert in its place 1 small piece of chicken liver. Place in the center. Cut the hard-boiled egg yolk in half and place on each side of egg. Put on top 1 or 2 chicken livers. Roll up carefully and sew with fine thread. Roll in waxed paper, then in cloth, and tie each end securely with string. Place in pan and just cover with water; bring slowly to a boil. Simmer very gently for 1½ hours. Remove and put a brick on top for a weight. Cool overnight in the refrigerator. Unwrap and carefully remove the thread. Cut in thin slices and serve as an hors d'oeuvre or with salad. This keeps very well.

POULET À LA KING
(Chicken à la King)

1 4-pound roasting chicken   *large lump butter or fat*
little sliced onion, carrot,   *4 thinly sliced, firm white mushrooms*
  and celery   *½ diced red pepper*
1 bay leaf   *½ diced green pepper*
few peppercorns   *2 or 3 level tablespoons flour*
salt   *½ teaspoon meat glaze*
handful grated Parmesan cheese

Place chicken in pan and just cover with water. Bring slowly to a boil and skim off all scum. Add the onion, carrot, celery, bay leaf, peppercorns and salt. Cook slowly for 40 minutes. Remove the chicken. Skin and remove all meat from bones and cut in shreds.

Melt a little butter or fat in a pan. Add the mushrooms and sauté a few minutes. Add the red and green peppers. Stir in the flour and the meat glaze. Remove from the fire and stir in 1½ cups of the liquid in which the chicken was cooked. Stir over the fire until the mixture comes to a boil. Put back the chicken. Arrange on a flat dish, sprinkle with grated cheese, dot with butter or fat and brown under the broiler. Serve with plain boiled dry rice.

POULET AU BLANC À L'ESTRAGON II
(Chicken with Tarragon)

1 4- or 5-pound boiling fowl   *large lump butter*
1 tablespoon sliced onion   *4 level tablespoons flour*
little sliced carrot   *cayenne pepper*
little sliced celery   *2 or 3 tablespoons cream*
bouquet of herbs   *1 egg yolk*
few peppercorns   *1 tablespoon milk*
salt   *few tarragon leaves*

Place fowl in a pan and just cover with water. Bring very slowly to a boil and skim off any scum. Add the onion, carrot, celery, herbs, peppercorns and salt and cook very, very slowly until just tender. Remove the skin, cut fowl up in neat joints, and arrange on a serving dish.

Melt 2 tablespoons butter in a pan. Stir in the flour, salt and cayenne pepper. Remove from the fire and add 1¾ cups of strained liquid in which the chicken was cooked. Stir over the fire until the mixture comes to a boil. Add, bit by bit, 2 or 3 tablespoons of cream and a small piece of butter and simmer to creamy consistency. Remove from the fire and add the egg yolk mixed into the milk. Pour over the chicken and decorate in the form of a branch or tree with tarragon leaves which have been dipped into boiling water.

CRÊPES NIÇOISES
(Pancakes Stuffed with Chicken)

4 tablespoons flour	5 or 6 sliced mushrooms
1 egg	large lump butter
1 egg yolk	¾ cup shredded cooked chicken,
1 tablespoon oil	veal, ham or tongue
½ cup milk	2 chopped, hard-boiled eggs
salt and pepper	1 teaspoon chopped parsley
cayenne pepper	3 or 4 tablespoons sour cream
	grated cheese

Place the flour, egg, egg yolk, oil, 4 tablespoons milk, salt and cayenne pepper in a bowl. Beat until smooth. Add enough milk to reduce to the consistency of thin cream. Cool in refrigerator for half an hour.

Sauté the mushrooms in a little butter. Add the chicken, veal, ham, or tongue, the hard-boiled eggs, parsley, salt, pepper and sour cream. Cook for a few minutes; keep warm.

Remove the batter from refrigerator; if too thick add a little milk. Heat a small pancake pan and grease with a little hot butter or oil. Cover the bottom with a very thin coating of batter. Brown carefully on one side, turn and brown the other. Cook remaining batter in the same way.

Place a spoonful of the filling in the middle of each pancake. Fold over and arrange overlapping on a hot serving dish. Pour over 3 tablespoons melted butter. Sprinkle well with grated cheese. Brown under the broiler.

POULET MARENGO II
(Chicken with Lobster and Fried Eggs)

1 4-pound chicken
large lump butter
1 tablespoon brandy
2 tablespoons sherry
1 tablespoon finely chopped onion
4 skinned, sliced tomatoes
1 teaspoon tomato paste
2 level tablespoons flour
1¼ cups light stock

3 small, white, thinly sliced
*   mushrooms*
2 baby hen-lobsters
salt and pepper
1 bay leaf
4 fried eggs, both sides golden
bread cut in croutons
little olive oil
freshly chopped chives .

Cut the chicken up as for casserole and brown in foaming hot butter. Add a little more butter. Cover pan with lid and sauté chicken over a slow fire until just tender (approximately 35 minutes). Shake occasionally. Remove chicken from pan. Place in the pan the brandy and sherry. Stir round the bottom of the pan until all the glaze has been mixed in. Add the onion and tomatoes and cook for 2 minutes. Stir in carefully the tomato paste, flour, and the stock. Stir over the fire until the mixture comes to a boil. Add the mushrooms and the meat from the cooked lobsters. Season with salt, pepper and the bay leaf. Put back the chicken. Simmer very gently for 5 minutes. Arrange on a serving dish. Garnish with fried eggs and croutons of bread fried in olive oil until golden. Sprinkle with freshly chopped chives and serve.

POULET MAJORCA
(Chicken with Orange and Pepper)

1 4-pound chicken
lump bacon fat
2 tablespoons Madeira or sherry
1 teaspoon tomato paste
½ teaspoon meat glaze
3 level teaspoons potato flour
1½ cups light stock
1 sprig tarragon
1 sprig parsley
salt and pepper

2 tablespoons olive oil
1 teaspoon chopped garlic
3 sliced mushrooms
½ diced red pepper
½ diced green pepper
2 skinned and pipped tomatoes,
  diced in large pieces
grated rind 1 orange
shredded rind 1 orange
potatoes

Cut chicken up carefully as for casserole and brown in a little hot bacon fat. Pour over the Madeira or sherry. Remove the chicken. Add to the pan the tomato paste, meat glaze and potato flour and pour on the stock. Stir over the fire until the mixture comes to a boil. Put back the chicken with the tarragon, parsley and a little salt and pepper. Cover and cook slowly for 35 minutes. Arrange chicken on a flat dish.

Heat the olive oil in a pan. Add the garlic and cook for 1 minute. Add the mushrooms and sauté for 1 to 2 minutes. Add the red and green peppers and the tomatoes. Shred finely the rind of 1 orange. Remove outer and inner skin of the 2 oranges and cut in thin slices. Add to the sauce. Pour over the chicken and garnish with sautéed potatoes.

POULET SAUTÉ AU MIREPOIX
(Chicken with White Grapes and Vegetables)

6 tablespoons butter	1 diced turnip
1 bay leaf	1 diced stalk celery
1 crushed clove garlic	1 diced leek
salt and pepper	1 handful diced green beans
1 3½-pound roasting chicken	½ cup shelled peas
2 tablespoons white wine	3 or 4 tablespoons cream
¼ cup water	bouquet of herbs
2 diced carrots	¾ cup skinned white grapes

Place a small lump of butter, the bay leaf and the garlic inside the chicken. Spread a little butter on top of the chicken; add salt and pepper. Place the chicken in a roasting pan and pour round the wine and water. Cover with waxed paper. Roast for 40 to 60 minutes in a moderate oven, turning and basting frequently. Remove paper about ¼ hour before chicken is cooked. Remove chicken and carve in 6 pieces. Cut legs off first and chop away the knuckle bone. Then remove wings and breast in one piece, slicing carefully in half. Keep warm.

In another thick pan melt 1 tablespoon butter. Blanch and drain the carrots, turnip, celery, leek, beans and peas and add to butter with salt and pepper. Cover with waxed paper and lid, place in a moderate oven and cook very slowly until tender (approximately 30 minutes). Arrange in the center of a serving dish. Arrange chicken on this and place in oven to keep warm. Strain the gravy from the pan; add salt, pepper and enough water or stock to make 1 cup; reduce to gravy consistency. Remove from the fire and add 3 or 4 tablespoons cream. Boil again. Reduce again, whisking well. Add the herbs and the grapes. Pour over the chicken and serve at once.

CÔTELETTES DE VOLAILLE VICOMTESSE
(Mousse of Chicken)

1 4-pound chicken
3 roughly beaten egg whites
1¼ cups cream
salt and pepper
4 chopped mushrooms

1 slice ham, chopped and diced
large lump butter
3 level tablespoons flour
1 egg yolk
1 tablespoon milk

Skin the chicken carefully and remove all meat from the bone. Put twice through the meat chopper. Mix in the egg whites slowly. Rub through a fine strainer. Place in a tin-lined saucepan over a bowl of ice. Beat in 1 cup cream slowly. Add salt and pepper to season. Beat a few minutes longer if mixture becomes a little thin when cream is added.

Grease 4 cutlet molds. Fill level with this chicken mousse mixture. Make small holes in centers with wet finger. Fill holes with the mushrooms, which have been sautéed, and the ham. Cover with a little more of the mousse. Drop molds into a pan of hot, seasoned water and allow to poach gently until set, without boiling (approximately 12 minutes). The chicken cutlets will slide out of their molds when cooked. Take out carefully. Dry lightly on a cloth and arrange overlapping around the serving dish. Pour over the following sauce: —

Sauce: Make a little stock from the bones of the chicken. Strain 1½ cups onto a tablespoon of melted butter, which has been stirred to a smooth paste with 3 level tablespoons of flour. Stir over the fire until the sauce comes to a boil. Add the rest of the cream and a small lump of butter. Simmer a few moments; then add 1 egg yolk mixed into 1 tablespoon of milk. Pour over the chicken and stick at each end of the cutlets a small côtelette frill.

ARMENIAN RICE WITH CHICKEN LIVER OR LAMB

12 chicken livers
4 tablespoons butter
2 tablespoons chopped onion
2 teaspoons chopped garlic
1/4 cup sliced mushroom stalks
1 shredded green pepper
2 1/2 cups rice
2 teaspoons meat glaze
2 tablespoons tomato paste
light stock
salt and pepper

little chili pepper
little dry mustard
2 tablespoons pineapple or
    peach preserves
1 eggplant
2 apples
2 onions
1/2 cup blanched almonds
3 tomatoes
1 finely sliced green pepper
little sliced pimento

bacon

Brown chicken livers very fast in hot butter. Remove livers and add chopped onion to pan; cook briskly with garlic for 1 minute. Add mushroom stalks and shredded pepper, cook for 2 minutes and add rice. Cook slowly for 2 or 3 minutes; then add meat glaze and tomato paste. Pour on enough stock to cover and cook until liquid is absorbed; add more stock as needed and continue until rice is tender. Add salt and pepper, chili pepper, dry mustard and preserves a few minutes before it is done. Continue cooking until all liquid is absorbed, then add eggplant, cut in rounds and fried golden in hot oil, skinned apples, cored and cut in thick slices and browned in butter, onions, cut thick and browned very dark in butter, almonds, cooked golden in hot oil, tomatoes, cut in thick slices, pepper, pimento and livers, which have been cut in thick slices. Cover and keep in a warm place for 10 minutes before serving. Garnish with strips of crisp bacon and serve very hot from a casserole.

CHICKEN LIVER SAUCE FOR SPAGHETTI

12 chicken livers
6 tablespoons butter
4 finely chopped cloves garlic
2 large, finely chopped onions
8 chopped mushrooms
salt and pepper
1 pinch dry mustard

1 tablespoon flour
½ teaspoon meat glaze
3 tablespoons tomato paste
¼ cup stock
2 tablespoons chopped, mixed fresh herbs
1 bowl grated cheese

5 skinned, coarsely chopped tomatoes

Brown the chicken livers very quickly in a little hot butter and remove. Place in the pan the remaining butter and the garlic; cook for 1 minute. Add the onions and cook fairly quickly until they begin to brown. Add the mushrooms and cook slowly for 5 to 6 minutes. Add salt, pepper, a little dry mustard and tomatoes; cook for 2 minutes. Remove from the fire and add carefully the flour, meat glaze and tomato paste. Add the stock and stir over the fire until the mixture comes to a boil. Simmer slowly for 3 to 4 minutes. Add the herbs and the finely chopped chicken livers. Simmer for 2 minutes. Serve on cooked, well-drained spaghetti. Serve separately a bowl of grated cheese.

RISOTTO MAISON

6 chicken livers
5 tablespoons butter
2 chopped onions
4 tablespoons sliced mushrooms

¾ cup good Patna rice
2 teaspoons tomato paste
2 cups stock
6 tablespoons grated cheese

Brown the livers in hot butter and remove from the pan. Cook the onions briskly in the pan until they begin to brown. Add the mushrooms and cook a little longer. Add the well-washed raw rice, the tomato paste, and the stock. Cook until the rice begins to absorb the stock. Add a little more stock and continue cooking until the rice has absorbed the stock; stir frequently. Slice the livers and mix into the rice. Sprinkle the top with the grated cheese and dot with butter. Cover with the lid and let stand a moment. Pile in deep fireproof dish and serve at once with a big bowl of grated cheese.

WILD DUCK MAISON
(Suitable also for tame duck)

2 ducks	1 bay leaf
4 tablespoons Marsala wine	5 mushrooms
2 tablespoons tomato paste	1 diced red pimento
2 tablespoons potato flour	½ diced green pepper
1½ cups chicken stock	little finely chopped orange rind
salt and pepper	3 tomatoes

orange sections

Cut ducks in pieces, brown all over in hot fat and pour over the wine. Remove duck and add to pan the tomato paste and flour. Blend well and pour on chicken stock. Let come to a boil and put back the duck; season with salt, pepper and the bay leaf and let simmer gently until tender. Slice the mushrooms and sauté them in chicken fat; add pimento, green pepper, orange rind, tomatoes and orange sections. Skin and shred tomatoes and a few orange sections and cook all together very gently. Remove the duck from its gravy, add more potato flour if too thin, add the orange mixture and pour over the duck on a platter. Garnish with stuffed baked potatoes and broiled tomatoes.

CANETON À L'ORANGE I
(Duck with Orange)

1 4½-pound duck	¼ cup red wine
3 tablespoons butter	1 tablespoon red currant jelly
4 tablespoons Marsala wine or brandy	1 bay leaf
2 finely chopped mushrooms	4 chicken livers
3 large oranges	3 large potatoes
salt and pepper	2 eggs
1 teaspoon tomato paste	3 tablespoons hot milk
½ teaspoon meat glaze	grated rind 1 orange
3 teaspoons potato flour	little flour
1½ cups stock	1 cup bread crumbs

Truss the duck carefully and brown all over very quickly in 1 tablespoon hot butter. Remove some of the fat from the pan in which the duck was browned, pour over the hot Marsala wine or brandy, and remove the duck. Add to the pan the mushrooms, the finely shredded rind of 1 orange, salt and pepper. Cook slowly for 6 minutes. Remove from the fire and add the tomato paste, meat glaze and potato flour; stir until smooth; add the stock. Stir over the fire until the mixture comes to a boil. Add the juice of 2 oranges, the red wine, jelly, salt and pepper. Cut the duck up in pieces and put it back in the pan with the bay leaf. Cover with the lid and cook very slowly until the duck is tender (about 1 hour). Arrange the duck on a long hot dish. If gravy is too thin, boil it down until thick and add the skinned sections of 2 oranges and the sautéed chicken livers, which have been sliced when cooked.

Skin and boil the potatoes until soft. Drain and dry over the fire. Rub through a fine strainer and beat in 1 egg, 2 tablespoons butter, the hot milk, salt, pepper, and the grated rind of 1 orange. Mix well. Form in small cork shapes, roll in flour, brush with beaten egg and roll in bread crumbs. Fry in hot fat until golden brown; remove and drain well on brown paper. Pile at each end of dish and serve.

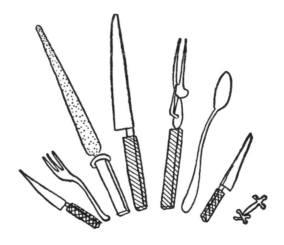

CANETON À L'ORANGE II
(Duck with Orange)

1 4½-pound duck	juice 2 oranges
5 tablespoons butter	¼ cup red wine
4 tablespoons Marsala wine or brandy	1 tablespoon red currant jelly
2 finely chopped mushrooms	1 bay leaf
finely shredded rind of 2 oranges	4 chicken livers
salt and pepper	skinned sections of 2 oranges
1 teaspoon tomato paste	3 large potatoes
½ teaspoon meat glaze	2 eggs
3 teaspoons potato flour	½ cup hot milk
1½ cups stock	handful bread crumbs

Carefully truss the duck and brown all over quickly in hot butter. Remove some of the fat from duck, pour over the hot Marsala wine or brandy and remove duck from the pan. Add to the pan the mushrooms, the finely shredded rind of 1 orange, salt and pepper. Cook slowly for 6 minutes. Remove from the fire and add the tomato paste, meat glaze, and potato flour; stir until smooth. Add the stock and stir over the fire until the mixture comes to a boil. Add the juice of 2 oranges, the red wine, jelly, salt and pepper. Cut the duck in pieces and return to the pan with the bay leaf. Cover with lid and cook very slowly until duck is tender (about 1 hour).

While duck is cooking, sauté the chicken livers. Arrange the cooked duck on a long, hot dish. If gravy is too thin, boil down until it becomes thick. Add the skinned sections of 2 oranges and the chicken livers.

Skin and boil the potatoes, drain and dry over the fire. Rub through a fine strainer and beat in 1 egg, 2 tablespoons butter, the hot milk, salt, pepper and the grated rind of 1 orange. Mix well. Form in small cork shapes, roll in a little flour, brush with beaten egg and roll in bread crumbs. Fry in hot deep fat until golden brown; remove and drain well. Pile at each end of dish and serve.

CANETON À L'ORANGE FROID
(Cold Duck with Orange)

1 quart jelly	*1 duck*
2 tablespoons gelatine	*few slices truffles*
½ cup sherry	*3 small, cooked carrots*
½ cup red wine	*12 small, cooked mushrooms*
2 blood oranges	*few small bundles water cress*
3 beaten egg whites	*1 tomato, cut into rings*

Mix the jelly, gelatine, sherry, red wine, grated rind and juice of the blood oranges, and egg whites. Clarify and when cool pour a little in a round or oval dish. When just set, arrange on top slices of duck, which has been previously cooked in a good stock until tender and then cooled.

Garnish with slices of truffles, the skinned pips of the blood oranges, small cooked carrots and mushrooms, all to be very cold and free from fat of any kind. Cover top with jelly which is on the point of setting. Leave until quite firm. Turn out and garnish with small bundles of water cress threaded through a ring of tomato and small molds of jelly, with the addition of grated orange rind in the jelly.

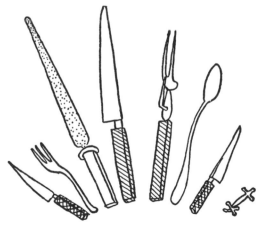

PAUPIETTES DE VEAU À LA GRECQUE
(Stuffed Veal Birds)

1½ pounds veal from leg
1 large, finely chopped onion
3 tablespoons butter
2 hard-boiled eggs, shelled and chopped
2 tablespoons mixed fresh herbs
salt and pepper

3 tablespoons sherry
1 teaspoon tomato paste
½ teaspoon meat glaze
2 teaspoons potato flour
1 cup stock
1 bay leaf

1 cup rice

Cut the veal in very thin slices. Place between 2 pieces of waxed paper and beat with a wooden mallet until very thin. Cook the onion in butter until soft without browning and add the eggs, herbs and seasoning. Spread on each slice of veal. Roll carefully and fasten at each end with thread. (These are called "paupiettes.") Brown quickly in hot butter. Pour on 2 tablespoons hot sherry and remove.

Stir in the pan the tomato paste, meat glaze and potato flour. Stir until smooth and add the stock. Season and stir over the fire until the mixture comes to a boil. Add the bay leaf, the veal and 1 tablespoon sherry. Cover and cook slowly for 20 minutes.

Boil the rice for 13 minutes in salted water; drain well and wash in hot water. Mix in the remaining butter with a fork and season. Grease a shallow round tin; gently press the rice into this. Remove onto a serving dish. Carefully remove thread from paupiettes. Arrange paupiettes on top of rice. Strain the gravy, pour over, and serve.

ESCALOPES DE VEAU ITALIENNE
(Scallops of Veal with Cheese)

1 pound veal from leg	1 bay leaf
2 tablespoons butter	salt and pepper
2 tablespoons sherry	2 pounds spinach
½ teaspoon tomato paste	2 tablespoons sour cream
½ teaspoon meat glaze	2 large cloves garlic, chopped
2 teaspoons potato flour	1 small chopped onion
1 cup stock	6 skinned, sliced tomatoes
6 thin slices Cheddar cheese	

Cut veal in very thin slices. Place between 2 pieces of waxed paper and beat with a wooden mallet until very thin. Brown both sides quickly in hot butter; pour over the sherry and remove the veal. Place in the pan the tomato paste, meat glaze and potato flour. Stir until smooth; add the stock, stir over the fire until the mixture comes to a boil. Add the veal, bay leaf and seasoning. Simmer gently for 15 minutes.

Wash the spinach well. Place in a pan with 1 dessertspoon butter, salt and pepper. Cook briskly for 5 to 6 minutes, stirring occasionally. Drain well and chop up coarsely. Mix in the sour cream and arrange on the serving dish. Place the veal on top.

Heat 1 tablespoon butter in a pan. Add the garlic and onion and cook briskly for 2 minutes. Add tomatoes and cook briskly for 5 minutes. Pour over the veal. Place on top the slices of Cheddar cheese. Strain over the gravy and brown under the broiler just before serving.

ESCALOPES DE VEAU MAINTENON
(Scallops of Veal with Smoked Tongue)

3 veal chops
4 shredded chicken livers
6 tablespoons butter
5 white, firm, sliced mushrooms
salt and pepper
5 slices shredded, smoked, cooked ham
3 tablespoons flour
cayenne pepper

1 cup milk
3 tablespoons grated cheese
½ teaspoon dry mustard
fat
½ teaspoon tomato paste
2 tablespoons sherry
6 tablespoons stock
4 large potatoes

Carefully remove meat from bones, and cut in thin slices. Place slices between 2 pieces of waxed paper and beat with a heavy mallet until thin. Brown one side only in butter.

In another pan brown the chicken livers quickly in butter. Remove and place the mushrooms, salt and pepper in the pan. Cook briskly for 3 to 4 minutes. Add the livers and the ham and cook for 1 minute. Arrange the veal, with this mixture on top, on a cookie sheet.

Melt in a pan 2 tablespoons butter; stir in the flour, salt and cayenne pepper. Add the milk and stir over the fire until the mixture comes to a boil. Add 2 tablespoons grated cheese and the mustard and simmer until thick. Pour 1 spoonful over each slice of veal. Sprinkle with grated cheese, dot with the fat and brown under the broiler. Arrange on a hot serving dish.

Add to the pan in which veal was browned the tomato paste, sherry, stock and seasoning. Boil and strain around dish.

Skin and cut the potatoes in very small balls with a potato cutter; dry well. Heat 3 tablespoons butter in a pan and add the potatoes, salt and pepper. Cover and shake over a brisk fire until golden brown. Pile up at each end of the dish and serve.

VEAU À LA CRÈME
(Veal with Cream)

2 pounds veal from shoulder or leg

2 tablespoons butter

2 tablespoons sherry

1 small, finely chopped onion

1 finely chopped clove garlic

4 skinned and sliced tomatoes

3 tablespoons flour

1 cup stock

¾ cup thin sour cream

salt and pepper

1 bay leaf

chopped chives

1 tablespoon tomato paste

Cut the veal in large squares, brown all over in the hot butter, and pour over the hot sherry. Remove the veal. Place in the pan the onion and garlic and cook for 2 minutes. Add the tomatoes and cook for 3 minutes. Remove from the fire and stir in the tomato paste and flour. Add the stock and stir over the fire until the mixture comes to a boil. Carefully mix in the sour cream and season; add the bay leaf and the veal. Cook slowly for ¾ hour, or until the veal is tender. Serve in a casserole. If sauce is too thin, boil down before pouring over. Sprinkle with chives and serve.

ESCALOPES DE VEAU VALENTINO
(Scallops of Veal with Asparagus Tips)

veal

½ cup butter

1 small dessertspoon flour

salt and pepper

¼ cup sherry

½ cup white wine

½ cup stock

¼ cup cream

1 teaspoon tomato paste

½ cup sliced mushrooms

12 cooked asparagus tips

lettuces

Cook the scallops of veal very slowly in about 4 tablespoons hot butter in a sauté pan; remove the veal. Place in the pan the flour, seasoning, sherry, white wine, stock and cream. Bring to a boil, add the tomato paste and simmer until reduced to the consistency of cream. Add the mushrooms, which have been sautéed in a little butter, and the asparagus tips. Place on braised lettuces and pour over a little cream. Glaze under the grill before serving.

RIZ DE VEAU JARDINIÈRE
(Sweetbreads with Vegetables)

1 pair sweetbreads
lemon juice
flour
salt and pepper
butter
chopped carrots, turnips, French beans

white wine
stock
bouquet of herbs
finely chopped mushroom
  peelings and stalks
reduced Marsala wine

bouquet of carrots, turnips and French beans

Blanch the sweetbreads in lemon juice and water; drain and press between 2 plates until cold. Roll in flour, season and brown lightly in a little butter; remove the sweetbreads. Add to the pan a handful of the chopped carrots, turnips and French beans. Brown lightly, adding a little flour; moisten with white wine, a little stock, bouquet of herbs and finely chopped mushroom peelings. Braise carefully for 30 to 40 minutes. Take up and arrange carefully on a *croûte* of bread. Reduce sauce, adding ½ cup reduced Marsala. Strain over dish and garnish round with bouquet of carrots, turnips and French beans boiled separately and tossed up in a little butter.

CÔTELETTE DE VEAU À LA BONNE FEMME
(Braised Cutlets of Veal)

3 tablespoons butter
4 veal chops
12 small white onions
2 cloves garlic
8 firm white mushrooms, quartered
1 teaspoon flour

½ teaspoon tomato paste
¾ cup dry white wine
½ cup light stock
salt and pepper
1 bay leaf
little freshly chopped parsley

Heat the butter in a pan, brown the chops quickly on each side and remove chops. Place the onions in the pan and brown well; add the finely chopped garlic and the mushrooms and cook for 1 to 2 minutes. Add the flour, tomato paste, wine and stock. Season and bring to a boil; add the bay leaf. Cover and cook in a 375° F. oven for 25 minutes. Remove, sprinkle with the parsley and serve in a casserole.

GOULASH DE VEAU HONGROISE
(Veal Goulash)

1½ pounds veal from leg or shoulder
2 tablespoons butter
2 sliced onions
2 sliced carrots
1 stalk celery
1 clove garlic
1 tablespoon paprika

1 shredded green pepper
1 shredded red pepper
1 tablespoon tomato paste
3 tablespoons flour
2 cups stock
salt and pepper
1 bay leaf

1 cup sour cream

Cut the veal in large squares; brown very quickly in hot butter and remove the veal. Place in the pan the onions, carrots and celery and the finely chopped garlic and cook slowly for 5 to 6 minutes. Add the paprika and cook slowly for 5 minutes. Add half the shredded red and green peppers; stir in the tomato paste, flour and stock. Stir over the fire until the mixture comes to a boil. Add salt, pepper to season, the veal and the bay leaf. Cover and cook slowly until the veal is quite tender; remove the veal. Strain the stock and return to the pan with a little more shredded red and green pepper. Reduce to thick consistency and pour over the veal, which has been placed in a casserole. Just before serving pour a little sour cream over the top.

Note: this may also be done with beef.

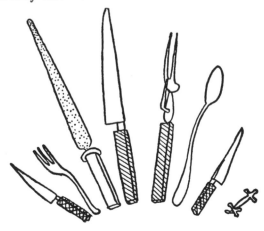

PAUPIETTES DE VEAU FONTANGES
(Veal Birds with Peas)

2 pounds veal from leg
4 chicken livers
8 firm, sliced, white mushrooms
4 tablespoons butter
salt and pepper
8 thin slices smoked tongue
3 tablespoons sherry
½ teaspoon tomato paste

½ teaspoon meat glaze
2 teaspoons potato flour
1 cup stock
1 bay leaf
2 tablespoons flour
2 cups strained cooked peas
   (purée)
½ cup cream

Cut the veal in thin slices. Put between 2 pieces of waxed paper and beat with a heavy mallet until very thin.

Brown the chicken livers and remove. Place the mushrooms in the pan and add a little more butter to that in which the livers were browned. Sauté the mushrooms for 5 to 6 minutes. Shred and add the chicken livers, salt and pepper. Place 1 slice of tongue on each slice of veal, and on top of the tongue put a little of the mushroom and chicken liver. Press down carefully. Roll each slice of veal and fasten each end with a fine thread (these are called "paupiettes"). Brown all over quickly in the pan in hot butter; pour over 2 tablespoons hot sherry and remove.

Place in the pan the tomato paste, meat glaze and potato flour and stir until smooth. Add the stock, season, and stir over the fire until the mixture comes to a boil. Add 1 tablespoon sherry; add the paupiettes and the bay leaf; cover and cook gently for 20 to 25 minutes.

Melt 2 tablespoons butter in a pan; add 2 tablespoons flour and brown slowly. When a good golden brown color, add the pea purée and cream. Add a little extra seasoning and stir over a slow fire until thick. Pour on the bottom of a serving dish. Remove string from veal and arrange paupiettes carefully on top of purée; strain over the gravy and serve.

VEAL PARISIENNE

4 pounds veal	*salt and pepper*
butter	*1 bay leaf*
3 tablespoons hot sherry	*2 pounds sorrel*
1 teaspoon meat glaze	*3 tablespoons fat*
1 teaspoon tomato paste	*1 tablespoon mixed herbs*
7 level tablespoons flour	*little creamy milk*
1½ cups beef stock	*3 tablespoons water*
½ cup sour cream	*1 teaspoon butter*

little lemon juice

Take veal cut from top of leg; cut in thin slices and brown each side quickly in hot butter. Pour on hot sherry and remove. Add meat glaze, tomato paste and 3 tablespoons flour to pan and pour on beef stock. Stir over the fire until the mixture comes to a boil; then add slowly and carefully the sour cream. Put the veal back with salt, pepper and bay leaf, cover and cook very slowly for 35 to 40 minutes. Put the sorrel, well dried, in the pan with fat, salt, pepper and herbs and cook briskly for 5 to 6 minutes, stirring occasionally. Drain, rub through a strainer and add to the following. —

Melt 2 tablespoons fat in a pan and add 4 tablespoons flour. Brown slowly and carefully, add to the sorrel with seasoning and milk. Cook for 5 minutes longer, arrange on a serving dish, put the veal on top, pour the sauce over and garnish with any seasonable vegetables such as carrots, peas, beans, baby onions, cooked as follows: —

Bring the vegetable to a boil quickly in cold water, drain and return to pan with water, butter and lemon juice; then cook until just tender, place in piles around meat and serve.

BREAST OF VEAL WITH RAISINS AND SOUR CREAM

3 pounds breast of veal
3 tablespoons butter
2 tablespoons hot sherry
¾ cup white sultana raisins
4 sliced mushrooms
1 teaspoon tomato paste
3 tablespoons flour

1½ cups beef stock
1 cup thin sour cream
1 tablespoon currant jelly
salt
cayenne pepper
corriander seed
1 bay leaf

Remove meat from bones, cut in small cubes and brown quickly in butter; then pour over hot sherry. Remove meat and add sultana raisins to the pan. Cook briskly for 2 to 3 minutes and add mushrooms, tomato paste and flour. When well blended pour on the beef stock. Stir over the fire until the mixture comes to a boil. Add slowly and carefully, beating steadily with a whisk, the sour cream, currant jelly, salt, cayenne pepper, corriander seed and bay leaf. Put back the veal and simmer gently until tender. Serve from the casserole with a bowl of boiled rice.

BOEUF EN DAUBE
(Braised Beef)

2½ pounds top round of beef
butter
1 tablespoon hot brandy
12 small mushrooms
24 stoned green olives
1 teaspoon tomato paste
3 tablespoons flour
2 cups stock

½ cup claret
1 tablespoon currant jelly
1 bay leaf
3 or 4 tomatoes
grated Swiss cheese
6 or 7 potatoes
1 egg
salt and pepper

milk (if necessary)

Cut beef in small pieces and brown very quickly on all sides in hot butter; pour on the hot brandy. Remove meat and add mushrooms to the pan. Brown quickly and add olives, tomato paste and flour; pour on the stock. Stir over the fire until the mixture comes to a boil; add claret and stir in jelly and bay leaf.

Put meat back and cook slowly until tender. Arrange meat on a long, flat dish, pour over the gravy and cover the top with tomatoes, thinly sliced. Sprinkle generously with cheese, dot with butter and surround with Duchess Potatoes.

Duchess Potatoes: Boil 6 or 7 potatoes, drain, dry and rub through a strainer. Beat with egg a good-sized lump of butter, salt, pepper and milk (if necessary). Fill in a pastry bag with rose tube and pipe around dish; put under the broiler to brown.

BOEUF PROVENÇALE

(Braised Beef with Green Peppers)

4 pounds top round of beef	*1½ cups strong stock*
¼ pound larding fat	*¼ cup red wine*
butter	*salt and pepper*
2 tablespoons hot sherry	*1 bay leaf*
1 teaspoon tomato paste	*2 cucumbers, peeled and cut diagonally*
1 teaspoon meat glaze	*8 mushrooms*
4 tablespoons flour	*6 green and 6 red peppers*

When the beef has been marinated, remove and dry on a cloth. Cut the larding fat in strips and lard the beef. Brown quickly all over in hot butter; pour over the sherry. Remove the beef and add to the pan the tomato paste, meat glaze and flour; stir until smooth. Add the stock and stir over the fire until the mixture comes to a boil. Add the red wine, seasoning, bay leaf and put back the beef. Cover and braise in the oven for 1½ hours, basting frequently. Cut as many thin slices off the beef as are required for 1 serving. Arrange overlapping on a serving dish. Strain sauce in which the beef was cooked; reduce and pour over the beef.

Scoop out the pits from the cucumbers. Chop the stalks of the mushrooms; cook the stalks in a little butter, salt and pepper for a few minutes. Put a little of this in the cucumbers. Cover with buttered waxed paper and bake in a moderate oven for 7 minutes. Sauté the mushroom heads in a little butter and seasoning and keep warm. Blanch the red and green peppers by bringing to a boil in cold water. Drain and carefully remove the pits; fill with the remaining chopped mushrooms. Arrange around the dish with the cucumber and peppers and serve.

BOEUF STRAGONOFF

(Fillet of Beef with Sour Cream)

1½ pounds fillet of beef   *1 cup sliced mushrooms*
juice 1 lemon   *handful flour*
large lump butter   *1 cup sour cream*
1 cup finely shredded onion   *12 small green olives*
12 small ripe olives

Cut the beef fillet in shreds. Sprinkle with lemon juice and leave for half an hour. Heat some of the butter in a pan and add the onion, cooking gently until brown. Remove the onion and replace with the mushrooms; cook for 5 minutes; remove the mushrooms. Reheat the pan. Add 2 tablespoons butter and, when sizzling, add the beef, which has been lightly floured. Shake over a brisk fire for 5 minutes. Add to the beef the mushrooms and onion and cook for 3 to 4 minutes. Pour on the sour cream. Garnish with small green and ripe olives and serve.

BOEUF BRAISÉ DUBARRY

(Braised Beef with Cauliflower)

4 pounds top round of beef   *4 tablespoons flour*
¼ pound larding fat   *1½ cups strong stock*
butter   *¼ cup red wine*
2 tablespoons hot sherry   *salt and pepper*
1 teaspoon tomato paste   *1 bay leaf*
1 teaspoon meat glaze   *2 cauliflowers*
4 tablespoons grated cheese

When the beef has been marinated in *marinade crue,* remove and dry on a cloth. Cut the larding fat in strips and lard the beef. Brown quickly all over in hot butter and pour on the sherry. Remove the beef. Place in the pan the tomato paste, meat glaze and flour. Stir until smooth. Add the stock and stir over the fire until the mixture comes to a boil. Add the red wine, seasoning, bay leaf and beef. Cover and braise for 1½ hours in the oven, basting frequently. Cut as many thin slices off the beef as are required for 1 serving. Arrange overlapping on a serving dish. Strain sauce it was cooked in, reduce it and pour over the dish.

Divide the cauliflowers in small bouquets and cook in salted water until just soft. Drain and squeeze dry in a cloth. Arrange on a cookie sheet, sprinkle the tops of each with grated cheese and a little melted butter. Brown under the broiler and use for garnish at each end of the meat dish.

BOEUF BOURGUIGNON
(Ragout of Beef with Onions)

2 pounds top round of beef	1 teaspoon meat glaze
2 tablespoons butter	3 tablespoons flour
2 tablespoons hot sherry	1 cup stock
24 small white onions	1 cup red wine
12 firm white mushrooms,	salt and pepper
quartered	bouquet of herbs
1 teaspoon tomato paste	freshly chopped parsley

Cut the beef in large squares and brown quickly in hot butter; pour over the hot sherry. Remove beef from the pan. Place the onions in the pan and brown quickly; add the mushrooms and cook for 1 minute. Add the tomato paste, meat glaze and flour and stir until smooth. Pour on the stock and stir over the fire until the mixture comes to a boil. Add ¼ cup of the red wine. Season and add the beef and herbs. Cook the beef very slowly until quite tender (approximately 1¾ hours). Add the remaining red wine slowly while cooking. Serve in a casserole and sprinkle with the parsley.

BRAISED SWEETBREAD GISMONDO
(With Spinach and Sour Cream)

6 pairs sweetbreads	*2 good cups stock*
butter	*salt and pepper*
2 tablespoons hot sherry	*tarragon or bay leaf*
1 teaspoon tomato paste	*3 pounds spinach*
3 teaspoons potato flour	*2 tablespoons fat*
5 tablespoons sour cream	

Blanch the sweetbreads, drain, remove all sinew, split in half lengthwise, dust lightly with flour and brown quickly in hot butter. Pour on the sherry; then remove breads and add to the pan the tomato paste and flour. Stir well until smooth and pour on the stock. Stir until the mixture comes to a boil; add salt, pepper and tarragon or bay leaf. Put back the breads, cover and cook slowly for 10 minutes. Remove and arrange on top of the following: —

Spinach with Sour Cream: Wash spinach well and put in the pot with fat, salt and pepper. Cook quickly, stirring occasionally, for 6 to 7 minutes. Drain well and chop finely in a wooden bowl; mix in the sour cream.

Arrange in loaf form on a serving dish, put sweetbreads on top, cover with sauce and serve very hot.

SWEETBREADS BRAISED WITH PEA PURÉE

4 pairs sweetbreads	*2½ cups chicken stock*
butter	*1 bay leaf*
4 tablespoons hot sherry	*3 tablespoons red wine*
5 or 6 mushrooms	*3 packages frozen peas*
salt and pepper	*1 tablespoon fat*
1 teaspoon tomato paste	*2 tablespoons flour*
3 teaspoons potato flour	*3 or 4 tablespoons cream*

Blanch the sweetbreads by bringing to a boil in cold water; drain, remove all skin and gristle. Brown very quickly in hot butter and pour over the sherry. Remove breads and add to the pan the mushrooms, which have been finely sliced (add butter if necessary); cook briskly for 3 or 4 minutes. Season with salt and pepper and stir in the tomato paste and flour. Blend well off the fire; then pour on chicken stock. Stir over the fire until the mixture comes to a boil; return breads with bay leaf and wine. Cover and cook gently for 15 minutes.

Pea Purée: Cook, drain and rub peas through a strainer. Melt the fat in a pan; remove from the fire and stir in the flour, salt and pepper. Brown slowly and add puréed peas; cook a few minutes and add cream.

Arrange on a serving dish in loaf form, lay sweetbreads on top, pour sauce over all and serve.

RISOTTO OF CHICKEN LIVERS AND LAMB KIDNEYS

½ pound chicken livers	*1 tablespoon tomato paste*
6 lamb kidneys	*1½ cups raw rice*
hot butter	*beef stock*
1 large sliced onion	*6 tomatoes*
6 sliced mushrooms	*grated cheese*

Slice livers, cut kidneys in half and brown very quickly in hot butter. Remove and add to the pan 1 sliced onion; brown slowly and add the mushrooms. Cook a little; then add tomato paste and rice and cover with stock. Cook slowly until the rice has absorbed liquid; add more stock from time to time until the rice is nearly cooked; then dice the liver and kidneys and add to the rice with skinned and sliced tomatoes. Put in an earthenware serving dish, sprinkle top with grated cheese and dot with butter, cover and leave in a warm place for 15 minutes. Sprinkle with more cheese and serve.

STEAK AND KIDNEY PIE

3 or 4 lamb kidneys	*2 tablespoons flour*
1½ pounds steak	*2 teaspoons tomato paste*
2 teaspoons vinegar	*1½ cups good stock*

Skin the kidneys, cut in half and remove the core; cut each kidney in 4 pieces. Cut steak in chunks and brown steak and kidneys very quickly in hot fat; then pour over the vinegar. Remove meat and add flour to the pan; work to a smooth paste and stir in tomato paste; pour on the stock. Stir over the fire until the mixture boils; return meat and kidneys to simmer for 1 hour. Put in a deep pie dish and cover with puff pastry ¾ inch thick. Decorate, brush with beaten egg and put in the refrigerator for a few minutes; bake in a hot oven for 15 minutes.

ROGNONS MOUTARDES

(Kidneys with Mustard Sauce)

8 lamb kidneys	*2 tablespoons flour*
large lump butter	*½ teaspoon meat glaze*
1 clove garlic	*½ cup red wine*
1 cup sliced mushrooms	*1 cup stock*
1 tablespoon mustard	*1 bay leaf*
½ teaspoon tomato paste	*handful freshly chopped chives*

Skin the kidneys; cut in half and remove the core; brown quickly in hot butter. Remove the kidneys and place the garlic in the pan; cook for 1 minute. Add the mushrooms with a little more butter and sauté a few minutes. Add the mustard and cook for 1 minute. Remove from the fire and stir in the tomato paste, flour, meat glaze, wine and stock. Stir over the fire until the mixture comes to a boil. Simmer a few minutes. Add the bay leaf and kidneys and cook slowly for 15 minutes. Place in a casserole and sprinkle the top with chives.

KIDNEYS IN MUSTARD SAUCE

5 lamb kidneys	1 teaspoon meat glaze
2 veal kidneys	3 tablespoons flour
3 tablespoons butter	1½ cups stock
little crushed garlic	3 tablespoons red wine
4 finely sliced mushrooms	2 tablespoons sour cream
1 tablespoon dry mustard	chopped fresh herbs

Skin kidneys, remove cores, slice rather thick and brown very fast in hot butter. When brown remove and add 2 teaspoons butter, garlic, mushrooms, mustard and meat glaze to the pan. Remove from the fire and add the flour and stock. Stir over the fire until the mixture comes to a boil; add the wine and sour cream. Cook slowly for 10 minutes; replace the kidneys and cook for 5 minutes more. Serve in a casserole and sprinkle the top with fresh herbs. This may be accompanied by a bowl of rice.

ROGNONS SAUTÉS TURBIGOS
(Kidneys with Onions and Red Wine)

8 lamb kidneys	3 teaspoons potato flour
large lump butter	1½ cups stock
12 small white onions	¼ cup red wine
8 firm white mushrooms, quartered	1 sprig parsley
½ teaspoon meat glaze	salt and pepper
½ teaspoon tomato paste	handful chopped parsley

Skin the kidneys; cut in half, and remove the core; brown very quickly in hot butter. Remove the kidneys and add the onions. Cook until fairly soft. Add the mushrooms and cook for 2 minutes. Remove from the fire and add the meat glaze, tomato paste, potato flour, stock and wine. Stir over the fire until the mixture comes to a boil and boil gently for 10 minutes. Add the sprig of parsley, seasoning and kidneys; cook gently for 15 minutes. Serve in a casserole; sprinkle with the chopped parsley.

PETITES CRÈMES DE FOIE À LA FOYOT
(Liver Creams)

½ pound ground calves' liver
2 beaten eggs
½ cup cream
salt and pepper
2 egg yolks

1 tablespoon tarragon vinegar
6 tablespoons thick cream
cayenne pepper
3 tablespoons butter
2 cups shelled peas

pinch freshly chopped mint

Mix the liver, eggs, 2 tablespoons cream, salt and pepper in a bowl. Rub through a fine strainer. Grease some cabinet pudding molds well and fill with the liver mixture. Place a piece of waxed paper on the bottom of a pan, place the molds on top and pour a little water around them. Bring to a boil. Cover with waxed paper and place in a moderate oven for 20 minutes. Remove and turn out of the molds into a hot serving dish.

Place the egg yolks, vinegar, 2 tablespoons cream, salt and cayenne pepper in a small bowl. Put the bowl in a pan of hot water and beat until the mixture begins to thicken. Add the butter, bit by bit, and 2 tablespoons more of the cream. Pour over the liver. Decorate dish with the peas which have been boiled, a little butter and the freshly chopped mint.

SAUTÉED CALVES' LIVER WITH ORANGE

6 small slices liver
salt and pepper
dry mustard
chili powder
2 dessertspoons butter
2 tablespoons dry wine
3 teaspoons butter or chicken fat
1 tablespoon chopped onion
2 teaspoons chopped garlic
1 tablespoon chopped herbs

3 tablespoons strong stock
2 tablespoons red wine
1 orange
hot oil
sugar
3 tablespoons fat
1 sliced onion
1 cup long-grain rice
stock, ½ inch above rice
little grated cheese

Dust slices of liver very lightly with flour and seasoning, including salt, pepper, mustard and chili powder. Heat in a pan

2 dessertspoons butter; this should be very hot. Brown both sides of the liver slices very quickly in this. Remove and add dry wine and butter or chicken fat to the pan. Add chopped onion and cook for 1 minute; add garlic and cook for 1 minute; then add herbs, stock and red wine. Pour sauce over the liver, which has been arranged on a serving dish. Cut 1 orange in thick slices with the skin on and brown quickly on both sides in hot oil and a sprinkling of sugar to make a glaze. Garnish the liver with this and serve with Rice Pilaf.

Rice Pilaf: Put fat in a heavy pan and add 1 sliced onion; cook briskly for 1 minute; then add rice, salt and pepper. Cook very slowly, stirring all the time, for 3 minutes. Cover with stock, ½ inch above rice; cover with waxed paper, put on the lid and cook in a 375° F. oven for 20 to 25 minutes. Remove and stir in a little grated cheese. This is a basic pilaf and may be varied in many ways.

CAILLES EN ASPIC MUSCATE
(Quails with Grapes)

2 quails	chervil
foie gras	butter
milk	whipped cream
salt and pepper	jelly
tarragon	pipped muscat grapes

Quails: Bone and stuff the quails with *foie gras*. Sew up the back with a needle and cotton thread. Poach for 5 minutes very carefully in a little milk, seasoning, tarragon and chervil. When cool, remove and dry very thoroughly. Have ready a very good white wine aspic.

Mousse de Foie Gras: To 1 part of *foie gras* add 2 parts butter and pound well. Season and add the whipped cream.

Lay the *mousse de foie gras* at the bottom of a large china dish or silver soufflé. Arrange the quail around the edge, set with a little jelly and garnish with pipped muscat grapes. Cover completely with jelly and serve very cold.

PÂTÉ MAISON
(Cold Meat Paté)

2 pounds ground calves' liver
2 pounds sausage meat
salt and pepper
6 slices bacon

2 shelled, hard-boiled eggs
6 ounces sliced liverwurst sausage
6 ounces cooked ham
6 ounces cooked tongue

6 chicken livers

Mix the liver and sausage meat together, adding plenty of salt and pepper to season. Grease a loaf mold well. Line with the bacon and half fill with the liver and sausage-meat mixture. Cut the eggs lengthwise and arrange down the center of the mold. Place the liverwurst sausage, ham, tongue and chicken livers on top. Cover with the rest of the liver and sausage-meat mixture and cover the whole with waxed paper. Put the mold in a pan surrounded by water and cook for 1½ hours in a moderate oven. Remove and press down the top with a brick. Cool in the refrigerator. Turn out of mold, cut in slices, and serve as a *pâté*.

CASSOULET
(Algerian Meat Dish)

2 small chickens
hot butter
½ cup diced, cold pork
2 teaspoons tomato paste
1¾ cups chicken stock
little garlic

1 pound white flageolet beans
¼ pound sliced garlic sausage
½ pound sliced liver sausage
6 chicken livers
3 tomatoes
½ cup diced, smoked tongue

Cut chickens up in portions and brown all over very well in hot butter. Remove and in same pan brown briskly the cold pork and tomato paste. When well blended pour on chicken stock and stir till the mixture comes to a boil. Then add garlic and beans, which have been previously soaked and half cooked for about 1 hour. Return chicken to the pan and add garlic and liver sausage. Then add the chicken livers, which have been sautéed and well seasoned. Cover and cook slowly until beans and chicken are tender. Just before serving add skinned and sliced tomatoes and smoked tongue.

CORNETS DE JAMBON LUCULLUS
(Cold Cornets of Ham)

thin slices of cooked ham	1 tablespoon tomato paste
¾ pound liver sausage	1 tablespoon tarragon vinegar
3 tablespoons butter	2 tablespoons red wine
salt and pepper	3 stiffly beaten egg whites
cayenne pepper	1½ cups rice
truffles or ripe olives	2 cups diced, cooked green beans
3 cups strong stock	and carrots
4 tablespoons gelatine	

Take as many cornet molds as there are people to serve. Line inside with a thin slice of cooked ham. Fill the center with liver sausage rubbed through a strainer and mixed with creamed butter, seasoned with salt, pepper and cayenne pepper. Fill into a pastry bag with a round tube and pipe into cornets. Put truffle or a ripe olive on top of each and cover with aspic.

Aspic: Put strong stock, cold and free from fat, in a pan; add gelatine, tomato paste, vinegar, wine and egg whites. Beat over a slow fire until the mixture comes to a boil; draw aside and let stand for 10 minutes. Pour through a cold, damp cloth, stir over ice until on the point of setting and put some in the refrigerator to chop later; cover cornets with the rest. Serve on a bed of Rice Salad.

Rice Salad: Boil rice for 13½ minutes in salted water, drain and wash well in cold water. Add diced vegetables, cool and mix with French dressing, fill into round cake tin and press down gently; turn out on a serving dish. Unmold the cornets and arrange in a crown on top of the rice; garnish with chopped aspic and serve.

LAPIN MOUTARDE
(Rabbit with Mustard Sauce)

1 4-pound rabbit
2 tablespoons lemon juice or vinegar
½ cup flour
salt and pepper
lump butter
1 finely chopped onion
2 finely chopped cloves garlic
4 sliced mushrooms

1 teaspoon meat glaze
1 teaspoon tomato paste
1½ cups stock
½ cup white wine
2 tablespoons dry mustard
½ cup thin sour cream
2 sprigs tarragon
little chopped, fresh tarragon

Cut the rabbit up in neat small joints. Soak in cold water with a little lemon juice or vinegar for 2 hours. Drain and dry on a cloth. Dust the joints lightly with flour, salt and pepper and brown well in sizzling hot butter. Remove the rabbit and add to the pan the onion and garlic. Cook a few minutes and add the mushrooms; cook for 2 minutes longer. Remove from the fire and add 3 tablespoons flour, the meat glaze and tomato paste. Stir until smooth; add the stock and wine and season; stir over the fire until the mixture comes to a boil. Mix the mustard into the sour cream and stir into the gravy. Add the rabbit with the sprigs of tarragon. Cover with the lid and cook slowly for 1 hour, or until the rabbit is quite tender. Place the rabbit in a deep casserole. If the gravy is too thin, boil it down until it is thick. Pour over the rabbit. Sprinkle top with a little chopped, fresh tarragon and serve.

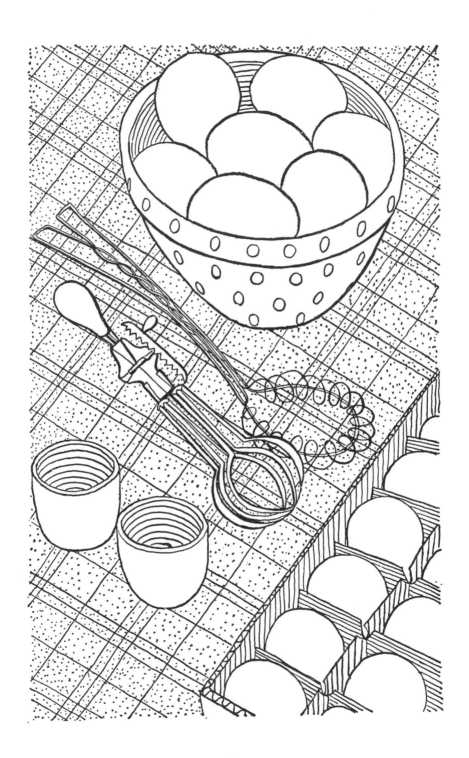

CHAPTER VIII

EGGS

Eggs boiled, poached and fried are favorites on the American breakfast table, yet they are seldom utilized in the luncheon or dinner menu except as ingredients in other dishes. More extensive and varied use of this nutritious and economical food should be encouraged. The egg is used in many attractive ways in the continental kitchen from a main dish omelet or soufflé to the garnish for the traditional *Poulet Marengo*.

Eggs should be strictly fresh for all purposes except the omelet. For this dish they should be at least two or three days old, for new-laid eggs curdle in the pan. The omelet and the *crêpe* are two dishes in egg cookery which require a special pan. This pan should be of cast aluminum or cast iron, preferably with a rounded base. It is never washed, for if water touches the surface at any time both omelet and *crêpe* stick to the pan. After each use it is wiped out carefully with a clean dry cloth.

Eggs as a protein food should always be stored in a cold place, for they deteriorate rapidly at room temperature.

The following recipes are favorites of French cooks; all of them are delicious and relatively simple to prepare.

OMELETS

For omelets it is necessary to have a cast-iron or aluminum pan. The metal must be of a porous nature; so copper, tin-lined or stainless steel pans are of no use for this purpose.

When the pan is new, rub over the surface with a piece of dry steel wool. Then clean pan thoroughly with oil. Never touch the pan with water at any time. When thoroughly clean fill with oil and leave for about 48 hours. Pour off the oil, which, of course, can be used again, and wipe the pan thoroughly. Get it very hot and then the pan is seasoned for use.

To make an omelet:

1 teaspoon butter	1 teaspoon cold water
3 eggs	salt and pepper

Test the heat of the pan by trying it with a small piece of butter. If the butter sizzles briskly without browning when it dissolves, the pan has reached the right temperature. Drop in at once 1 teaspoon butter and 3 eggs, which have been beaten with 1 teaspoon cold water, salt and pepper until they mix without being frothy. Stir quickly with a fork and shake the pan until the eggs begin to set. Then stir more slowly on the top of the set eggs for a minute or two. Leave for a second. Fold over the omelet to the edge of the pan. Turn out at once onto a hot serving dish.

OMELETTE FINES HERBES
(Herb Omelet)

3 eggs	tarragon
1 teaspoon cold water	fresh thyme
salt and pepper	onion
parsley	garlic
chives	1 teaspoon butter

Beat the eggs with 1 teaspoon cold water, add the salt and pepper and beat well but not too frothy. Mix herbs and chop very finely with onion and garlic. Add this to the hot butter just before adding the eggs. Finish off as in usual omelet. Small croutons of fried bread can be added to the herbs if desired.

POTATO OMELET

potatoes	3 eggs
crisp fried onions	salt and pepper
1 tablespoon butter	

Sauté the thinly sliced potatoes. Mix with onions and mix into egg mixture just before making the omelet.

SORREL OMELET

finely shredded sorrel	*whipped cream*
salt	*cayenne pepper*

Mix all ingredients and stuff into omelet before folding over.

OEUFS POCHÉS À LA SOUBISE
(Eggs on Onion Purée)

6 eggs	*few peppercorns*
salt and pepper	*1 bay leaf*
vinegar	*large lump butter*
4 finely sliced onions	*2 tablespoons flour*
1½ cups milk	*cayenne pepper*
1 crushed clove garlic	*2 tablespoons cream*
	little hot oil

Fill a saucepan ¾ full with hot water, season with salt, and color lightly with vinegar. Then stir violently with a spoon until you make a little whirlpool. Drop in the egg and poach gently for 3 minutes. Take out and put into hot water until ready for use. Continue until all 6 eggs are done in this way. Arrange neatly in a hot serving dish and pour over the following Soubise Sauce: —

Soubise Sauce: Slice the 4 onions finely and put in a pan with 1½ cups milk. Crush the clove of garlic, few peppercorns, salt and 1 bay leaf. Simmer until the onions are quite soft. Then push through a fine strainer and pour onto the following thickening: —

Melt 2 tablespoons butter in a pan and stir in 2 tablespoons flour, salt and cayenne pepper. Stir this over the fire with the liquid until the mixture comes to a boil. Add a small lump of butter and 2 tablespoons cream. Simmer for a few moments and pour this sauce over the eggs. Garnish with thick onion rings, which have been dipped in a little flour and some seasoning, fried until golden in hot oil and dried well on brown paper before placing on dish.

OMELETTE D'ÉPINARD
(Spinach Omelet)

spinach	*salt and pepper*
butter	*3 eggs*
sour cream	*paprika*

Wash the spinach well and cook in a little butter for 3 to 4 minutes. Drain well and chop coarsely. Mix with a little sour cream and seasoning. Put into omelet just before folding over. Serve with sour cream and a little paprika on top of the omelet.

OEUFS FARCIS MAISON (PLAT FROID)
(Cold Stuffed Eggs)

3 hard-boiled eggs	*½ cup sliced, cooked string*
½ cup strained, cooked peas	*beans*
6 tablespoons butter	*freshly ground black pepper*
2 tablespoons grated Parmesan cheese	*lemon juice*
salt	*little oil and vinegar*
2 cups boiled dry rice	*few ripe olives and gherkins*
2 tablespoons cooked, sliced tongue	*1 bunch water cress*
2 tablespoons cooked, sliced ham	*4 firm tomatoes*

Filling: Cut the eggs in half lengthwise. Scoop out the yolks and put the whites aside. Rub the yolks through a wire strainer and add to the strained peas with the creamed butter and grated Parmesan cheese; season and mix thoroughly.

Rice Salad: Place the rice in a bowl with the tongue, ham and string beans. Add the salt, freshly ground black pepper, little lemon juice, oil and vinegar. Mix well with 2 forks. Arrange round the sides of a bowl. Lay the whites of the hard-boiled eggs firmly on the rice and fill them with the filling mixture, using a pastry bag with a rose pipe or plain pipe. Decorate each egg with a slice of gherkin or ripe olives. Fill the center with water cress and surround the edge of the dish with quarters of the skinned tomatoes, which have had the pips removed.

OEUFS BROUILLÉS MARIETTE
(Scrambled Eggs with Shrimps)

4 eggs	1 sliced mushroom
salt and pepper	½ cup sliced, cooked shrimps
2 tablespoons cream	2 skinned, sliced tomatoes
4 tablespoons butter	buttered toast
1 small chopped onion	2 tablespoons grated cheese

Break the eggs in a bowl and mix well with the seasoning and the cream. Melt the butter in a pan, add the onion and mushrooms, and simmer for 4 to 5 minutes. Add the shrimps and tomatoes. Shake over the fire for 1 to 2 minutes. Add the egg mixture. Stir slowly with a metal spoon until thick and creamy. Arrange some squares of buttered toast on a hot dish for serving and place eggs on top. Serve at once, well dusted with the grated cheese.

OEUFS BROUILLÉS MALTAISE
(Scrambled Eggs with Oranges)

2 oranges	1 teaspoon tomato paste
4 eggs	2 tablespoons dry sherry
1 tablespoon cream	5 tablespoons butter
salt and pepper	2 slices stale white bread

Peel the rind of 1 orange finely, cut in shreds and bring to a boil in cold water. Remove outer and inner skin of the other orange and cut out the sections.

Beat the eggs in a bowl, add the cream and season. Add the shredded orange rind, the tomato paste and the sherry. Add to 3 tablespoons butter melted in a pan and stir slowly over a low fire until thick and creamy. Place on a hot serving dish.

Cut the bread in squares, 2 for each person. Melt 2 tablespoons butter in a pan and add 1 tablespoon orange juice. Add the bread and cook briskly until brown and sticky on both sides. Arrange at one end of the serving dish. Warm the orange sections and arrange at the other end of the dish.

OEUFS SUR LE PLAT FLAMENCO
(Baked Eggs with Sausages)

2 potatoes
4 tablespoons butter
3 frankfurters, skinned and cut in slices
salt and pepper
2 tablespoons cooked peas
2 red pepper caps, diced in large pieces

tomatoes
chopped parsley
4 eggs
freshly ground black pepper
2 tablespoons cream
cayenne pepper

Peel the potatoes, place in a pan and cover with cold water. Bring slowly to a boil, drain and dry in a cloth. Cut in small, even cubes and add to the melted butter and frankfurters. Shake over a moderate fire until the potatoes begin to brown. Add salt, pepper, peas and the red peppers and cook a little longer. Add the tomatoes and parsley. Place on the bottom of a flat earthenware dish; break the eggs on top; season them with a little salt and freshly ground black pepper. Place in a moderate oven until set. Pour over the cream and sprinkle the top with a very little cayenne pepper. Serve at once.

OEUFS SUR LE PLAT MARIANNE
(Baked Eggs with Lima Beans)

1½ pounds young Lima beans
2 tablespoons butter
1 sliced onion
1 teaspoon chopped parsley

salt and pepper
1 skinned, sliced tomato
4 eggs
3 tablespoons cream

2 tablespoons grated cheese

Shell the Lima beans, simmer until tender in a little salted water, and drain. Melt the butter in a pan, add the onion and simmer for 4 minutes without browning. Add the beans, parsley, seasoning and the tomato. Shake over the fire for 1 to 2 minutes. Turn onto a well-buttered, flat, fireproof dish. Break the eggs on top and pour the cream over the yolks; sprinkle with the grated cheese. Place in the oven for 7 to 10 minutes; remove and serve.

OEUFS POCHÉS CLAMART (PLAT FROID)
(Cold Poached Eggs with Peas)

1 cup flour	cayenne pepper
5 tablespoons butter	little lemon juice
5 egg yolks	¾ cup salad oil
2 tablespoons grated cheese	4 tablespoons cream
salt and pepper	2½ cups cooked peas
paprika	4 eggs
handful rice	little chopped mint
2 tablespoons vinegar	freshly ground black pepper
1 teaspoon French mustard	little water cress

Pastry: Put the flour on a marble slab. Make a well in the center and place in the hole the butter, 3 egg yolks, grated cheese, salt, pepper and a little paprika. Work these ingredients to a smooth paste; work in the flour. Roll out fairly thin, cut in large rounds with a fluted cutter, and line into small tartlet tins. Press a little piece of waxed paper, with a small smear of butter on the back side of it, into each tartlet. Fill with raw rice or split peas to keep the shape of the tartlet while cooking. Bake in a 375° F. oven for 20 minutes. Remove paper and rice; remove the tart carefully from the tin and cool on a rack.

Mayonnaise Sauce: Place 2 egg yolks in a bowl. Stir in the vinegar, mustard, salt, cayenne pepper and a few drops of lemon juice. Beat in the oil very slowly. Add 2 tablespoons cream and 2 tablespoons cooked peas, rubbed through a fine strainer. Keep cool.

Poached Eggs: Fill ¾ of a small, deep pan with hot water and color with vinegar. Bring to a boil. Turn down the fire so that the water is just simmering. Stir with a spoon until you form a whirlpool. Drop in an egg and poach gently for 3 minutes. Slip eggs into a basin of cold water to wash away the vinegar.

Filling: Mix with the remaining peas 2 tablespoons cream, a little chopped mint, salt and a little freshly ground black pepper.

Serve: Place the tartlet shells on a flat dish and fill each shell with the peas. Set a neatly trimmed egg on top and pour over the sauce. Decorate at each end with water cress.

OEUFS POCHÉS GEORGETTE
(Poached Eggs in Baked Potatoes)

4 large potatoes
4 tablespoons butter
salt and pepper
¾ cup milk or stock
1 sliced onion
½ pound cooked, shelled shrimps,
*   cut in pieces*

1 cup flour
2 tablespoons cream
3 large tomatoes, skinned, pipped
*   and shredded*
1 teaspoon chopped, mixed herbs
4 eggs
2 tablespoons grated cheese

1 bunch water cress

Potatoes: Scrub the potatoes well without skinning, dry on a cloth and rub with a little salt. Bake for 45 to 60 minutes in a moderate oven. Cut the tops off lengthwise. Scoop out most of the inside, rub through strainer and beat in a small lump of butter. Season and add 1 or 2 tablespoons milk. Fill a pastry bag with small rose pipe and keep it warm.

Shrimps: Melt 2 tablespoons butter in a pan; add the onion and simmer 4 to 5 minutes without browning; season. Add the shrimps and sprinkle with a little flour. Add the tomatoes; rub the seeds and pulp of the tomatoes through a strainer and add the juice. Add the herbs. Bring to a boil, draw aside and keep warm.

Sauce: Add the milk or stock to 1 tablespoon butter and 2 tablespoons flour melted in a pan. Stir over the fire until the sauce comes to a boil; then add the remaining butter, bit by bit. Add the cream. Simmer a few minutes and keep warm.

Poached Eggs: Fill a small deep pan three-quarters full with hot water, color with vinegar and bring to a boil. Turn down the fire so that the water is just simmering. Stir with a spoon until you form a whirlpool. Drop in an egg and poach gently for 3 minutes. Remove the egg and slip into a basin of warm water to wash away vinegar.

Serve: Put a teaspoon of the shrimp mixture in the bottom of each potato. Drain the eggs, trim them and dry lightly on a cloth. Fit one into each potato and cover with the sauce. Surround the edge of each potato with the mashed potato and scatter with the grated cheese. Dot with a little butter and brown quickly under the broiler. Garnish the dish with water cress just before serving.

OEUFS EN SURPRISE
(Poached Eggs in Cheese Omelet)

3 level tablespoons butter
3 level tablespoons flour
salt
cayenne pepper
¾ cup milk

½ Camembert cheese
3 tablespoons grated Cheddar cheese
½ teaspoon dry mustard
8 eggs
1 egg white

Melt the butter in a pan, stir in the flour, salt and cayenne pepper, pour on the milk and stir over the fire until the mixture thickens. Rub the Camembert cheese through a strainer and add to this mixture with the grated Cheddar cheese. Then add the dry mustard, 4 egg yolks and 5 stiffly beaten egg whites. Grease a flat glass baking dish and half fill with the soufflé mixture. Make four evenly spaced wells with a spoon in the soufflé mixture, fill each well with a raw egg, cover with the rest of the soufflé mixture and bake in a very hot oven for 15 minutes. Remove and serve at once.

OEUFS POCHÉS À L'ESTRAGON
(Cold Poached Eggs in Tarragon Aspic)

6 eggs
4 cups strong beef stock, cold
   and free from fat
3 level tablespoons gelatine
salt and pepper

1 tablespoon tomato paste
¼ cup red wine
3 stiffly beaten egg whites
2 bunches fresh tarragon
cooked smoked tongue or ham

1 bunch water cress

Poach the eggs the same way as for Oeufs Pochés Clamart (p. 215), but put them in a bowl of cold instead of hot water. Put the stock in a tin-lined copper pan with the gelatine, salt, pepper, tomato paste, red wine and stiffly beaten egg whites. Beat over a slow fire until the mixture comes to a boil, draw aside and allow to stand for ten minutes. Pour through a cold, damp cloth and stir over ice until on the point of setting. Run a little cold water through a rind mold, and half fill the mold with the jelly on the point of setting. Drain the eggs and dry carefully on a dry cloth; space them evenly on the top of the aspic, having first decorated where the eggs are to be placed with tarragon leaves. Between the eggs put thin rounds of smoked tongue or ham, cover with the rest of the gelatine and put in the refrigerator. Remove, dip quickly into a bowl of warm water and turn out onto a serving dish. Set the rest of the aspic and chop finely on a piece of waxed paper. Decorate around the dish with this aspic, a few tarragon leaves and the water cress and serve.

OEUFS POCHÉS AU BEURRE NOIR
(Poached Eggs in Black Butter)

½ cup vinegar
4 eggs
3 cups shelled peas
6 tablespoons butter

2 tablespoons flour
½ cup cream
salt and pepper
2 tablespoons capers

3 tablespoons white wine

Fill a small, deep pan three-quarters full with hot water. Add the vinegar, bring to a boil, lower the fire, and stir with a spoon until you form a whirlpool. Drop an egg into the whirlpool and allow it to poach gently for 3 minutes. Take it out and put in a pan of hot water. Continue until all the eggs are poached. Cook the peas until soft in a little salted water. Drain and rub through a strainer. Melt 1 tablespoon butter in a pan, stir in the flour, and stir over a slow fire until it browns. Add the peas with the cream, salt and pepper and cook for 5 to 6 minutes. Arrange on the bottom of a serving dish, place the poached eggs on the top and pour over the following sauce: —

Sauce: Put the rest of the butter in a shallow pan and cook slowly until it is a dark brown color. Add the capers, white wine, salt and pepper. Pour over the eggs and serve.

OEUFS À LA TALLYRAND
(Hard-Boiled Eggs with Spaghetti)

3 cups cooked spaghetti	cayenne pepper
4 tablespoons butter	1 cup milk
6 hard-boiled eggs	¼ cup cream
3 level tablespoons flour	2 raw egg yolks
salt and pepper	little grated Parmesan cheese
	paprika

When the spaghetti is cooked, drain and mix in 1 tablespoon hot butter. Arrange on the bottom of a serving dish. Slice the hard-boiled eggs and arrange on the top. Pour over the following sauce: —

Sauce: Melt 2 tablespoons butter in a pan, stir in the flour, salt and cayenne pepper. Pour on the milk and stir over the fire until the sauce comes to a boil. Then add the cream and, bit by bit, 1 tablespoon butter. Simmer for 5 to 6 minutes and add the egg yolks mixed into 1 tablespoon milk. Pour over the eggs, sprinkle the top with a little Parmesan cheese and a little paprika and serve.

OEUFS À LA TRIPE
(Hard-Boiled Eggs with Onions)

6 large onions
3 tablespoons oil
6 hard-boiled eggs
bread crumbs
2 tablespoons butter
3 level tablespoons flour

salt and pepper
1 cup milk
3 tablespoons grated Gruyère and
    Parmesan cheeses mixed
½ teaspoon dry mustard
¼ cup cream
little fat

Skin the onions and cut in thin slices; cook until soft, without browning, in the hot oil. Cut the hard-boiled eggs in thin rounds. Grease a small, narrow, deep glass baking dish and line with a few bread crumbs. Put a layer of onions in the bottom, then a layer of hard-boiled eggs alternately until all the materials have been used. Cover the top with the following sauce: —

Sauce: Melt the butter in a pan; stir in the flour, salt and pepper. Pour on the milk and stir over the fire until the sauce comes to a boil. Add the grated cheese, dry mustard and cream. Simmer for 5 or 6 minutes, pour over the dish, sprinkle the top with a little more grated cheese, a few bread crumbs and dot with fat. Brown under the broiler.

OEUFS POCHÉS FLORENTINE
(Hard-Boiled Eggs with Spinach)

½ cup vinegar
4 eggs
2 pounds spinach
1 tablespoon fat
salt and pepper
3 tablespoons sour cream
2 tablespoons butter

3 level tablespoons flour
1 cup milk
4 tablespoons grated Gruyère and
    Parmesan cheeses mixed
½ teaspoon dry mustard
¼ cup thin cream
1 egg yolk

Fill a small deep pan three-quarters full of water, add the vinegar and bring to a deep boil. Lower the heat and stir with a spoon until you form a whirlpool. Drop the egg into the whirlpool and allow to poach gently for 3 minutes. Remove and put in a bowl of warm water.

Wash the spinach and put in a pan with 1 tablespoon fat, salt and pepper. Cook for 6 minutes, stirring occasionally; drain well and chop in a wooden bowl. Arrange on a serving dish and mix in the sour cream. Carefully place the eggs on the top and pour over the following sauce: —

Sauce: Melt the butter, stir in the flour, pour on the milk and add the salt and pepper. Stir over the fire until the sauce comes to a boil; then add the cheese, mustard and cream. Simmer for 5 or 6 minutes. Lastly add the egg yolk, mixed with 1 tablespoon of milk. Pour over the eggs, sprinkle the top with a little more cheese and broil under the broiler.

OEUFS CARMALITE

(Hot Stuffed Eggs)

4 hard-boiled eggs	bread crumbs
3 ounces foie gras	3 egg yolks
2 tablespoons grated cheese	1 tablespoon tarragon vinegar
salt and pepper	2 tablespoons cream
1 beaten egg	little dry mustard
little flour	4 tablespoons butter

Cut the hard-boiled eggs across in half, carefully remove the yolks and rub through a strainer. Mix in the *foie gras*, grated cheese, salt and pepper. Fill the eggs with this mixture, reshape, brush with beaten egg, roll in flour, brush with beaten egg again and roll in bread crumbs. Fry in hot fat until golden brown. Arrange on a hot serving dish on a napkin and serve separately the following Hollandaise Sauce: —

Hollandaise Sauce: Put two egg yolks in a bowl with the tarragon vinegar, cream, mustard, salt and pepper. Put the bowl over another pan of hot water over a slow fire and beat until the sauce begins to thicken. Then add, bit by bit, the butter and, lastly, a drop of lemon juice.

POACHED EGGS CLAMART

4 cups peas	*½ cup cream*
2 tablespoons fat	*4 tablespoons butter*
3 level tablespoons flour	*¼ cup dry white wine*
salt and pepper	*2 tablespoons capers*

Cook peas until just soft, drain and rub through a strainer. Melt the fat in a pan and stir in flour, salt and pepper. Brown slowly, add to the peas and mix in cream. Reheat and arrange on the bottom of a serving dish. On top of this place as many poached eggs as people to serve and pour over the following: —

Black Butter with Capers: Brown butter very slowly; add wine, salt, pepper and capers.

To Poach Eggs: Fill a small pan ¾ full with water and add salt, and vinegar enough to color water; bring to a boil, then lower flame, and stir water until you get a whirlpool. Drop eggs one at a time in the middle of the whirlpool, increase the flame a little and cook for 3½ minutes. Remove with a perforated spoon and keep warm in a bowl of hot water. Each egg is a separate operation, but they can be cooked ahead of time and kept perfectly in a bowl of hot water.

EGGS À LA TRIPE

2 large Spanish onions	*1½ cups milk*
6 hard-boiled eggs	*3 tablespoons grated cheese*
2 tablespoons chicken fat	*1 level teaspoon dry mustard*
3 tablespoons flour	*¼ cup cream*
salt	*1 egg yolk*
cayenne pepper	*1 tablespoon milk*
	butter

Skin and slice the onions and cook in hot fat until golden. Shell and slice the hard-boiled eggs. In an earthenware dish arrange alternate layers of onions and eggs, using all; then pour over the following sauce: —

Mornay Sauce: Melt chicken fat; stir in flour, salt and cayenne pepper; then pour on the milk. Stir over the fire until the sauce comes to a boil and add cheese, mustard and cream. Simmer for 5 minutes and add egg yolk mixed with milk. Pour over eggs, sprinkle with grated cheese, dot with butter and put under the broiler to brown. Serve from the dish in which they were cooked.

EGGS ZEPHYR CHAMPIGNONS

5 eggs	*3 tablespoons grated cheese*
1 tablespoon butter	*1 diced dill pickle*
salt	*mushrooms*
cayenne pepper	*oil*
1 tablespoon cream	*chopped parsley*

Beat eggs lightly and put in the top of a double boiler with butter, salt, cayenne pepper, cream and grated cheese. Stir over the fire until just set; then add diced pickle. Use as many mushrooms as people to serve; wash, season, put a little oil on top and broil. Arrange eggs on a serving dish, place mushrooms on top, sprinkle with chopped parsley and serve.

CHEESE SOUFFLÉ

2 tablespoons butter	*3 tablespoons grated Parmesan cheese*
3 level tablespoons flour	*2 sections Camembert cheese*
salt	*1 teaspoon dry mustard*
cayenne pepper	*4 egg yolks*
¾ cup milk	*5 stiffly beaten egg whites*

Melt the butter in a pan, stir in the flour, salt and cayenne pepper, pour on the milk and stir over the fire until the mixture thickens; do not allow it to boil. Remove and stir in the cheese, which has been put through a strainer. Add mustard, egg yolks and stiffly beaten whites. Grease a soufflé dish, tie a band of wax paper on the outside, fill with the mixture and bake for half an hour in a 375° F. oven. Serve at once very hot.

CHAPTER IX
VEGETABLES

There are so many vegetables to cook and so many ways to cook them that whole books have been written on the subject. It is a sad fact, however, that with the numerous types of vegetables available, many of them the year round, home and restaurant menus do not reflect the same variety. Yet how easy it is to tempt the eyes and the appetite with the natural colors and flavors of fresh vegetables. What could be more appetizing than the deep, gleaming purple of eggplant served as *aubergine farci?* Or perhaps an artichoke freshly prepared with dried mushrooms and ripe tomatoes. Sorrel with its piquant flavor, the fresh tang of dandelion greens when in season, tender beet tops, or the clean bite of fragrant water cress will all add originality and new savor to the luncheon or dinner menu.

It is poor economy to buy stale or wilted vegetables. Small, very young vegetables may cost a little more, but their return in flavor, appearance and food value far outweighs the extra pennies.

We know that vegetables are a valuable source of body-building vitamins and minerals, but these vitamins need careful treatment for they are quickly destroyed by overcooking and too much exposure to air. Minerals also should be conserved for they readily dissolve in cooking water. Therefore it is logical when boiling vegetables to cook them quickly in a small amount of water (with the exception of cabbage and cauliflower which are cooked uncovered in large amounts of boiling salted water to eliminate cooking odors). When a small amount of water is used, any liquid remaining after cooking should be utilized in soups, sauces and gravies. A little added lemon juice when cooking green vegetables will help them keep their flavor and fresh color. We know, too, that vegetables retain their vitamin content better in a slightly acid solution.

Of all national *cuisines*, the Chinese consistently excel in vegetable cookery. No doubt the Chinese method of rapid precooking in hot fat, followed by quick steaming with a little added water, is largely responsible for the outstanding quality of their cooked vegetables. The French also use this method very often and many of these recipes are included in this chapter.

Numerous and exciting are the ways of preparing vegetables, and when cooked correctly they add not only color and nutriment to meals but unique and superb flavor as well.

DOLMAS DE CHOUX
(Stuffed Cabbage Leaves)

1 large green cabbage	2 tablespoons strong stock
4 tablespoons oil	2 teaspoons chopped, fresh herbs
butter	2 chopped, hard-boiled eggs
1 finely chopped onion	½ cup boiled rice
1 large chopped mushroom	1 tablespoon flour
½ pound chopped beef	1 crushed clove garlic
tomato paste	1½ cups light stock

1 chopped, skinned tomato

Put the cabbage in a pot and bring slowly to a boil; remove and carefully take off the large outer leaves and remove the stalks. Fill with the following: —

Filling: Heat 2 tablespoons oil and 1 tablespoon butter; add the onion and cook until golden; add the mushroom and cook a little longer; then add chopped beef. Cook briskly for 6 or 7 minutes and add 1 teaspoon tomato paste. Mix in strong stock; then add herbs, hard-boiled eggs and rice. Season well and put a good tablespoon of mixture in each leaf. Fold up, dust with flour, and pack in a deep pan or casserole; pour over a little light stock to moisten the pan, cover with waxed paper, put on the lid and cook slowly for 20 minutes. Meanwhile prepare the Tomato Sauce.

Tomato Sauce: Melt 2 tablespoons oil and stir in 1 tablespoon tomato paste and flour. Add garlic and pour on 1½ cups light stock. Stir over the fire until the sauce comes to a boil; then add, bit by bit, 1 teaspoon butter and 1 chopped, skinned tomato. Simmer for 10 minutes. Arrange well-drained leaves on a dish, pour sauce over all and serve.

AUBERGINES À LA BOSTON
(Eggplant with Mushrooms and Cheese Sauce)

2 eggplants	*cayenne pepper*
salt and pepper	*¾ cup milk*
3 level tablespoons flour	*4 tablespoons grated Gruyère and*
4 tablespoons oil	*Parmesan cheeses mixed*
2 sliced onions	*¼ cup cream*
6 tablespoons butter	*1 teaspoon dry mustard*
6 sliced mushrooms	

Cut the eggplants in half and make a few incisions with a sharp knife. Sprinkle well with salt and let stand for half an hour. Squeeze out the water and salt and dry on a cloth. Dust the top lightly with flour. Put tops-downward in a frying pan of hot oil. Cover with lid and cook slowly for 10 minutes on each side.

Cook the onions slowly until soft, without browning, in a little butter, salt and pepper. Melt 2 tablespoons butter in a pan. Remove from the fire and add the flour, salt and cayenne pepper. Stir in the milk and stir over the fire until boiling; then add 2 tablespoons grated cheese, 3 tablespoons cream and the dry mustard. Add to the onions. Add a little extra cheese and the mushrooms, sautéed in a little butter. Scoop out the meat from the fried eggplants, chop roughly in a wooden bowl and add to the mixture. Fill the eggplant skins. Sprinkle well with the remaining grated cheese; melt the remaining butter and pour over the top. Brown under the broiler and just before serving pour over the remaining cream, which has been seasoned with a little salt.

AUBERGINES À L'AUVERNAISE
(Eggplant Stuffed with Dried Mushrooms)

4 tablespoons dried mushrooms	8 tablespoons cooking oil
6 tablespoons butter	6 firm, skinned, thickly sliced
2 chopped cloves garlic	tomatoes
salt	little tarragon
2 medium-sized eggplants	3 tablespoons fat
little flour	2 Spanish onions, cut in thick rings
	chopped thyme

Soak the mushrooms overnight in water, drain well and shred. Heat a little butter in a pan, add garlic and salt and cook for 1 minute. Add the mushrooms, cover with lid and cook very slowly for 20 minutes.

Cut the eggplants in half lengthwise, then in slices ¼ inch thick. Arrange on a flat platter, sprinkle with salt and let stand for 20 minutes. Drain off the water and salt and dry well on a cloth. Crush the garlic and salt into a smooth paste. Spread a little on the slices of eggplant. Dust them gently in flour. Fry on each side in hot oil until golden brown and remove from pan. Fry the tomatoes in the same oil and add the chopped fresh tarragon.

Arrange layers of eggplant, tomatoes and mushrooms on a shallow dish for serving. Put in the oven for 5 to 6 minutes. Dust the onion rings lightly with flour and fry in deep fat until golden brown and crisp; drain well on brown paper. Arrange onion rings on top. Sprinkle with thyme and serve piping hot.

AUBERGINES FARCIES PROVENÇALES
(Stuffed Eggplant)

2 medium-sized eggplants	4 skinned, chopped tomatoes
salt and pepper	little grated cheese
4 tablespoons salad oil	few brown bread crumbs
2 tablespoons butter	6 anchovy fillets
4 medium-sized sliced onions	little chopped, mixed fresh herbs

Cut the eggplants in half lengthwise and make a few incisions with a sharp knife. Sprinkle well with salt, let stand for half an hour, squeeze out salt and water and dry on a cloth. Place face-downward in hot oil, cover with lid and cook for 10 to 12 minutes on each side. Add more oil if necessary. Scoop out meat and chop coarsely in a wooden bowl. Melt the butter in a shallow pan, add the onions and cook slowly until soft without browning. Add the tomatoes and the eggplant meat. Cover with lid and cook slowly for 5 minutes. Fill the eggplant skins with the mixture and sprinkle with the cheese and bread crumbs. Cut the fillets of anchovy in strips and place them latticewise on top. Pour over a little melted butter, brown well under the broiler and sprinkle with chopped herbs.

AUBERGINES FARCIES ITALIENNES
(Stuffed Eggplant)

2 medium-sized eggplants	12 chopped string beans
salt and pepper	1 cup finely chopped mushrooms
little cooking oil	1 dessertspoon tomato paste
6 tablespoons butter	12 tablespoons diced cooked ham
2 medium-sized, finely chopped	3 tablespoons bread crumbs
onions	3 skinned, shredded tomatoes
1 finely chopped carrot	grated cheese
freshly chopped chives or parsley	

Cut the eggplants in half lengthwise. Make a few incisions with a sharp knife, sprinkle well with salt and let stand for half an hour. Squeeze out the salt and water and dry on a cloth. Heat 5 or 6 tablespoons of oil in a pan. Put in eggplants face-side-down, cover and cook for 10 to 12 minutes on each side until thoroughly soaked through. Scoop out all the meat from egg-plants and chop finely.

Melt in a pan 3 tablespoons butter and add the onions, carrots and string beans. Cook very slowly with salt and pepper until quite soft. Add the mushrooms and cook a moment. Add the tomato paste and cooked ham, bread crumbs and a little extra seasoning. Cover the pan with lid and cook for 5 minutes. Add the tomatoes and the eggplant meat and mix well. Fill eggplant skins, sprinkle the tops with the grated cheese and melted butter and brown under the broiler. Arrange on a long, flat, hot dish. Sprinkle the top with chives or parsley just before serving.

ARTICHAUDS À LA BARIGOULE
(Stuffed Globe Artichokes)

4 globe artichokes
2 tablespoons lemon juice
1 cup finely chopped mushrooms
4 tablespoons shredded, cooked ham
4 tablespoons shredded, cooked tongue
4 tablespoons butter
2 small, finely chopped onions
2 teaspoons tomato paste
handful chopped parsley

handful bread crumbs
4 slices bacon
2 tablespoons oil
½ cup white wine
½ cup stock
1 tablespoon sherry
2 level tablespoons flour
salt
cayenne pepper

1 crushed clove garlic

Boil the artichokes in salt and water with a little lemon juice until tender. Drain, pull out the small center leaves and remove the choke.

Place in a pan the mushrooms, ham, tongue and 3 tablespoons melted butter and cook for a few minutes. Add the onion, 1 teaspoon tomato paste, the parsley and 1 tablespoon bread crumbs and cook for 1 to 2 minutes. Fill the artichokes, sprinkle top with bread crumbs and pour over a little melted butter. Tie around each artichoke a slice of bacon.

Stand the artichokes in a buttered, fireproof dish. Pour over the oil and cook in a moderate oven for 2 minutes. Add the wine, stock, sherry and 1 teaspoon tomato paste. Cover with buttered waxed paper and return to the oven for 40 minutes; remove and keep warm.

Melt 1 tablespoon butter in a pan. Remove from the fire and add the flour, salt and cayenne pepper. Stir until smooth. Strain and add the liquid in which the stuffed artichokes were cooked. Stir over the fire until the mixture comes to a boil. Add the crushed garlic and simmer for 1 to 2 minutes. Pour on the bottom of a hot serving dish. Remove the slices of bacon and arrange the artichokes on top; sprinkle with a little chopped parsley and serve.

ARTICHAUDS VINAIGRETTE
(Artichokes with Vinaigrette Sauce)

artichokes
little vinegar
1½ teaspoons lemon juice
salt and black pepper
½ teaspoon onion salt
1 teaspoon crushed black and
white peppercorns
½ teaspoon sugar
½ teaspoon dry mustard
½ teaspoon Worcestershire
sauce

1 finely chopped clove garlic
2 teaspoons finely chopped onion
2 tablespoons finely chopped, mixed
parsley, chives, marjoram, tarragon
1 teaspoon finely chopped green olives
½ teaspoon finely chopped gherkin
4 tablespoons tarragon vinegar
1 cup olive oil
1 finely chopped, hard-boiled egg

To boil artichokes, strip off the larger outside leaves, cut off the stalks and trim bases neatly. Rub with lemon to prevent their getting black. Snip off the end of each leaf with a pair of kitchen scissors within a couple of inches of the base. Remove the inner chokes and tie a thread around the largest circumference of the artichoke. Blanch head-down in fast-boiling water, to which some vinegar, lemon juice and a little salt have been added. Leave to simmer for 15 minutes. If the leaves will come off easily the artichoke is fully cooked. Then drain well, dry and cool; arrange on a napkin and serve cold with a Vinaigrette Sauce.

Vinaigrette Sauce: Put in the bottom of a ½-pint, screw-top bottle 1 teaspoon salt, onion salt, black pepper, peppercorns, sugar, mustard, lemon juice, Worcestershire sauce, garlic, onion, herbs, olives, gherkin, tarragon vinegar, olive oil and hard-boiled egg. Serve ice cold.

TOMATE FARCIE À LA BAYONNE
(Stuffed Tomatoes)

4 large, firm tomatoes
salt and pepper
6 tablespoons butter
2 finely sliced onions
½ cup finely chopped mushrooms
¾ cup cooked, chopped ham
½ cup chopped, cooked tongue
1 small, chopped frankfurter

little chopped parsley
little grated Parmesan and
*   Gruyère cheeses mixed*
handful bread crumbs
2 level tablespoons flour
2 tablespoons tomato paste
1½ cups stock or water
1 crushed clove garlic

Skin the tomatoes by plunging in boiling water for 1 minute; remove the skins. Cut a thin slice off the tops and scoop out the pulp, putting it aside. Dry well with a cloth and place on a fireproof dish. Season the inside of each tomato with a little salt and pepper and pour in 1 tablespoon melted butter. Cook in a moderate oven for 4 minutes; keep warm.

Melt 3 tablespoons butter in a pan. Add the onions, salt and pepper and cook for a few minutes. Add the mushrooms and cook for 3 minutes. Add the ham and tongue. Simmer the frankfurter in water for 6 minutes and add. Add a little extra salt and pepper and a little chopped parsley and simmer for a few minutes. Stuff the tomatoes with this mixture. Sprinkle the tops with a little grated cheese and bread crumbs, pour over 1 tablespoon melted butter and brown under the broiler. Remove and arrange on a flat dish for serving.

Melt 1 tablespoon butter in a pan. Stir in the flour, salt, pepper and tomato paste. Add the stock or water. Stir over the fire until the mixture comes to a boil. Add the garlic and 1 teaspoon butter and simmer for 10 to 15 minutes. Strain and pour around the tomatoes. Sprinkle the tops with chopped parsley and serve.

ÉPINARD EN BRANCHES PARMESAN
(Spinach with Cheese)

3 pounds spinach
6 tablespoons butter
salt and pepper
2 tablespoons flour
cayenne pepper

½ cup cream
5 tablespoons grated Parmesan cheese
½ teaspoon dry mustard
2 tablespoons sour cream
croutons

Wash the spinach well. To remove all the grit first plunge into cold water, then into warm salted water, and lastly into cold water again. Drain well and put in pan with 2 tablespoons butter, salt and pepper. Cover with lid and cook slowly for 5 to 6 minutes, stirring occasionally. Drain and press well. Return to the pan and dry a little longer over the fire. Keep warm.

Melt in a pan 2 tablespoons butter. Remove from the fire and add the flour, salt, cayenne pepper and stir until smooth. Strain on all the liquid from the spinach and add the cream. Stir over the fire until the mixture comes to a boil. Add the cheese, bit by bit, the remaining butter and dry mustard. Draw aside and simmer for a few minutes. Mix in the spinach. Arrange on a hot dish and pour over the sour cream. Surround the dish with croutons of bread, fried until golden in butter.

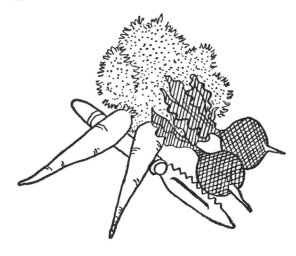

ÉPINARD À LA HAMBOURG
(Spinach with Mornay Sauce)

2 pounds spinach
4 tablespoons butter
salt and pepper
1 cup small diced croutons of bread,
  fried until golden in butter
2 tablespoons flour

cayenne pepper
1 cup milk
½ teaspoon dry mustard
3 tablespoons Parmesan cheese
2 tablespoons Gruyère cheese
3 tablespoons cream

Wash the spinach well. To remove all the grit, first plunge the spinach into cold water, then into warm salted water, and lastly into cold water again. Drain well and put into a pan with 1 tablespoon butter, salt and pepper. Cook slowly for 6 to 7 minutes, stirring occasionally; drain well. Chop up coarsely in a wooden bowl; mix in the croutons of bread; arrange on a flat dish.

Melt 2 tablespoons butter in a pan. Stir in the flour, salt and cayenne pepper, until smooth; add the milk. Stir over the fire until the mixture comes to a boil. Mix in the mustard, 2 tablespoons Parmesan cheese, the Gruyère cheese and the cream. Simmer slowly for 8 to 9 minutes. Pour over the spinach and sprinkle the top with the remaining Parmesan cheese. Dot with butter and brown quickly under the broiler.

PAIN D'ÉPINARD À LA CRÈME
(Spinach Cream)

1½ pounds spinach
4 tablespoons butter
salt and pepper
3 tablespoons flour
croutons

¾ cup stock
½ cup cream
2 eggs
1 egg yolk

Wash the spinach well. Place it in a pan with 2 tablespoons butter, salt and pepper and cook for 3 to 4 minutes, stirring occasionally. Drain well and return to pan to dry. Rub through a fine strainer.

Melt the remaining butter in a pan. Remove from the fire and add the flour, salt and pepper. Strain on the liquid in which the spinach was cooked. Stir over the fire until the mixture thickens. Add 2 tablespoons cream and bring to a boil. Cool and add to the spinach the 2 beaten eggs and 1 egg yolk. Add 1 more table-spoon cream and a little extra salt and pepper. Butter well a ring or dome mold, pour in the mixture, put a piece of buttered waxed paper on the bottom of the pan and the mold on this. Half fill the pan with cold water and bring slowly to a boil on top of the fire. Cover the pan with greaseproof paper and the lid, and finish setting in a moderate oven for 20 minutes, or until firm to the touch. Remove from the oven and the water jacket and leave for about 5 minutes. Slide a knife around the edge to be sure it is not sticky. Turn out on a hot dish for serving. Pour round the rest of the cream and surround with croutons of bread, fried till golden in butter.

CONCOMBRES À LA TOSCANA
(Cucumbers with Mushrooms and Mint)

3 small cucumbers	*4 tablespoons finely sliced mushrooms*
4 tablespoons butter	*1 egg yolk*
2 tablespoons flour	*¼ cup cream*
salt	*2 teaspoons chopped fresh mint*
cayenne pepper	*2 slices bread*

Peel 2 of the cucumbers and slice all 3 in slices 1 inch thick. Bring to a boil in cold water; drain, reserving the cucumber stock. Melt 2 tablespoons butter in a pan. Remove from the fire and stir in the flour, salt and cayenne pepper. Stir until smooth. Pour on 1 cup of the cucumber stock. Stir over the fire until the mixture comes to a boil. Add the mushrooms, cucumbers and a little more salt and cayenne pepper. Simmer gently until the cucumbers are just soft. Mix the egg yolk into the cream. Remove from the fire and add this to the vegetables. Add the mint. Serve in a deep casserole, surrounded by fingers of the bread, which have been toasted and buttered.

ÉPINARD À L'ITALIENNE
(Spinach with Pine Kernel Nuts)

2 pounds spinach
4 tablespoons butter
3 tablespoons olive oil
3 finely chopped cloves garlic
salt

cayenne pepper
4 tablespoons stoned raisins
4 tablespoons pine kernel nuts
handful coarsely grated Parmesan
    cheese

Wash the spinach well, drain, and cut in coarse shreds. Plunge into boiling water, remove and drain. Heat in a pan 2 tablespoons butter and the olive oil; add the garlic, salt and cayenne pepper. Cook over a moderate fire for 2 to 3 minutes. Add the raisins and the pine kernel nuts; cook for 2 minutes. Mix this into the spinach until it is well blended. Arrange on a hot, flat serving dish. Scatter the cheese over the top. Melt the remaining butter, pour over and brown quickly under the broiler.

Note: this recipe can be made with broccoli as well.

LAITUES BRAISÉES AU JUS
(Braised Lettuce)

4 firm heads of Boston lettuce
2 slices fat bacon
1 finely chopped, small onion
1 finely chopped, small carrot

¾ cup strong stock
salt and pepper
handful chopped parsley
3 tablespoons butter

Remove the outside leaves of the lettuce and wash; keep the rest cold. Place in a pan, cover with cold water and bring to a boil. Strain and plunge into ice water. Dry well on a cloth and cut in half. Butter a fireproof dish well and place the bacon on the bottom. Sprinkle the onion and carrot over the bacon. Fold under the tops of the lettuces and place on top; pour over the stock. Add salt and pepper. Cover with buttered waxed paper. Cook in a moderate oven for 45 minutes. Remove the lettuces and arrange on a hot dish for serving. Strain and reduce the liquid in which they were cooked. Pour over the lettuces and sprinkle with chopped parsley just before serving.

BROCCOLI SAUCE BÉARNAISE

1 bunch broccoli
juice ½ lemon
3 egg yolks
1 tablespoon tarragon
   vinegar
2 tablespoons cream
salt
cayenne pepper

4 tablespoons butter
2 tablespoons chopped, mixed, fresh
   herbs — parsley, tarragon,
   chives, thyme, basil
¼ teaspoon finely chopped garlic
1 teaspoon finely chopped onion
1 teaspoon finely chopped green olive
¼ teaspoon meat glaze

Wash the broccoli well. Plunge into a pan of boiling salted water with a little lemon juice or vinegar. Cook until just soft; broccoli will lose its color if overcooked. Drain well and arrange carefully around a hot serving dish.

Mix well in a bowl the egg yolks, vinegar, cream, salt and cayenne pepper. Place this bowl in a shallow pan of hot water over a slow fire. Stir until the mixture begins to thicken. Add, bit by bit, the butter. Mix in the herbs, garlic, onion, olives and meat glaze. Pour over the broccoli and serve at once.

POMMES DE TERRE BOULANGÈRE
(Potatoes Boulangère)

1 pound potatoes
¼ pound Gruyère cheese
1 pound onions
salt and pepper

½ cup stock
handful bread crumbs
handful grated cheese
4 tablespoons butter

French mustard

Butter a fireproof dish well. Put a layer of sliced, peeled potatoes on the bottom; add a layer of thin slices of Gruyère cheese and a layer of thin slices of the onion. Sprinkle with salt and pepper and repeat until the dish is full. Press down well and pour over the stock. Sprinkle with bread crumbs and a little grated cheese; pour over the melted butter. Cover with a piece of buttered waxed paper and cook in a moderate oven for 30 to 35 minutes. Remove the paper after 20 minutes and serve.

POMMES DE TERRE MOUSSELINE
(Potatoes Mousseline)

2 pounds potatoes	2 tablespoons butter
2 egg yolks	salt and pepper
½ cup hot milk	

Peel the potatoes and cut in half. Put in a pan of cold water with plenty of salt and bring to a boil. Simmer until soft, strain, and return to the pan. Dry well over the fire. Rub through a fine strainer. Beat in thoroughly the egg yolks, butter, salt, pepper and milk. The mixture should be of a fairly soft consistency.

POMMES DE TERRE MONTROUGE

4 potatoes	2 tablespoons fat
4 carrots	2 tablespoons sour cream
1 egg	salt and pepper
3 tablespoons grated cheese	little dry mustard

Take equal parts of potatoes and carrots and cut in longish slices. Put in a pan, cover with salted water and cook until really soft. Drain and rub through a strainer. Beat in the egg, grated cheese, fat, sour cream, salt, pepper and mustard. Arrange on a serving dish and sprinkle with grated cheese. Dot with butter and brown under the broiler. This may also be served plain as mashed potatoes.

POMMES DE TERRE BONNE FEMME

6 or 7 good-sized potatoes	salt and pepper
2 onions	3 slices finely shredded,
3 good tablespoons fat	raw bacon

Skin and slice the potatoes and onions. Put in a heavy pan with fat, salt and pepper and put shredded raw bacon on top. Cover and cook briskly for 20 to 25 minutes. (Cook fast and shake once or twice; do not stir with spoon or fork.) Arrange on a serving dish, sprinkle with paprika and serve.

ORANGE POTATOES

2 pounds potatoes	*salt and black pepper*
grated rind 1 large orange	*2 tablespoons butter*
2 large eggs	*2 tablespoons hot milk*

Peel the potatoes and cut in half. Place in a pan and cover with cold water; season well and bring to a boil. Simmer slowly until soft. Strain and return to the pan to dry well over the fire. Rub through a fine strainer. Add the orange rind. Beat in thoroughly 1 whole egg, salt, black pepper, butter and hot milk. Fill a pastry bag with a rose tube attachment and pipe out in small rosettes onto a well-greased cookie sheet. Bake in a hot oven until golden brown. Remove from oven, carefully sliding a spatula under each rosette, and arrange on a hot serving dish.

Note: this recipe can also be finished off in the following manner: When the potato purée is finished, form in small cork shapes between well-floured hands, roll in flour, brush with beaten whole egg, roll in white dry bread crumbs and fry in hot fat until golden brown.

POMMES DE TERRE ANNA
(Potatoes Anna)

2 pounds potatoes	*¾ cup butter*
salt and pepper	*1 pinch French mustard*

Butter well a small pancake pan or shallow tin. Peel the potatoes and cut enough of them in thin slices to line the bottom of the pan, slightly overlapping. Sprinkle with a little salt and dot with melted butter. Put a layer of finely sliced potatoes on top and a pinch of French mustard. Arrange in layers, seasoned, until the pan is full. Pour over the remaining melted butter and press down well. Bake in a hot oven for 40 to 50 minutes, or until the potatoes begin to come away from the side of the pan. Remove from the fire a few moments. Slide a thin knife carefully around the side of the pan and give it a small knock on the side of the stove. Turn out on a hot, flat dish and serve.

POMMES DE TERRE HONGROISE

4 or 5 potatoes	1 tablespoon flour
1 tablespoon chicken fat	2 cups water
1 tablespoon paprika	1 crushed clove of garlic
2 tablespoons tomato paste	sprig tarragon

Slice potatoes finely and add to the following: —

Paprika Sauce: Melt chicken fat and stir in paprika. Cook for a few minutes; then add tomato paste and flour. Blend well and pour on water and crushed clove of garlic. Stir over the fire until the sauce boils; then put in the potatoes with a sprig of tarragon. Simmer gently until soft and serve.

POMMES DE TERRES BOUCHANT

8 medium-sized potatoes	2 tablespoons fat
2 eggs	little dry mustard
2 tablespoons grated cheese	bread crumbs

Boil potatoes in salted water until soft. Drain well and dry over the fire. Rub through a strainer and beat in 1 egg, grated cheese, fat and mustard. Form in cork shapes with lightly floured hands. Brush with beaten egg, roll in crumbs and fry in deep fat until golden.

POMMES DE TERRE SAUTÉES

(Sautéed Potatoes)

2 pounds potatoes	1 tablespoon chopped, fresh rosemary or
5 tablespoons butter	other herb
	salt and pepper

Peel the potatoes and place in a pan. Cover with water and bring to a boil. Drain and dry well in a cloth. Cut in thick slices. Melt the butter in a thick frying pan. Add the salt, pepper and potatoes. Shake over the fire until they begin to brown. Add the rosemary and fry until done. Pile on a hot serving dish, sprinkle with more rosemary and serve.

POMMES DE TERRE NOISETTE
(Noisette Potatoes)

2 pounds old potatoes or　　　　　　*6 tablespoons butter*
1 pound very small new potatoes　　*salt and pepper*

Peel the old potatoes and hollow them out with a small round potato cutter; scrape the new potatoes. Cover with cold water in a pan and bring to a boil. Drain and dry well on a cloth. Heat the butter, without browning, in a thick pan, adding the salt, pepper, and potatoes. Cover with the lid. Shake over a slow fire until brown all over, and just soft, but not mushy. Drain off the butter just before serving.

PETITS POIX À LA JOHN SCOVILLE
(Peas John Scoville)

1 cup small pearl onions　　　　　*lemon juice*
2 cups shelled peas　　　　　　　*4 tablespoons olive oil*
½ pound small white mushrooms　*salt and pepper*

Bring the onions to a boil in cold water and drain. Bring the peas to a boil in cold water and drain. Wash the mushrooms in lemon juice and water and cut in thick slices. Sauté in the hot oil. Add the peas, onions, salt and pepper. Cover with the lid and shake over a slow fire for 10 to 15 minutes, or until the peas are just soft but not mushy. Serve in a casserole.

PEAS, SCALLIONS AND LETTUCE

1 pound fresh peas, shelled　*salt and pepper*
1 bunch scallions　　　　　　*1 cup water*
½ head shredded lettuce　　*1 level teaspoon butter*
2 slices bacon, cut up　　　*2 level teaspoons flour*

Put peas in a pan with scallions, shredded lettuce, bacon, salt and pepper. Pour over 1 cup water, bring to a boil and thicken with worked butter and flour. Add, bit by bit, to the peas, simmer gently until tender and serve.

PETITS POIX À LA BONNE FEMME
(Peas Bonne Femme)

3 to 4 pounds peas
1 Boston lettuce, cut in 8 pieces
12 small scallions, cut in half
2 ounces diced bacon or salt pork
1 cup stock or water

salt and pepper
3 tablespoons butter
1 tablespoon flour
bouquet of herbs

Shell the peas and bring to a boil in cold water. Drain the peas and add the lettuce, scallions, bacon or salt pork, the stock or water and seasoning. Bring to a boil. Work the butter and flour to a smooth paste and add bit by bit. Simmer gently, until the peas are just soft, with a bouquet of fresh herbs. Remove the herbs and serve in a casserole.

BRUSSELS SPROUTS WITH CHESTNUTS

1 pound chestnuts
2 tablespoons hot butter
2 tablespoons sherry
1 teaspoon meat glaze
1 teaspoon tomato paste

2 teaspoons potato flour
1 cup light stock
1 bay leaf
1 pound sprouts
lemon juice

Cover the chestnuts with cold water, bring to a boil and boil for 2 to 3 minutes. Then shell, skin and brown quickly in hot butter. Pour over sherry. Remove nuts and stir into pan the meat glaze, tomato paste and potato flour and pour on light stock. Stir over the fire until boiling, then put back the nuts with bay leaf. Simmer gently until just soft.

In the meantime boil the sprouts in salted water with lemon juice added. Drain and mix with the nuts at the last minute before serving. This should be served in a casserole.

BROCCOLI WITH SAUTÉED TOMATOES

4 or 5 tomatoes	*cayenne pepper*
2 tablespoons hot oil	*1 tablespoon tarragon vinegar*
chopped fresh marjoram or	*1 tablespoon cream*
dried marjoram and fresh parsley	*1 teaspoon tomato paste*
broccoli	*2 tablespoons butter*
2 egg yolks	*½ teaspoon meat glaze*
salt	*1 tablespoon fresh herbs*

drop of lemon juice

Skin tomatoes, cut in very thick slices and cook briskly in hot oil. Sprinkle with chopped marjoram. Arrange on a serving dish, place sprigs of cooked broccoli on top, and pour on the following sauce: —

Sauce: Put yolks in a bowl with salt, cayenne pepper and vinegar; add cream and tomato paste. Beat with a whisk over a slow fire in a pan of hot water until the sauce begins to thicken; then add butter bit by bit. Lastly add meat glaze, herbs and lemon juice. Pour over the broccoli and serve.

CARROTS POULETTE

6 large carrots	*2 cups chicken stock*
lemon juice	*½ cup cream*
2 tablespoons fat	*2 teaspoons butter*
3 tablespoons flour	*1 tablespoon chopped parsley*
salt	*little chopped chives*
cayenne pepper	*2 egg yolks*

2 tablespoons milk

Skin carrots, cut in small thick pieces and cook until tender in salted water with lemon juice added; then add to: —

Poulette Sauce: Melt fat and stir in flour, salt and cayenne pepper. When blended pour on chicken stock. Stir over the fire until the sauce comes to a boil and add cream and butter, bit by bit. Mix and add parsley, chives, egg yolks and milk. Add carrots and serve as a vegetable dish.

MUSHROOM SOUFFLÉ

2 level tablespoons fat

3 tablespoons flour

salt

cayenne pepper

¾ cup milk

½ cup sautéed, sliced mushrooms

3 or 4 egg yolks

2 tablespoons grated cheese

5 stiffly beaten egg whites

Melt fat, remove from the fire, and stir in flour, salt and cayenne pepper. When well blended pour on milk and stir over the fire until the mixture thickens. Then add the mushrooms, egg yolks and grated cheese and fold in beaten egg whites. Grease a soufflé dish and tie waxed paper on the outside. Pour in the mixture and bake for half an hour in a 400° F. oven.

BROCCOLI SOUFFLÉ

3 tablespoons fat

3 level tablespoons flour

salt

cayenne pepper

¾ cup milk

2 tablespoons grated Parmesan cheese

1 teaspoon dry mustard

3 egg yolks

1 cup broccoli

4 beaten egg whites

sweet butter

Melt the fat and add flour, salt, cayenne pepper and, when well blended, pour on the milk. Stir until the mixture thickens; add grated Parmesan cheese, mustard, egg yolks, and broccoli, cooked and strained. Then fold in beaten egg whites.

Grease a soufflé dish and tie a band of waxed paper on the outside several inches higher than the dish. Pour in the mixture and bake for half an hour in a 400° F. oven. Remove, take off the paper and put a few curls of sweet butter on top.

FENNEL WITH MUSTARD MAYONNAISE

4 stalks fennel
2 large egg yolks
2 teaspoons dry mustard

2 tablespoons cream
2 tablespoons tarragon vinegar
2 good tablespoons butter or fat

Remove outside pieces of fennel, cut in half and cut off the tops. Cook in salted water until just soft and drain. Arrange on an oven dish and pour over Mustard Mayonnaise: —

Mustard Mayonnaise: Put egg yolks, mustard, cream and vinegar in a bowl, place in a pan of hot water over a slow fire and beat well with a whisk until the sauce begins to thicken; then add butter or fat, bit by bit. Continue beating till light and fluffy. Pour over the fennel and serve.

OYSTER PLANTS ITALIENNE

8 sticks oyster plant
juice ½ lemon
2 tablespoons butter
1 chopped onion
2 chopped mushrooms
2 tablespoons cooked, chopped ham
1 tablespoon flour

1 teaspoon tomato paste
salt and pepper
¼ cup white wine
1 cup stock
2 skinned and quartered tomatoes
some chopped herbs or parsley
grated Parmesan cheese

Wash well, trim and scrape the oyster plant. Simmer in boiling salted water with the lemon juice until tender (about 45 to 50 minutes). Melt the butter in a casserole. Add the onion, mushrooms, and ham. Cook slowly for 7 to 10 minutes, stirring frequently. Remove from the fire and mix in the flour, tomato paste, seasoning, wine and stock. Bring slowly to a boil and simmer for 15 to 20 minutes with the lid off. Add the oyster plant and tomatoes and cook for 5 minutes. Serve in a casserole or fireproof dish. Sprinkle with the chopped herbs or parsley and serve a bowl of grated Parmesan cheese with it.

Note: Jerusalem artichokes, sea kale and small new potatoes are excellent cooked in this way.

CAULIFLOWER POLONAISE

2 small cauliflowers
lemon juice
6 teaspoons oil
2 teaspoons butter

3 tablespoons bread crumbs
2 teaspoons chopped onion
3 finely chopped, hard-boiled eggs
salt and pepper

Remove most of outer leaves of cauliflowers and plunge into hot water seasoned with salt and lemon juice. Boil until tender. Remove, place on a hot serving dish and pour over the following sauce: —

Sauce: Heat oil and butter in a pan and add bread crumbs and chopped onion. Cook for 1 minute; then add hard-boiled eggs, salt and pepper. Cook another minute, spread thickly over the cauliflower and serve.

MUSHROOMS WITH SHERRY

2 cups mushrooms
butter

salt and pepper
1 tablespoon sherry

1 tablespoon finely chopped dill

Slice mushrooms finely and put in very hot butter. Season with salt and pepper and cook briskly for 2 to 3 minutes. Then pour over the sherry and chopped dill and serve with any chicken dish.

FENNEL WITH MUSTARD SAUCE

4 stalks fennel
butter
salt and pepper
1 tablespoon flour

1 dessertspoon dry mustard
1 cup liquor
1 dessertspoon chopped, fresh dill
1 tablespoon cream

Parmesan cheese

Split fennel in half, blanch, drain and return to pan with a little butter, salt and pepper. Cover and cook slowly until tender.

Mustard Sauce: Melt 1 tablespoon butter, stir in flour, mustard, salt and pepper. Pour on the liquor the fennel was blanched in.

Stir over the fire until the sauce comes to a boil and add chopped dill and cream. Arrange fennel on a flat serving dish, pour over the sauce, sprinkle with Parmesan cheese and brown under the broiler.

BRAISED CHESTNUTS AND BRUSSELS SPROUTS

1½ pounds chestnuts
4 tablespoons oil
1 sliced onion
1 sliced carrot
1 small stalk celery, sliced
1 sliced clove garlic
3 tablespoons flour
few mushroom peelings and stalks
1 teaspoon tomato paste

2 cups strong stock
¼ cup red wine
1 tablespoon sherry
1 tablespoon red currant jelly
1 bay leaf
salt and pepper
little butter
1 pound Brussels sprouts
1 teaspoon lemon juice

Put the chestnuts in a pan and cover with cold water. Bring to a boil and boil for 6 to 7 minutes. Then remove both inner and outer skins and brown quickly all over in a little hot oil; remove from the oil. Place in the pan the onion, carrot, celery, and garlic and brown slowly. Add the flour and brown very slowly. Add the mushroom peelings and stalks and cook for another 1 to 2 minutes. Add the tomato paste and stock and stir until smooth. Stir over the fire until the mixture comes to a boil. Add the red wine, sherry, jelly and bay leaf. Simmer down to a creamy consistency, adding salt and pepper. Strain and add the chestnuts. Simmer very gently until the chestnuts are just cooked. If the liquid becomes too thick, add a little more stock.

Wash the Brussels sprouts well and bring to a boil in cold water. Drain and return to the pan with a little butter, lemon juice and 2 tablespoons water. Season, cover with the lid and cook gently until just soft. Do not overcook them or they will lose their color. Add them at the last moment to the chestnuts. Serve in a casserole.

HARICOTS VERTS PARISIENNE
(Green Beans Parisienne)

1 pound young green beans *salt*
3 tablespoons butter   *cayenne pepper*
1 teaspoon lemon juice *4 tablespoons water*

Cut the beans in very thin slices diagonally. Bring slowly to a boil in cold water and drain. Melt the butter in a thick pan; add the lemon juice, salt, pepper and 4 tablespoons water. Add the beans. Cover with a lid and cook very gently, stirring occasionally, until just soft (approximately 20 minutes). Drain and serve.

TOMATO AND DILL SALAD

5 skinned tomatoes   *½ teaspoon dry mustard*
sugar   *little chili pepper*
2 tablespoons chopped fresh dill *grated rind 1 lemon*
1 egg yolk   *1 crushed clove garlic*
salt   *½ cup oil*
cayenne pepper   *3 tablespoons cream*
1 stiffly beaten egg white

Cut tomatoes in thick slices, sprinkle with a very little sugar, let stand for a few minutes and add chopped dill. Pour over the following dressing: —

Put into a bowl 1 egg yolk, salt, cayenne pepper, mustard, chili pepper, grated rind of 1 lemon and garlic. Mix well and add oil slowly. Then mix in cream, salt and beaten egg white. Mix lightly with tomatoes and serve.

SALADE DE LEGUMES MAISON
(Raw Vegetable Salad)

1 firm white cabbage
juice 1 lemon
3 large sliced onions
1 shredded red pepper
1 shredded green pepper
white pepper
black pepper
salt
½ teaspoon French mustard
1 teaspoon chopped herbs and
   garlic
2 or 3 sprigs tarragon
1 tablespoon wine vinegar

1 dessertspoon tarragon vinegar
4 tablespoons oil
2 sweet apples, peeled, quartered,
   and cored
3 large carrots, peeled and
   coarsely grated
1 raw beet, peeled and coarsely
   grated
2 bunches water cress
4 tomatoes, peeled, quartered and
   pipped
grated Gruyère cheese
cayenne pepper

Cut the cabbage in half; remove and discard thick stalks; cut in fine shreds. Soak in ice cold water with the lemon juice for 1 hour. Bring the onions to a boil in cold water; boil for 5 minutes, drain, cool and dry. Bring the peppers to a boil in cold water; boil for 5 minutes, drain, cool and dry.

Dressing: Mix the seasoning, herbs, garlic and vinegar together. Stir in the oil vigorously.

Drain the cabbage and dry well. Mix the apple and cabbage with a small quantity of the dressing. Mix the carrots, beet, onions and peppers with a little dressing. Arrange the cabbage and apple on one side of a large salad bowl and around the sides the beets, carrots, onions and peppers. Put a bunch of water cress in the middle and outline the different vegetables with sprigs of water cress. Arrange the tomatoes around the edge of the bowl. Sprinkle over the remaining dressing and cool in the refrigerator.

Cut some very thin slices of stale white bread. Arrange on a cookie sheet, sprinkle with grated Gruyère cheese and a little cayenne pepper and brown in the oven. Serve.

FRENCH DRESSING
(For one quart)

4 teaspoons salt

2 teaspoons onion salt

2 teaspoons pepper

4 teaspoons crushed black and
    white peppercorns

2 teaspoons dry mustard

1 teaspoon sugar

1 crushed clove garlic

2 teaspoons lemon juice

½ teaspoon Worcestershire sauce

12 tablespoons vinegar

4 cups oil

1 chopped, hard-boiled egg

little chopped capers

little chopped olives

little chopped herbs

Into a 1-quart, screw-top jar put the salt, onion salt, pepper, peppercorns, mustard, sugar, garlic, lemon juice, Worcestershire sauce, vinegar and oil. Screw top on securely and shake until thoroughly mixed.

Vinaigrette Sauce: For Vinaigrette Sauce add hard-boiled egg, capers, olives and herbs.

HOT BISCUITS WITH BACON AND CHEESE

2 cups flour

4 level tablespoons baking powder

1 teaspoon salt

4 tablespoons fat

½ cup buttermilk or sour milk

1 beaten egg

few slices bacon

few small slices red cheese

Place in a bowl the flour, baking powder, salt and fat; work these to a paste. Add the buttermilk or sour milk; work the milk into the paste; then roll out, not too thick. Cut in rounds with a cookie cutter. Place half the rounds on greased cookie sheet. Brush tops with beaten egg. Place on tops a small piece of bacon and a small slice red cheese. Cover with remaining rounds and brush again with beaten egg. Bake for 15 minutes.

GNOCCHI PARISIENNE

1 cup water	3 eggs
4 tablespoons butter	1 teaspoon dry mustard
salt	1 cup grated cheese
cayenne pepper	1½ cups milk
1½ cups flour	3 tablespoons cream
	1 egg yolk

Place in a thick pan the water, 2 tablespoons butter, salt and cayenne pepper. Bring slowly to a boil and when boiling add the flour. Beat in the eggs one at a time and season with a little more salt and cayenne pepper. Add ½ teaspoon dry mustard and 4 tablespoons grated cheese. Fill a pastry bag, having a large, plain tube in it, and pipe out in 1-inch-long pieces in a pan of hot, salted water. Simmer without boiling until the *gnocchis* are set (about 20 minutes). Drain and arrange on a flat dish.

Melt 2 tablespoons butter in a pan. Remove from the fire and stir in 3 tablespoons flour, a little salt and cayenne pepper; add 1 cup milk. Stir over the fire until the mixture comes to a boil. Add 3 tablespoons grated cheese, ½ teaspoon dry mustard and the cream. Simmer for 10 minutes. Add the egg yolk mixed into 2 tablespoons milk. Pour over the gnocchis. Sprinkle with a little more grated cheese and dot with butter. Brown under the broiler and serve.

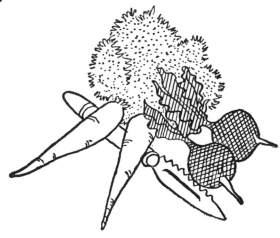

RUSSIAN GNOCCHI

¼ pound pot cheese	*pinch chili pepper*
2 cream cheeses	*1 tablespoon sour cream*
salt	*¾ cup cake flour*
cayenne pepper	*butter*
paprika	

Rub the pot cheese and cream cheese through a strainer and mix in salt, cayenne pepper, chili pepper and sour cream. Then carefully mix in the cake flour. Roll out in a long sausage on a floured board, cut in wedge-shaped pieces ¾ of an inch thick and drop into a pan of salted water, which has been brought to a boil and just stopped. Poach gently for 15 to 20 minutes until firm. Drain well and arrange on a long, flat platter. Pour over a little hot butter, sprinkle with paprika and bake in a moderate oven for 15 minutes. These should be served with Beef Stroganoff.

GNOCCHI ROMANA NAPOLITANA

2 cups water	small lump butter
10 tablespoons white or yellow corn meal	4 tablespoons grated Parmesan and Gruyère cheeses, mixed
salt and pepper	6 tablespoons olive oil
1 egg	2 chopped cloves of garlic
	4 skinned, sliced tomatoes

Put the water in a thick pan and slowly mix in the corn meal; add salt and pepper. Stir over the fire until the mixture comes to a boil. Continue stirring over a slow fire until the mixture is soft and comes clean away from the sides of the pan (about 20 to 25 minutes). Remove from the fire and beat in the egg, butter, 4 tablespoons Parmesan and Gruyère cheeses mixed. Form in egg shapes with two dessertspoons, drop into a pan of hot seasoned water and simmer gently, without boiling, until firm. Drain and arrange on a serving dish. Heat the oil; cook the garlic for 1 minute. Add the tomatoes and cook for 1 minute. Pour over the gnocchi and serve.

CHAPTER X

DESSERTS

Entremets or desserts, both hot and cold, add the finishing touch to the luncheon and dinner menus. The type of menu determines the entremet as a general rule. When the meal has been light, a rich *gâteau*, mousse or *bavaroise* may be served. Most of these desserts may be prepared in advance and permit many variations. If choux paste is stored in the refrigerator, it may, for example, be used with a rum pastry cream and again with a chocolate cream, creating the illusion of two entirely different entremets. Similarly, the mousses and *bavaroises* are basic recipes which may be used with different flavors and garnished with a number of fruits for variation.

To end a fairly substantial meal, a light entremet such as macédoine of fruits is suitable. The French custom of ending a meal with a basket of fresh fruit on the table is a pleasant one. The French choose their fruits wisely, however, using only those in season, for they know that fruit grown out of season is not only expensive but does not have the full, true flavor as when ripened naturally in the sun. In the United States, with its variety of climate and excellent refrigerating methods, it is possible to enjoy much longer seasons for fresh fruit than is possible in Europe.

APPLE PIE

2 cups flour	6 or 7 large apples
4 egg yolks	2 teaspoons lemon juice
4 tablespoons fat	grated rind 1 lemon
5 or more tablespoons sugar	2 tablespoons peach or apricot jam
salt	ground cinnamon
1 beaten egg	1 cinnamon stick

little confectioners' sugar

Put the flour on a slab or pastry board. Make a well in the center and put in it the egg yolks, fat, 4 tablespoons sugar and a pinch of salt. Work center ingredients to a smooth paste; work in the flour quickly. Roll out, not too thick, and line a shallow pie dish. Trim off neatly and brush the edges with beaten egg.

Skin, core, and slice the apples thickly. Put in a pan with the lemon juice and grated lemon rind, the peach or apricot jam and 1 tablespoon sugar. Half cook the apples. Cool a little. Fill the lined pie dish. Sprinkle top with a little ground cinnamon. Stick in the top a small piece of cinnamon stick. Cover with remaining pastry and trim off neatly. Stick down the edges with a pointed knife. Brush all over top with beaten egg and sprinkle with granulated sugar. Bake for 35 to 40 minutes in a moderate oven until golden brown on the top. Remove and cool. Dust with confectioners' sugar and serve.

SWISS PLUM TART

2 cups flour	½ teaspoon ground ginger
2 hard-boiled eggs	grated rind 1 lemon
4 eggs	salt
2 tablespoons browned almonds	bread crumbs
1 cup granulated sugar	1 pound plums
4 tablespoons fat	handful ground or grated pecans or
1 teaspoon ground cinnamon	walnuts

little confectioners' sugar

Put the flour on a pastry board or slab. Make a well in the center and in it put the yolks of the 2 hard-boiled eggs, which have been pushed through a strainer, 3 raw egg yolks, 2 tablespoons browned almonds, 4 tablespoons sugar, 4 tablespoons fat, 1 teaspoon ground cinnamon, ½ teaspoon ground ginger, the grated rind 1 lemon, and a pinch of salt. Work the center ingredients to a smooth paste. Work the flour in quickly. Roll out, not too thin. Place a flan ring on a cookie sheet. Line it with the pastry and trim off neatly. Sprinkle the bottom with bread crumbs and brush edges with beaten egg.

Cut the plums in quarters. Mix in a handful ground pecans or walnuts and a little sugar. Fill the tart and cover with the remaining pastry. Trim off neatly and press down edges with tip of knife. Brush over the top with beaten egg and sprinkle with granulated sugar and grated or ground pecans or walnuts. Bake for 35 to 40 minutes in a moderate oven. Remove, cool and dust with confectioners' sugar. Serve.

TARTE AUX QUICHES

2 cups flour	handful bread crumbs
4 egg yolks	1 pound plums, split
4 tablespoons sugar	6 tablespoons red currant jelly
4 tablespoons fat	1 tablespoon water
	salt

Short Pastry: Put the flour on a pastry board or slab. Make a well in the center and in the well put the egg yolks, 4 tablespoons sugar and the fat. Mix center ingredients to a smooth paste with a pinch of salt and quickly work in the flour. Roll out, not too thin. Place a flan ring on a cookie sheet. Line the flan ring with the pastry and trim off neatly. Sprinkle bottom with a few bread crumbs and cover with the plums. Bake in a hot oven about 35 minutes. Remove and take off the flan ring and cool.

Put the currant jelly in a pan with 1 tablespoon water. Stir over the fire until the jelly dissolves and is of thick syrupy consistency. Cool a little and brush all over the top of tart. Cool and serve.

LEMON MERINGUE PIE

2 cups flour	handful uncooked rice
4 egg yolks	grated rind and juice of 2 large lemons
2½ cups sugar	6 tablespoons butter or fat
4 tablespoons fat	3 eggs
salt	4 egg whites

Short Pastry: Put the flour on a pastry board or slab. Make a well in the center and in the well put the egg yolks, 4 tablespoons sugar, a pinch of salt and the fat. Mix the center ingredients to a smooth paste and quickly work in the flour. Roll out, not too thin. Place a flan ring on a cookie sheet, carefully line the flan ring with the pastry and trim off neatly. Line with waxed paper and put a little uncooked rice on top of the waxed paper. Bake in a 350° F. to 400° F. oven for 30 to 35 minutes until golden brown on top. Remove paper and rice and cool. Fill with the following lemon curd: —

Lemon Curd: Put in the top of a double boiler the grated rind and juice of 2 large lemons, 6 tablespoons butter or fat, 1 cup sugar and 3 beaten eggs. Stir over a slow fire until mixture thickens and coats back of spoon. Cool and fill in the pie.

Stiffly beat 3 or 4 egg whites in a bowl. When dry, carefully fold in 6 tablespoons sugar. Fill pastry bag with a rose tube and cover the top of pie. Sprinkle with a little granulated sugar and put to set in a slow oven until golden brown. Remove, cool and serve.

TARTE AUX PÊCHES
(Peach Tart)

2 cups flour	1 pound half-ripe peaches or pears
4 egg yolks	1 cup whipped cream
4 tablespoons sugar	little vanilla
4 tablespoons fat	2 or 3 tablespoons peach or apricot jam
salt	2 tablespoons water
handful uncooked rice	handful shredded blanched almonds

Short Pastry: Place the flour on a pastry board or slab. Make a well in the center and in the well put the egg yolks, 4 tablespoons sugar, a pinch of salt and the fat. Mix center ingredients to a smooth paste and quickly work in the flour. Roll out not too thin. Place a flan ring on a cookie sheet; carefully line the pastry into the flan ring and trim off neatly. Line with waxed paper and put in a little rice on top of the waxed paper. Bake in a 350° F. oven for 30 to 35 minutes, until golden brown on top. Remove paper and rice and cool. Fill level with whipped cream, which has been flavored to taste with vanilla. Cover the top with half-ripe peaches or pears.

Put the jam and 2 tablespoons water in a pan and cook to a syrupy consistency. Rub through a strainer. Cool a little and brush all over the top of peaches or pears. Sprinkle top with shredded blanched almonds, which have been baked in the oven until golden brown.

HONEY TART

2 cups flour	handful bread crumbs
2 strained, hard-boiled egg yolks	4 Philadelphia cream cheeses
3 raw egg yolks	½ cup cottage cheese
8 tablespoons granulated sugar	5 tablespoons honey
5 tablespoons fat	2 tablespoons raisins
grated rind 1 lemon	2 tablespoons sour cream
	confectioners' sugar

Put the flour on a pastry board or marble slab. Make a well in the center and into the well put the 2 hard-boiled egg yolks, which have been forced through a strainer, 3 raw egg yolks, 5 tablespoons sugar, the fat and the grated lemon rind. Work the center ingredients into a smooth paste; quickly work in the flour. Roll out not too thin and line a shallow pie dish or flan ring. Trim off neatly and sprinkle with a few bread crumbs.

Cream the Philadelphia cream cheeses. Add the cottage cheese with 2 tablespoons sugar, the honey, raisins and sour cream. Fill the pie and cover top latticewise with strips of the remaining pastry. Sprinkle top with the rest of the granulated sugar. Bake in a 350° F. oven for 35 to 40 minutes. Cool thoroughly. Carefully remove the ring or loosen from pie dish and arrange on a flat wooden board. Dust the top with confectioners' sugar and serve.

LINTZER TARTE
(Spiced Raspberry Tart)

1½ cups flour	grated rind 1 lemon
3 strained, hard-boiled egg yolks	1 teaspoon cinnamon
4 raw egg yolks	½ teaspoon nutmeg
7 tablespoons fat	handful bread crumbs
7 tablespoons sugar	2 cups well-reduced raspberry jam
2 tablespoons finely ground coffee	confectioners' sugar

Put the flour on a pastry board or marble slab. Make a well in the center and into the well put the 3 hard-boiled egg yolks, which have been pressed through a strainer, the 4 raw egg yolks, fat, sugar, coffee, lemon rind, cinnamon and nutmeg. Work center ingredients into a smooth paste and quickly work in the flour. Roll out not too thin and line into a shallow pie dish or flan ring. Trim off neatly and sprinkle the bottom with bread crumbs. Fill level with the jam. Cover the top latticewise with the remaining pastry cut into strips. Brush with the beaten egg and dust with granulated sugar. Bake in a 375° F. oven for 40 minutes. Put in the refrigerator and let it get quite cold. Carefully remove the flan ring or loosen from pie dish. Dust with confectioners' sugar and serve.

NAPOLEON
(Puff Paste)

1 cup flour	3 tablespoons sugar
level teaspoon salt	1 tablespoon dry gelatine
½ to ¾ cup ice water	1 teaspoon vanilla
1 cup butter	¾ cup hot milk
1 egg	2 tablespoons rum
1 egg yolk	2 stiffly beaten egg whites
3 heaping tablespoons flour	¾ cup whipped cream

Put 1 cup flour on a slab or pastry board and make a well in the center; add salt; then work quickly to a paste with ice water. Roll out to the size of a man's handkerchief. In the middle place the butter. Fold up like a package and put in the refrigerator for

15 minutes. Remove and roll out into a long strip. Fold in thirds with open edges out; roll again; fold and wrap in a napkin and put in the refrigerator for half an hour. Repeat this 3 times. It is well to leave the paste in the refrigerator several hours before using. On the last time, roll very thin and cut in 3 long strips, the length of a cookie sheet by 3 inches wide. Place on cookie pans, which have been moistened with water and set in the refrigerator for ¼ hour; then bake until golden brown in a 400° F. oven for about 15 minutes. At the same time bake all scraps of leftover paste to be used later for topping. Remove from the oven, let cool and sandwich with Cream Filling.

Cream Filling. Put 1 egg and 1 egg yolk, 3 heaping tablespoons flour and 3 tablespoons sugar in a bowl. Beat well; then mix in gelatine and vanilla. Pour on hot milk and stir over the fire until the mixture just comes to a boil; remove and stir over ice until it begins to thicken. Add rum, stiffly beaten egg whites and whipped cream. After sandwiching layers, spread a thin coating of the cream on top layer, sprinkle with crumbled bits of baked scraps of pastry and dust generously with confectioners' sugar. Serve in a long strip or cut into individual portions.

ALMOND TART

1½ cups flour	*¾ cup browned, chopped almonds*
3 egg yolks	*1 whole egg*
3 tablespoons shortening	*3 tablespoons sugar*
3 tablespoons sugar	*little rum*
pinch salt	*1 stiffly beaten egg white*

Put flour on a pastry board and make a well in the center for egg yolks, shortening, sugar and salt. Mix center ingredients into smooth paste with fingers, then work quickly into flour. Roll, cut into rounds and put into small flat tart tins. Fill with almonds, egg, sugar, rum, all well mixed; then add stiffly beaten egg white. Fill shells level, sprinkle top with granulated sugar and bake until golden brown in a 350° F. oven. Dust with confectioners' sugar and chopped nuts.

TARTE AUX FRAISES
(Strawberry Tart)

2 cups flour	2 teaspoons gelatine
5 egg yolks	¾ cup hot milk
7 tablespoons sugar	2 stiffly beaten egg whites
4 tablespoons fat	2 to 3 tablespoons whipped cream
salt	vanilla or rum to flavor
handful uncooked rice	strawberries
1 egg	6 tablespoons red currant jelly
3 tablespoons flour	1 tablespoon water

Short Pastry: Put 2 cups flour on a pastry board or slab. Make a well in the center and in the well put 4 egg yolks, 4 tablespoons sugar, a pinch of salt, and the fat. Mix the center ingredients to a smooth paste and quickly work in the flour. Roll out, not too thin. Place a flan ring on a cookie sheet. Carefully line the flan ring with the pastry and trim off neatly. Line with waxed paper and put a little rice on top of the waxed paper. Bake in a 350° F. to 400° F. oven for 30 to 35 minutes until golden brown on top. Remove paper and rice and cool.

Put in a small bowl 1 egg, 1 egg yolk, 3 tablespoons sugar and 3 tablespoons flour. Beat until fluffy and light. Mix in the gelatine. Pour on ¾ cup hot milk. Stir over the fire until the mixture comes to a boil. Stir over ice until it begins to cool. Mix in 2 stiffly beaten egg whites and 2 or 3 tablespoons whipped cream. Flavor with a little vanilla or rum. Fill tart level. Cover top carefully with the strawberries.

Put in a pan the jelly and 1 tablespoon water. Stir over the fire to thick, syrupy consistency. Cool a little and brush all over top of strawberries. Serve.

CRÊPES SUZETTES

4 heaping tablespoons flour
1 egg
1 egg yolk
1 tablespoon cooking oil
3 or more tablespoons milk
5 tablespoons butter
juice 3 oranges

2 teaspoons grated orange rind
4 tablespoons sugar
3 tablespoons orange curaçao,
Cointreau, brandy or rum
finely shredded rind 1 orange
peeled sections 2 small oranges

Put in a small bowl the flour, egg, egg yolk, cooking oil and 3 tablespoons milk. Stir until quite smooth. Add enough milk to reduce it to a thin consistency. Place in the refrigerator for at least half an hour. Remove and add enough milk to reduce it to a thin consistency again. Heat a small pancake pan and, when very hot, wipe out with a piece of buttered waxed paper. Cover bottom of pan with a very thin layer of batter. Cook until golden brown on one side; turn over and cook until golden brown on the other.

Cream 3 tablespoons butter in a bowl. Mix in the juice of ½ orange, 2 teaspoons grated orange rind, 2 tablespoons sugar, 2 teaspoons orange curaçao, Cointreau, brandy or rum. Spread on each pancake. Fold in thirds. Arrange overlapping on a serving dish.

Put in a pan the juice of 2 oranges, finely shredded rind 1 orange, 1 tablespoon butter, 2 tablespoons sugar, 2 tablespoons orange curaçao, Cointreau, rum or brandy. Cook this to syrupy consistency; then add the peeled sections of 2 small oranges.

Pour this over the pancakes. At last moment pour over hot liqueur, which has been heated in a small pan. Ignite liqueur with a match just before pouring it over the pancakes.

APPLE CHARLOTTE

handful granulated sugar
bread
10 or 12 large green apples or
  good cooking apples

grated rind 1 lemon
2 or 3 tablespoons apricot jam
2 tablespoons butter

Butter well and dust out with granulated sugar a small round cake tin about 8 inches in diameter. Cut several fingers of bread about 1 inch wide and a little longer than the depth of the tin. Fry them golden in a little hot butter or oil, on one side only. Line the bottom and sides of the tin, brown side next to the tin, with these fingers of bread.

Skin, core and cut the apples in thick slices and put in a pan with the grated lemon rind, jam and 1 tablespoon butter. Cook over a slow fire until nearly soft. Fill the lined mold and cover the top with the remaining fried bread. Bake in a hot oven for half an hour. Cool a little before turning out onto a hot serving dish. Serve with Sabayon Sauce (p. 284).

CRÊPES FOURRÉS
(Pancakes Stuffed with Apples)

4 heaping tablespoons flour
1 egg
1 egg yolk
1 tablespoon cooking oil
1 cup milk
4 or 5 large cooking apples
6 tablespoons peach or apricot jam

grated rind 2 lemons
4 tablespoons granulated sugar
grated rind 1 orange
juice 1 lemon and 1 orange
½ cup water
handful shredded, blanched,
  browned almonds
confectioners' sugar

Put in a small bowl the flour, egg, egg yolk, cooking oil, and 3 tablespoons milk. Stir until quite smooth. Add enough milk to reduce to thin consistency. Put in the refrigerator for at least half an hour. Remove and add enough milk to reduce to thin consistency once again.

Heat a small pancake pan and, when very hot, wipe out with

piece of buttered waxed paper. Cover bottom of pan with a very thin layer of batter. Cook until golden brown on one side. Turn and cook until golden brown on the other.

Skin, core and cut the apples in thick slices. Put in a pan with 2 or 3 tablespoons peach or apricot jam, the grated rind of 1 lemon and 1 tablespoon sugar. Cook slowly until soft. Sandwich into your pancakes. Shape like a cake and cut in quarters. Reheat in the oven.

Put in a pan the grated rind of 1 orange, 1 lemon, the juice of both orange and lemon, 3 tablespoons apricot or peach jam, 3 tablespoons sugar and ½ cup water. Cook to a syrupy consistency and pour over the pancakes. Sprinkle top with shredded, blanched, browned almonds, dust with confectioners' sugar and serve at once.

POMMES PARISIENNE

1 small, or ½ large, apple for each person	*1 egg yolk*
4 tablespoons peach or apricot jam	*3 level tablespoons flour*
½ cup corn syrup	*3 level tablespoons sugar*
grated rind 1 lemon	*2 teaspoons dry gelatine*
grated rind and juice 1 orange	*¾ cup strong coffee and milk mixed*
1 egg	*2 stiffly beaten egg whites*
rum	

Carefully core 1 apple for each person. Wash in lemon juice and water but do not peel. Plunge for 1 minute in hot water; then cook in the following syrup: —

Syrup: Put jam, corn syrup, lemon and orange rind in a pan and cook to a syrupy consistency. Put in apples and cook until just soft but not mushy. Allow to cool, arrange on a long serving dish and pipe the top of each with Pastry Cream.

Pastry Cream: Put 1 egg, 1 egg yolk, flour and sugar in a bowl and beat well; stir in the gelatine. Put coffee and milk mixture in a pan and bring to a boil; add to the mixture. Stir over the fire until the mixture comes to a boil; stir over ice until it cools. Add egg whites and flavor with a little rum. Fill into a pastry bag with rose tube, pipe into apples over which the syrup is poured and serve.

APPLE STRUDEL

2 cups flour	2 tablespoons vanilla
1 tablespoon oil	2 tablespoons brown sugar
1 egg	grated rind 1 lemon
¾ cup lukewarm water	½ cup ground walnuts
1 cup bread crumbs	½ cup raisins and currants **mixed**
4 tablespoons fat or butter	2 teaspoons cinnamon
3 pounds peeled, cored, sliced	1 teaspoon allspice
apples	confectioners' sugar

Put the flour on a marble slab and make a well in the center. Put the oil and the beaten egg in the center and work up a soft dough with the lukewarm water. Beat on the slab until very light. Place on a lightly floured board and brush top of dough mixture with oil. Cover with a bowl and put in a warm place for 1 hour.

Spread a cloth over a large table and sprinkle lightly with flour. Place the dough on top and roll out into a square the size of a large pocket handkerchief. Pull it out carefully and gently with the hands until it covers the whole table. Allow to dry. Sprinkle with oil and arrange the following mixture at one end of the pastry: —

Mixture: Fry the bread crumbs in hot fat and place at one end of the pastry. Soak the apples in the vanilla and brown sugar for half an hour. Drain off the liquid and arrange the apples on top of bread crumbs with the grated rind of 1 lemon. On this put the nuts, raisins and currants, cinnamon and allspice. Fold the edges over and roll up like a jelly roll. Place on a well-greased cookie sheet and bake in a hot oven for 35 minutes. Baste frequently with fat. Cool a little. Cut small piece off each end. Place on a long wooden board, sprinkle well with confectioners' sugar and serve with whipped or thick cream.

STEWED APPLES WITH COFFEE CREAM

4 large apples	*3 tablespoons flour*
4 tablespoons apricot jam	*2 teaspoons coffee essence*
little shredded orange rind	*¾ cup hot milk*
6 tablespoons sugar	*1 stiffly beaten egg white*
½ cup water	*2 tablespoons rum*
1 egg	*1 tablespoon whipped cream*
1 egg yolk	*shredded, browned almonds*

Carefully skin and halve the apples and remove center with seeds with a potato scoop. In the meantime put jam, orange rind, 3 tablespoons sugar and ½ cup water in a pan and cook to a syrupy consistency. Put apples in and poach gently until just tender. Cool, arrange on a flat serving dish and fill centers with Coffee Rum Cream.

Coffee Rum Cream: Put 1 egg, 1 egg yolk, 3 tablespoons sugar and flour in a bowl and beat with a whisk until smooth; then beat in gelatine and add the coffee essence. Pour on hot milk and stir over the fire until the mixture comes to a boil. Remove from the fire and stir over ice until cool; mix in beaten egg white and rum. When quite stiff add whipped cream. Fill into a pastry bag with rose tube and pipe onto top of apples; pour over the syrup in which the apples were cooked and scatter a few almonds over the top. This makes a delicious simple dessert by omitting the cream filling.

PINEAPPLE IN PORT WINE SYRUP

1 pineapple	*5 tablespoons sugar*
rind 1 orange	*½ cup pineapple juice*
rind ½ grapefruit	*½ cup port wine*

Skin, slice and core pineapple and put into the following syrup: —

Syrup: Put finely shredded orange and grapefruit rind in a pan with sugar, pineapple juice and wine. Cook until rind is clear; remove from fire, put in the sliced fruit and allow it to cool in the syrup. Place in a glass bowl and serve cold

POIRE FONDUE
(Pear Dessert)

5 pears	1 egg yolk
1 cup sugar	3 tablespoons flour
3 tablespoons apricot jam	2 good teaspoons gelatine
½ cup water	¾ cup hot milk
little lemon juice	3 stiffly beaten egg whites
1 egg	2 tablespoons cream

rum to taste

Skin, halve and remove cores of 5 pears with a potato scoop. Put in a pan ¾ cup sugar, jam, water and lemon juice and cook to a thin syrup. Put in the pears and simmer gently for 7 to 8 minutes. Remove and cool. Arrange the pears on a serving dish, saving the syrup, and fill the centers with Pastry Cream.

Pastry Cream: Put 1 egg, 1 egg yolk, 3 tablespoons sugar and flour into a bowl and beat very well. Add gelatine; then pour on the milk. Stir over the fire until just on the point of boiling. Remove from the fire and stir over ice until cold. Add egg whites, cream and rum. Fill into pears through a pastry bag, pour the syrup on top and serve.

POIRES MERINGUES AU CHOCOLAT À LA FOYOT
(Pears with Meringue and Chocolate Sauce)

5 pears	rind and juice 1 lemon
3 tablespoons apricot jam	2 tablespoons chopped, mixed, candied
½ cup sugar	fruit
¼ cup water	2 egg whites
2 tablespoons sherry	2 ounces dark, sweet chocolate

Skin and core pears but keep whole and cook in the following syrup: —

Syrup: Put jam, ¼ cup sugar, water, sherry and lemon in a pan and cook to a syrupy consistency. Put in the pears and turn around in the syrup until well immersed. While pears are simmering gently, soak the candied fruit in rum or sherry. Remove pears when tender, not soft, fill hole with chopped fruit and cover with the following meringue: —

Meringue: Put 2 egg whites in a bowl with 6 level tablespoons sugar. Beat until stiff; then fill into a pastry bag with rose tube and cover top of pears; put in a very slow oven to brown. Remove and serve with Chocolate Sauce.

Chocolate Sauce: Break up the chocolate. Add to the syrup in which the pears were cooked, stir over a slow fire until dissolved and pour around the dish or serve separately. Both fruit and sauce should be hot.

POIRES MERINGUES AU CHOCOLAT
(Pears with Chocolate and Meringue)

4 tablespoons apricot jam	*6 ripe pears*
¼ cup sugar	*rum*
½ cup water	*2 egg whites*
2 tablespoons chopped, mixed,	*5 tablespoons sugar*
candied fruit	*3 ounces dark sweet chocolate*

Put the apricot jam, ¼ cup sugar and ½ cup water in a pan. Cook to a syrupy consistency. Peel the pears carefully, removing the core, and keeping them whole. Add to the syrup and cook gently for 15 minutes, basting frequently. Remove the pears and fill the centers of the pears with the candied fruit, which has been mixed with a little rum. Arrange on a serving dish.

Beat the egg whites until stiff. Fold in 4 tablespoons sugar. Fill a pastry bag with rose tube and pipe the egg whites around the top of the pears. Sprinkle with another tablespoon sugar. Brown in a moderate oven for 3 minutes. Cut up the chocolate and add it to the syrup. Stir over a slow fire until it dissolves. Pour around the dish just before serving.

CHOCOLATE SPONGE

½ pound dark sweet chocolate
2 tablespoons butter
½ cup evaporated milk
4 egg yolks

4 stiffly beaten egg whites
1 teaspoon gelatine
¼ cup warm water
3 tablespoons whipped cream

Melt the chocolate with the butter and evaporated milk. Remove from fire and mix in the egg yolks. Cook very slowly for 1 minute. Fold in the stiffly beaten egg whites with the gelatine, which has been dissolved in ¼ cup warm water. Mold in a deep brown crock mold and set in a cool place. Serve in the crock with whipped cream.

COLD ORANGE MOUSSE

3 eggs
2 egg yolks
3 tablespoons granulated sugar
grated rind 1 large orange
1½ packets plain gelatine

juice 1 large orange
1 or 2 tablespoons whipped cream
2 skinned sections of orange
3 tablespoons red currant or apple jelly

2 tablespoons water

Break in a bowl the 3 eggs and 2 egg yolks. Add 3 tablespoons granulated sugar and the grated rind 1 large orange. Place the bowl over another bowl of hot water and beat until very thick and frothy. Dissolve in a pan the gelatine and the juice of 1 large orange; stir over a slow fire until entirely dissolved. Mix this carefully into the egg mixture in the bowl. Add 1 or 2 tablespoons whipped cream. Pour into a serving bowl and place in the refrigerator to set. Remove and arrange on top 2 skinned sections of orange.

Put the jelly in a pan with 2 tablespoons water and cook to a syrupy consistency. Cool thoroughly and pour over the orange sections.

CHOCOLATE MOUSSE

5 eggs   5 tablespoons cold water
½ pound dark sweet chocolate   2 teaspoons rum

Separate the yolks and whites of the 5 eggs. Break the chocolate in small pieces and place in a thick pan with the cold water. Stir over a low fire until it dissolves. Remove from fire and mix in carefully the 5 egg yolks and 2 teaspoons rum. Add the 5 stiffly beaten egg whites and mix thoroughly. Fill into small glasses or jars. Place in refrigerator for at least 4 hours. Remove and serve. This will make 8 small cups.

RON FROMAGE
(Danish Cheese)

1 level tablespoon gelatine   4 egg yolks
1 cup milk   ¼ cup granulated sugar
1 cup cream   2 or 3 tablespoons Jamaica rum
salt   ½ cup powdered sugar
                    ½ cup cold water

Dissolve the gelatine in a little of the milk. Gently heat the rest of the milk, the cream and a pinch of salt. Beat the egg yolks in a bowl, add the granulated sugar and beat well until quite fluffy and light. Pour on the hot cream, milk and salt mixture, beating all the time. Return to the fire and stir until thick. Cook a little longer. Be very careful the custard mixture does not curdle. Remove from the fire; if cooked in a double boiler remove from the water. Add gelatine and stir in the rum. Cool a little and pour into a mold. Chill for several hours, if possible, overnight.

Put ½ cup powdered sugar in a thick pan with ¼ cup cold water. Dissolve sugar slowly. Then turn up the fire and cook to a light caramel. Remove at once from the fire. If the caramel should be a little too dark, place the pan in another pan of cold water. Stir into the caramel ¼ cup cold water. Mix well and cool. Pour over the Danish cheese.

Note: the caramel mixture can be kept for a long time in a tightly closed bottle.

MOUSSE DE POMMES CALVADOS
(Cold Applejack Mousse)

2 pounds apples, peeled, cored and sliced	*3 tablespoons granulated sugar*
grated rind 1 lemon	*1 tablespoon gelatine*
2 tablespoons brown sugar	*juice 1 lemon*
5 tablespoons apricot jam	*2 tablespoons whipped cream*
2 tablespoons butter	*2 liqueur glasses applejack*
3 eggs	*skinned sections 2 oranges*
2 egg yolks	*apricot syrup*
	3 tablespoons water

Cook the apples to a purée with a little grated lemon rind, 2 tablespoons brown sugar and 2 tablespoons apricot jam. Add 2 tablespoons butter and mash well. Put in a bowl 3 eggs, 2 egg yolks and 3 tablespoons granulated sugar. Beat until thick either over another bowl of hot water or in an electric beater. Add 1 tablespoon of gelatine, melted down in a little lemon juice and water.

Carefully mix in the apple purée, well cooled, with 2 tablespoons whipped cream and 2 liqueur glasses applejack. Pour the mixture into a bowl for serving. Put to set in a cool place and decorate the top with skinned sections of oranges and thin slices of raw, sweet apple. Cover the top with a little clear Apricot Syrup.

Apricot Syrup: Put 3 tablespoons apricot jam in a pan with 3 tablespoons water. Boil down to a syrupy consistency, strain and cool.

CRÈME BRÛLÉE

2 cups thick cream
½-inch vanilla bean

4 egg yolks
1 cup granulated sugar

Heat the cream slightly with vanilla bean over a very slow fire. Beat the egg yolks in a bowl with 4 tablespoons sugar until very creamy and light. Mix in the warm cream very carefully and slowly. Return to a thick pan. Place on a slow fire and stir until the mixture coats the back of a wooden spoon. Pour into a very shallow glass dish. Place in the refrigerator to set overnight. Next day cover top completely with granulated sugar so that none of the cream shows. Place the dish on a bowl of crushed ice and place under broiler until the sugar caramelizes. Place in the refrigerator for 3 minutes just before serving.

CRÈME CARAMEL
(Caramel Custard)

2 whole eggs
3 egg yolks
pinch of salt
4 tablespoons granulated sugar

1 small vanilla bean
1½ cups milk
1 cup lump sugar
1 tablespoon syrup glucose

½ cup water

Break the eggs and egg yolks in a bowl, add the granulated sugar and pinch of salt, and beat the whole thoroughly. Mix in the vanilla bean and slowly pour on the hot milk, stirring all the time. Put the lump sugar in a pan with the syrup glucose and ½ cup water. Melt it slowly without stirring; then turn up the heat and continue cooking until you have a good dark caramel. Pour this in a soufflé dish and turn the dish around until the whole of the inside has been lined. Fill the dish with the egg and milk mixture, place the crème caramel in a pan surrounded with water and put into a very slow oven (250° F.) to set for about 1 hour. Remove and let it get quite cold before turning it onto a serving dish.

BAVARIAN CREAM TRIFLE
(Emily's Teeth)

stale cake	1 tablespoon dry gelatine
rum	1½ cups hot, creamy milk
5 egg yolks	3 stiffly beaten egg whites
4 tablespoons sugar	whipped cream
½ to ¾ cup almonds	

Break stale cake in pieces and soak liberally in rum. Then mix into the following: —

Bavarian Cream: Put egg yolks in a bowl with sugar. Beat well; then mix in dry gelatine and pour on hot, creamy milk. Stir over the fire until the mixture thickens but does not boil. Stir over ice until on the point of setting and add stiffly beaten egg whites and 2 tablespoons whipped cream. Mix in the cake, fill into a bowl for serving and put in the refrigerator to set. Just before serving cover the top with thick mounds of whipped cream. Decorate with almonds, split and stuck close together all over the top. They should be stuck upright in the cream. A ring of fresh strawberries will add a striking note.

FRESH RHUBARB MOUSSE

1 bunch rhubarb	4 tablespoons sugar
lemon juice	grated rind 1 lemon
little sugar	2 tablespoons gelatine
5 whole eggs	1 cup cooked rhubarb
4 egg yolks	grape jelly

Cut rhubarb in pieces, put in an earthenware dish and sprinkle with lemon juice and sugar. Bake for 15 minutes in a moderate oven. Put in a bowl the eggs, egg yolks, sugar and rind of 1 lemon and beat until very stiff in an electric mixer. Carefully add the gelatine, which has been dissolved in lemon juice and water; beat very hard with a wooden spoon while adding gelatine; then add cooked rhubarb. Pour into a bowl for serving and put in the refrigerator to set. When firm garnish the top with the rest of the rhubarb and spread over all some grape jelly, which has been thinned over the fire with a little water.

PRALINE MOUSSE

4 whole eggs	5 tablespoons water
3 egg yolks	4 tablespoons crushed praline
4 tablespoons sugar	whipped cream
2 tablespoons gelatine	1 tablespoon rum
	chopped nuts

Beat whole eggs, egg yolks and sugar until stiff in an electric mixer or over hot water; when stiff stir in the gelatine, which has been dissolved over the fire in 5 tablespoons water. Then add crushed praline, 2 tablespoons whipped cream and rum. Fill into a bowl for serving and put in the refrigerator to set. Garnish with whipped cream and sprinkle the top with chopped nuts. Serve quite cold.

CARAMEL MOUSSE WITH FRESH STRAWBERRIES

4 whole eggs	¼ cup water
3 egg yolks	1 tablespoon glucose syrup
sugar	4 tablespoons hot water
2 tablespoons gelatine	whipped cream
grated rind 1 lemon	currant jelly
½ cup caramel	fresh strawberries

Beat whole eggs, egg yolks and 5 tablespoons sugar in an electric mixer at high speed until very stiff; then mix gelatine and grated lemon rind in carefully, beating hard. (Dissolve the gelatine first in water over the fire.) Add ½ cup caramel, made as follows; this can be made while the mousse is in the mixer: —

Caramel: Put ¼ cup sugar, water and glucose syrup in a pan and cook quickly without stirring until dark caramel. Then add 4 tablespoons hot water.

Add the caramel to the mousse, stirring vigorously; pour in a bowl to set in the refrigerator. When firm remove and spread with whipped cream. Decorate with crisscross lines of currant jelly. Make rosettes of cream all around the edge and place a fresh strawberry in each rosette.

SOUFFLÉ AU CARAMEL FROID
(Cold Caramel Soufflé)

¾ cup sugar	3 egg yolks
1 tablespoon syrup glucose	2 level tablespoons gelatine
water	juice 1 lemon
4 eggs	¾ cup whipped cream
grated nut meats	

Put ½ cup sugar in a thick pan with the syrup glucose and ¼ cup water. Dissolve over the fire slowly. Turn up the fire and cook without stirring until it makes a good dark caramel. Add 4 tablespoons water and cool a little. Put in a bowl or an electric beater the eggs and yolks with ¼ cup sugar and beat until stiff. (If you have no machine, place your bowl over a pan of hot water and beat until very stiff with a rotary beater.) Mix in the caramel and the gelatine, dissolved in the lemon juice and a little water. Add 2 tablespoons whipped cream.

Oil a soufflé dish. Tie a band of oiled waxed paper around the outside. Pour in the mixture so that it comes up above the edge of the dish and place in the refrigerator to set. Remove outside paper. Stick around the edge a few grated nuts and decorate top with the remaining cream forced through a pastry bag with a rose pipe.

This can be made with chocolate by adding to the mixture, instead of the caramel, 3 ounces dark sweet chocolate, which has been dissolved in 2 tablespoons water over a slow fire and cooled.

This can also be made with fresh fruit, such as strawberries and raspberries, by using a cup of fresh fruit pulp.

LEMON SOUFFLÉ

2 tablespoons butter	4 egg yolks
3 level tablespoons flour	4 tablespoons sugar
¾ cup milk	5 stiffly beaten egg whites
juice and grated rind 1 lemon	

Melt butter and stir in the flour; when blended pour on the milk. Stir over the fire until thick but not boiling; then add lemon juice and grated lemon rind. Mix in the egg yolks and sugar and lastly fold in the stiffly beaten egg whites.

Grease a soufflé dish. Dust with sugar and tie waxed paper on the outside to form a cuff. Fill with the mixture and bake for ¼ hour in a 350° F. oven. Remove the paper. Dust the top with sugar and serve at once.

HOT CHOCOLATE SOUFFLÉ

2 tablespoons butter	5 tablespoons sugar
3 level tablespoons flour	2 tablespoons rum
¾ cup milk	5 egg yolks
4 ounces dark sweet chocolate	5 stiffly beaten egg whites
½ ounce bitter chocolate	confectioners' sugar
3 tablespoons water	1 egg
2 tablespoons Marsala wine	

Melt the butter in a small thick pan, stir in the flour and pour on the milk. Stir over the fire until it thickens; it must not boil. Add the chocolate, dissolved in 3 tablespoons cold water over a slow fire. Add 3 tablespoons sugar and rum. Beat in 4 egg yolks and 5 stiffly beaten egg whites. Grease a soufflé dish, tie a band of greased waxed paper around the outside and dust out with granulated sugar. Pour in the soufflé mixture, place in a pan of hot water and bake in a 375° F. oven for 45 minutes. Carefully remove the paper and dust with confectioners' sugar.

Put in a small bowl 1 egg, 1 egg yolk, 2 tablespoons sugar and the Marsala. Put the bowl in another pan of hot water and beat over a slow fire with a rotary beater until thick. Serve this sauce at once, separately, with the soufflé.

APRICOT SOUFFLÉ

2 tablespoons butter   3 or 4 egg yolks
3 level tablespoons flour   3 or 4 tablespoons sugar
¾ cup milk   5 stiffly beaten egg whites
2 teaspoons lemon juice
        ½ cup apricot jam or 1 cup cooked apricot pulp

Melt butter and stir in the flour. When blended pour on the milk. Stir over the fire until thick; it must not boil. Then add lemon juice and apricot jam or cooked apricot pulp; mix in egg yolks and sugar and lastly fold in stiffly beaten egg whites.

Grease a soufflé dish. Dust with sugar and tie waxed paper outside to form a cuff. Fill with the mixture and bake for half an hour in a 350° F. oven. Remove paper, dust with sugar and serve immediately.

HOT LEMON SOUFFLÉ

2 level tablespoons butter   5 egg yolks
3 level tablespoons flour   5 stiffly beaten egg whites
¾ cup milk   salt
grated rind and juice 1 lemon   confectioners' sugar
1 cup sugar   1 egg
            2 tablespoons sherry

Melt the butter in a pan, stir in the flour, add the milk and stir over the fire until the mixture thickens; it must not boil. Stir in the grated rind and juice of 1 lemon, 3 tablespoons sugar, 4 egg yolks and 5 stiffly beaten egg whites. Fold in the latter very carefully with a pinch of salt. Butter a soufflé dish, dust out with sugar and tie a band of buttered paper around the outside. Pour in the soufflé mixture and bake for half an hour in a 375° F. oven. Remove and carefully take off the paper. Dust quickly with confectioners' sugar.

Put in a bowl 1 egg, 1 egg yolk, 2 tablespoons sherry and

3 tablespoons sugar. Put the bowl in a pan of hot water over a slow fire and beat until the mixture thickens. Serve at once with the soufflé.

MARMALADE SOUFFLÉ

2 tablespoons butter
3 level tablespoons flour
¾ cup milk
grated rind 2 lemons
grated rind 1 orange
4 tablespoons bitter marmalade
salt

2 tablespoons sugar
3 egg yolks
5 stiffly beaten egg whites
cup grated pecan nuts
little confectioners' sugar
¾ cup thick sour cream
1 teaspoon grated nutmeg

Melt the butter in a pan, stir in the flour, pour on the milk and stir over the fire until the mixture thickens. Add the grated rind of 1 lemon and 1 orange and the marmalade. Fold in carefully a pinch of salt, 1 tablespoon sugar, 3 egg yolks and 5 stiffly beaten egg whites. Butter a soufflé dish. Dust out with grated pecan nuts and a little sugar. Fill and bake in a 375° F. oven for half an hour. Remove and dust with confectioners' sugar.

Mix into ¾ cup thick sour cream 1 tablespoon sugar, the grated rind of 1 lemon and 1 teaspoon grated nutmeg. Serve separately, ice cold.

CAFÉ LIÉGEOISE
(Coffee Cream)

4 large egg yolks
½ cup sugar

¼ cup water
3 tablespoons coffee essence
2 cups cream

Put egg yolks in a bowl and beat well. Then put sugar and water in a pan and cook until it forms a thread. Pour onto the yolks and beat in an electric mixer until stiff; add coffee essence and cream. Pour into a freezer and turn until set. Serve in tall glasses and top with whipped cream. This makes 1½ pints.

FRENCH ICE CREAM

Vanilla (one quart): Put ½ cup sugar in a pan with ¼ cup water. Cook to a light thread. Pour onto 3 large, beaten egg yolks and continue beating until very stiff. Add 1 inch of vanilla bean scraped out and 3½ cups thick cream. Pour into an ice cream freezer and turn until set.

Other Flavors

Chocolate: Add to the above mixture in place of the vanilla, 6 ounces of dark sweet chocolate and ½ ounce bitter chocolate dissolved over a slow fire. Freeze in the usual manner.

Brown Bread: When the vanilla ice cream is set add ¾ cup crisp brown bread crumbs, dried in the oven, and flavor with good rum.

Fruit: Add a cup of any fresh fruit pulp to the vanilla ice cream.

Coffee: Add 2 tablespoons coffee essence to the above mixture in place of vanilla. When set, add 2 tablespoons rum.

MONT BLANC AUX MARRONS
(Chestnuts with Meringue)

3 egg whites	*vanilla*
10 tablespoons sugar	*1 cup corn syrup*
1 pound chestnuts	*rum*
½ milk and ½ water	*coarsely grated chocolate*

Beat egg whites very stiff; then fold in sugar carefully. Fill a pastry bag with plain tube at the end. Put a piece of waxed paper on a cookie sheet and drop meringues on this; sprinkle with sugar and bake in a very slow oven (225° F.) until firm and light golden brown. Cool and cover with the following: —

Chestnut Purée: Shell chestnuts and put in a pan with cold water to cover. Bring to a boil and boil for 2 to 3 minutes. While hot peel off skins. Put the chestnuts in a saucepan and cover with ½ milk and ½ water flavored with vanilla; simmer until soft.

Drain and put through a strainer and beat in the following syrup: —

Syrup: Put corn syrup in a pan and cook to a fine thread; flavor with rum and mix carefully into nuts to consistency of mashed potatoes. Fill a pastry bag with very small, round tube (the size of spaghetti). Pipe carelessly in mounds onto meringues and on top of that pipe rosettes of whipped cream. Sprinkle with coarsely grated chocolate. Arrange on a serving dish and serve.

VACHERIN AUX PÊCHES
(Macaroon with Peaches)

whites 3 large eggs	1 cup thick cream
10 tablespoons granulated sugar	1 tablespoon granulated sugar
6 tablespoons ground nuts	rum or vanilla to flavor
2 tablespoons cool, melted butter	1 pound sliced ripe peaches,
3 tablespoons sifted flour	strawberries or pears
little confectioners' sugar	

Whip the egg whites until stiff. Carefully fold in the sugar, ground nuts, butter and flour and mix well. Butter 3 cookie sheets and dust them lightly with flour. Mark a circle in the middle of each, roughly 10 inches in diameter. Divide the mixture evenly among the 3 cookie sheets. Spread out evenly and smooth with a spatula. Bake until golden brown in a moderate oven. Remove and loosen at once with a spatula. Place a saucepan lid the same size on top of each. Trim off edges with a small, sharp knife. Lift lids off the cookie sheets. Cool on cake racks.

Put the thick cream in a bowl and place the bowl over another bowl of cracked ice. Beat with a wire whisk until the cream begins to thicken. Add 1 tablespoon sugar, flavor with a little rum or vanilla and continue beating until stiff. Mix in carefully the peaches, strawberries or pears. Sandwich the mixture into the 3 rounds of cake and reshape. Garnish with confectioners' sugar, some of the best slices of the fruits, and a little plain whipped cream squeezed through a pastry bag with a rose pipe.

RIZ AUX FRAISES
(Strawberries with Rice Cream)

2 cups milk	2 egg yolks
4 tablespoons rice	1 egg white
2 teaspoons gelatine	2 cups sliced strawberries
1 small lemon	1 cup whipped cream

Put the milk in a thick pan with the rice and stir over a slow fire until the mixture comes to a boil. Cook very slowly, stirring occasionally, until the rice is quite soft. Melt the gelatine with the juice of the lemon and a very little water over a slow fire; add to the rice. Remove from the fire and stir in the egg yolks. Stir over a bowl of crushed ice until the mixture is quite cold. Mix in carefully the stiffly beaten egg white, the strawberries and lastly the whipped cream. Place in a serving bowl and serve ice cold.

BABA AU RHUM
(Rum Baba)

9 tablespoons flour	½ cup water
2 yeast cakes	3 tablespoons rum
6 tablespoons lukewarm milk	1 egg yolk
3 large eggs	3 tablespoons flour
3 tablespoons creamed butter	3 tablespoons sugar
4 tablespoons sugar	3 teaspoons gelatine
salt	¾ cup hot milk
3 tablespoons currants	2 stiffly beaten egg whites
¾ cup sugar or white corn syrup	3 or 4 tablespoons whipped cream

Put 9 tablespoons flour in a warm bowl. Mix to a smooth paste the yeast cakes, dissolved in 6 tablespoons lukewarm milk. Add 2 large eggs. Beat lightly with the hand until the mixture is thoroughly blended. Cover with a plate and put in a warm place for three-quarters of an hour to rise. Add 3 tablespoons creamed butter, 1 dessertspoon sugar, a pinch of salt and 3 tablespoons currants, which have been dusted with a little flour. Grease well and quarter fill some cabinet-pudding molds. Leave in a warm place until mixture rises to tops of molds. Bake in a 475° F. oven for 10 minutes.

Rum Syrup: Put ¾ cup sugar or white corn syrup in a pan with ½ cup water and 3 tablespoons rum. Cook to 200° F. Soak the *baba* in it and just before serving sprinkle with rum, or pour lighted rum over the top.

Pastry Cream: Beat together thoroughly in a bowl 1 egg, 1 egg yolk, 3 tablespoons flour and 3 tablespoons sugar. Stir in 3 teaspoons gelatine. Pour on ¾ cup hot milk. Stir over the fire until the mixture comes to a boil. Stir over ice until it begins to cool. Mix in the 2 stiffly beaten egg whites with 3 or 4 tablespoons whipped cream and flavor with rum.

Note: The *baba* can be baked in a ring as well as cabinet-pudding molds and soaked in the same syrup. The center can be filled with fresh fruit as well as pastry cream. With red fruit add a little red currant jelly; with white fruit apricot jam.

DENTS DE LION
(Lion's Teeth)

3 eggs	1½ cups strawberries
2 tablespoons granulated sugar	¾ cup thin red currant jelly
2 tablespoons butter	little confectioners' sugar
1½ cups whipped cream	½ cup rum

Separate the eggs. Mix 1 tablespoon granulated sugar into the yolks of the egg and beat well. Then beat the egg whites until stiff and mix them into the yolks. Heat an omelet pan, and when hot, put in it a small piece of butter and about 2 tablespoons of the egg mixture and spread it out with a spatula. Cook it until golden brown on one side and then hold it under the grill for a second to set the top. When all the egg mixture is used in this way, put a tablespoon of sweetened whipped cream in the center of each. Fold over the omelet and stick around the edge the hulled strawberries, which have been dipped in the red currant jelly. Arrange all the omelets on a hot serving dish and sprinkle the tops generously with the confectioners' sugar; at the last moment pour around rum and light it.

PUDDING SANS SOUCI

3 tablespoons butter	*4 egg yolks*
3 tablespoons flour	*2 apples*
¾ cup milk	*3 egg whites*
vanilla bean	*1 whole egg*
6 tablespoons sugar	*2 tablespoons sherry*

Melt the butter and stir in the flour. When well blended pour on ¾ cup milk, which has been heated with a vanilla bean; stir over the fire until thick; do not boil. Remove and mix in 4 tablespoons sugar and 3 egg yolks. Skin, core and cut the apples in small pieces and fry in a little hot butter until golden brown. Add to the mixture and, lastly, the stiffly beaten egg whites. Grease an oval cake tin, dust with sugar and fill with the mixture. Put in a pan of hot water, cover with waxed paper and the lid and steam for half an hour until firm to touch. Remove from the water and let stand for 4 minutes before turning out on a hot serving dish. Serve with the following sauce: —

Hot Sabayon Sauce: Put 1 egg and 1 egg yolk, sherry and 2 tablespoons sugar in a bowl. Beat until stiff over a bowl of hot water; then pour over the pudding and serve.

GINGER ROLL

1 cup flour	*⅓ cup molasses*
1 teaspoon ground ginger	*⅓ cup sugar or light corn syrup*
1 teaspoon cinnamon	*1 well-beaten egg*
1 teaspoon nutmeg	*½ cup hot water*
1 teaspoon allspice	*little confectioners' sugar*
1 teaspoon baking soda	*½ cup corn syrup*
⅓ cup dissolved fat or butter	*2 stiffly beaten egg whites*
2 or 3 tablespoons whipped cream	

Mix the flour, ginger, cinnamon, nutmeg, allspice and baking soda in a bowl. Add the fat, molasses, ⅓ cup sugar or light corn syrup, 1 well-beaten egg and ½ cup hot water. Mix well together. Butter a cookie sheet, line with waxed paper and grease again.

Spread the mixture easily over the top. Bake for 15 minutes in a moderate oven, or until just set. Remove and cover with a cloth that has been wrung out in cold water. Cool in the refrigerator. Remove the cloth and dust well with confectioners' sugar. Turn out on waxed paper and carefully peel the paper off the top.

Put in a pan ½ cup corn syrup. Cook it to a light thread (the syrup should be thick enough to form a thread between the finger and thumb). Pour slowly on 2 stiffly beaten egg whites, beating slowly all the time. Continue beating until thick. Spread mixture on pastry. Roll up like a jelly roll and serve on a long, narrow wooden board. (This roll can be filled with whipped cream, as with the chocolate and nut roll.)

JELLY ROLL

5 eggs	*3 tablespoons cake flour*
4 tablespoons sugar	*4 tablespoons stiff red currant jelly*

Separate the eggs. Add the sugar to the yolks and beat well. Stir in carefully the sifted flour and the stiffly beaten egg whites. Grease a cookie sheet; cover with waxed paper and grease again. Spread mixture evenly on top. Bake in a 400° F. oven for 12 minutes, or until it is a light golden brown on top. Loosen roll from cookie sheet and sprinkle top with a little granulated sugar. Turn it onto a piece of waxed paper and carefully remove the under paper. Roll up and place in the refrigerator to cool. Remove, unroll and spread with jelly. Roll up tightly again and serve.

ROULAGE LÉONTINE

(Chocolate Roll)

5 large eggs
1 cup sugar
6 ounces dark sweet chocolate

3 tablespoons cold water
little grated chocolate or cocoa
1 cup cream

vanilla

Separate the eggs. Beat into the yolks ¾ cup sugar; beat to light, creamy consistency. Break up the chocolate in pieces and put in a pan with 3 tablespoons cold water. Stir over a slow fire until it dissolves; do not let it get too hot. Cool the chocolate a little and mix into the sugared egg yolks. Stir in the stiffly beaten egg whites; mix well. Butter a cookie sheet; cover with waxed paper and butter again. Spread the mixture evenly on top. Bake for 10 minutes in a moderate oven and then for 5 minutes in a slightly cooler oven. Remove and cover top with a cloth which has been wrung out in cold water. Cool and place in the refrigerator for 1 hour. Remove the cloth carefully and loosen the roll from the tin. Dust the top heavily with grated chocolate or cocoa. Turn out on a piece of waxed paper and carefully peel the paper off the top.

Place 1 cup thick cream in a bowl over another bowl of crushed ice. Beat with a whisk and, when it begins to thicken, add a little sugar and vanilla to taste and continue beating until the cream is thick enough to spread.

Spread the top with whipped cream. Roll up like a jelly roll and serve on a long, narrow wooden board.

NUT ROLL

6 large eggs
¾ cup sugar or
  1 cup light or dark corn syrup
1½ cups ground pecans or walnuts

1 teaspoon baking powder
little confectioners' sugar
3 cups heavy cream, whipped
1 tablespoon sugar
½ teaspoon vanilla

Separate the 6 eggs. Beat into the yolks ¾ cup sugar or 1 cup light or dark corn syrup. Mix in 1½ cups ground pecans or walnuts and the baking powder and stiffly beaten egg whites. Butter a cookie sheet, cover with waxed paper and butter again. Spread the mixture on top. Bake for 15 or 20 minutes in a 375° F. oven until golden brown on top. Remove and cover with a cloth that has been wrung out in cold water. Cool in the refrigerator. Loosen with a spatula from the cookie sheet. Remove cloth from the top and dust well with confectioners' sugar. Turn out on waxed paper and carefully peel paper off the top. Spread with whipped cream which has been flavored with vanilla and 1 tablespoon of sugar. Roll up like a jelly roll and serve on a long, narrow wooden board.

SABLIS
(Shortbread Cookies)

1 cup flour
4 hard-boiled egg yolks
6 level tablespoons butter

6 level tablespoons sugar
grated rind 1 lemon
pinch salt

Put flour on a pastry board and make a well in the center. Put in egg yolks passed through a strainer with butter, sugar, lemon and salt. Mix center ingredients to a smooth paste. Work in the flour, roll out not too thin, cut in small rounds, arrange on an ungreased cookie sheet and bake for 15 minutes in a 350° F. oven.

CHOCOLATE JELLY ROLL

4 large, or 5 small, eggs
¾ cup granulated sugar
3 tablespoons sifted flour
6 ounces dark sweet chocolate
½ ounce bitter chocolate

3 tablespoons cold water
2 or 3 tablespoons butter
2 or 3 tablespoons rum
½ cup coarsely shredded sweet
*   chocolate*

confectioners' sugar

Separate 4 large, or 5 small, eggs. Mix into the yolks 4 or 5 tablespoons sugar and 3 tablespoons sifted flour. Mix in the stiffly beaten egg whites. Oil a cookie sheet, line with waxed paper and butter the waxed paper. Spread evenly on top and bake until just golden brown in a 350° F. oven. Remove and loosen from cookie sheet. Sprinkle the top well with granulated sugar. Turn out on waxed paper and carefully peel off the paper on top. Roll up and put on the refrigerator to cool.

Put in a pan 6 ounces dark sweet chocolate broken up, ½ ounce bitter chocolate and 3 tablespoons cold water. Stir over a slow fire until the chocolate dissolves. Stir in carefully 2 or 3 tablespoons butter and the rum. Stir over ice until it begins to cool.

Remove roll from the refrigerator. Unroll and spread chocolate mixture on top. Roll up and cover the top with remaining chocolate filling. Cover all over with coarsely shredded sweet chocolate. Dust with confectioners' sugar and serve.

CIGARETTES

1 egg white
4 tablespoons sugar

2 tablespoons sifted flour
1 tablespoon cool, melted butter

Put egg white and sugar in a bowl and beat until very white. Add the flour and melted butter. Grease a cookie sheet; spread the mixture on with a spatula very thinly in 2½-inch squares. Bake to golden brown in a moderate oven. Take from the pan at once and roll around a pencil.

PROFITEROLES AU CHOCOLAT
(Chocolate Cream Puffs)

1 cup water	*little confectioners' sugar*
2 tablespoons butter	*little vanilla*
1¼ cups flour	*½ ounce bitter chocolate*
5 eggs	*6 tablespoons water*
1 cup whipped cream	*6 ounces dark sweet chocolate*

1 tablespoon rum

Put the water and butter in a thick pan and bring slowly to a boil. When bubbling add the sifted flour. Remove from the fire and beat until smooth. Beat in, 1 at a time, 4 eggs. Cool in the refrigerator for 1 hour. Butter a cookie sheet well and place the mixture on the cookie sheet in very small balls or with a pastry bag and small round tube. Brush tops with beaten egg. Bake in a 375° F. oven for 20 minutes and then in a 300° F. oven for 5 minutes. They should be a good golden-brown color and firm to the touch. Cool and make a small hole in the bottom with a small knife. Fill with whipped cream, which has been flavored with a little sugar and vanilla. Pile on a serving dish and sprinkle well with confectioners' sugar.

Break up the chocolate and put in a thick pan with 6 tablespoons water. Stir over a slow fire until it dissolves. Add the rum and cook a little longer. Serve separately, piping hot.

BISCUIT MILANESE
(Sponge Cake)

5 eggs	sifted cake flour
sugar	grated rind 1 lemon
potato flour	2 or 3 tablespoons currants
little confectioners' sugar	

(Amount of sugar should correspond to weight of the 5 eggs. Amount of cake flour should equal weight of 1 egg. Amount of potato flour should correspond to or equal the weight of 1 egg.)

Break and separate the eggs. Add to the bowl containing the yolks the sugar and the 2 flours and beat for 15 minutes. Then add the stiffly beaten egg whites to the mixture with the grated lemon rind and the currants, which have been dusted with a little flour. Grease a cake tin, lining the bottom with waxed paper, and grease again. Dust out with flour and bake for 40 to 50 minutes in a 350° F. oven. Remove; allow to wait a few minutes before turning out. Dust with confectioners' sugar and serve.

GÂTEAU FAVORITE

½ cup water	2 teaspoons gelatine
2 level teaspoons butter	¾ cup milk
½ cup flour	3 ounces sweet chocolate
5 eggs	3 tablespoons water
blanched, shredded, browned almonds	2 cups whipped cream
3 tablespoons flour	2 tablespoons rum
3 tablespoons granulated sugar	confectioners' sugar

Put the water in a small, thick pan with the butter and bring slowly to a boil. When bubbling, add ½ cup flour. Remove from the fire and beat until smooth. Add, 1 at a time, 2 whole eggs. Grease a cookie sheet and mark on it a large circle. Fill this paste into a pastry bag with a large, plain tube and cover the circle on the cookie sheet with this paste. Brush with beaten egg and sprinkle the top generously with blanched, shredded, browned almonds. Bake for 25 to 30 minutes in a 375° F. oven, until well-risen and golden brown all over. Remove, cool, carefully split across in half, and fill the center with the following: —

Chocolate Pastry Cream: Put 1 egg and 1 egg yolk in a bowl, 3 tablespoons flour and 3 tablespoons sugar and beat until smooth; then add 2 teaspoons gelatine. Pour on ¾ cup hot milk and stir over the fire until the mixture comes to a boil. Stir over ice until it is on the point of setting. Add the chocolate, which has been melted down with 3 tablespoons of water over a slow fire; stir this in with the other mixture and, when cool and thick, add 1 stiffly beaten egg white and 2 tablespoons whipped cream and the rum. Fill this into the bottom of the cake. Cover the top with whipped cream. Cover with the other half of the cake, dash well with confectioners' sugar and serve.

MAPLE CAKE

½ cup vegetable shortening	2 teaspoons baking powder
1 cup granulated sugar	4 stiffly beaten egg whites
4 egg yolks	2½ cups maple syrup
1½ cups cake flour	¾ cup egg whites
½ cup milk	few chopped pecan nuts

Cream the vegetable shortening, add the sugar and beat until very smooth; beat in the 4 egg yolks. Sift the flour and add alternately with the milk. Add the baking powder. Fold in the 4 egg whites, stiffly beaten. Grease 2 shallow layer-cake tins with vegetable shortening. Line the bottoms with waxed paper and grease again. Divide the cake batter in the two tins and bake in a 350° F. oven for 15 minutes, until the cakes are a golden brown on top. Turn out on waxed paper; cool slightly.

Put the maple syrup in a pan and cook to a light thread (225° F.). Pour on ¾ cup egg whites, stiffly beaten, and continue beating until very thick. Spread between the layers and cover the cake generously and decorate the top with the chopped nuts.

CHOCOLATE CAKE

5 eggs
9 tablespoons granulated sugar
5 level tablespoons flour
11 ounces dark sweet chocolate
8 tablespoons water

4 egg yolks
¾ cup corn syrup
1¼ cups creamed butter
2 tablespoons rum
shredded, browned almonds

confectioners' sugar

Put 5 whole eggs and the sugar in an electric mixer and beat until stiff. Fold in the sifted flour and 5 ounces dark sweet chocolate, which has been melted down in 4 tablespoons water. Grease a deep, loose-bottomed cake tin, line with waxed paper, fill with mixture and bake for 45 minutes in a 350° F. oven. Remove, turn out and cool. Cover with the following frosting: —

Frosting: Beat 4 egg yolks in a bowl, cook the corn syrup to a thread, pour onto the egg yolks and continue beating until stiff. Add the creamed butter and 6 ounces dark sweet chocolate, which has been melted down in 4 tablespoons water and cooled. Add the rum, cover the cake with this mixture, sprinkle all over with the shredded, browned almonds, dust with a little confectioners' sugar and decorate with the rest of the butter frosting through a pastry bag and rose tube.

GLOSSARY

GLOSSARY

Artichauds. Globe artichokes.

Aubergines. Eggplant.

Béchamel. White sauce.

Baking Powder. Royal Baking Powder has been used in preparing the recipes in this book.

Basting. Covering a roast of meat or game, or a braised fish, with the juice in which it was cooked.

Blanching. Bringing to a boil from cold water.

Bread crumbs. Can be either white or brown. The white are used for coating and frying in deep fat fish or meat, etc., and are made by carefully drying stale white bread in a slow oven until quite dry and then rubbing through a wire sieve. These can be stored in an airtight jar. The brown bread crumbs are made in the same way except that the bread is browned in the oven and is used for sprinkling over the top of *gratin* dishes, etc.

Beards of mussels. These are the small, narrow, black frills found on the edge of the mussels. As they are rather tough it is better to remove them.

Bouillon. A stock made of veal or beef bones, giblets, and flavoring vegetables. It can also be made of vegetables only.

Bouquet of Herbs. The bouquet of herbs is always fresh and consists of parsley, tarragon, chives and thyme. This bouquet is used for most meats and fowl. For fish, parsley, chives, marjoram and chervil. For wild game the same as for fish but adding a fresh bay leaf and basil.

Braising. The meats, fowl, fish, etc. are first browned in butter on the top of the stove. Then add a little flour, tomato paste, flavoring, vegetables and fish, meat, or game stock and put to cook in the oven.

Bouillabaise. A Marseille fish stew made with eels, scallops, lobsters, mackerel, cod, red and gray mullet, mussels, etc.

Cheese. Grated. The best combination is Gruyère and Parmesan, mixed in equal quantities, the Parmesan giving flavor and the Gruyère melting power.

Clarify. For stocks, aspics, etc., add stiffly beaten egg white, tomato paste and wine, and beat over the fire until the mixture comes to a boil. For butter, simply dissolve over a slow fire. For fat, to clarify and clean, add to 4 cups of fat 1 cup of water, 1 skinned and sliced potato, 1 sliced apple, with its skin on. Bring to a boil, strain, cool and pour off the fat.

Caramel. Sugar cooked in a little water and glucose to a dark brown.

Carcass. Fish or game bones.

Chaud froid sauce. A very creamy white sauce thickened with aspic or gelatine and used for coating cold chicken, fish, etc.

Court bouillon. Fish stock for cooking shellfish or fish.

Croutons. Small diced bread fried in hot butter or oil until golden brown.

Cuisson. Stock in which meat, fowl, fish or vegetables have been cooked.

Demi-glacé or brown sauce. A partially clear, brown sauce.

Farce. A stuffing made with minced, cooked, raw meat or fish.

Fish fumet. Fish stock.

Foie gras. Goose liver *pâte*.

Fat. Any tasteless vegetable fat is most often used for deep fat frying; beef fat is the best.

Glazing or glazed. To glaze under the broiler means that the only ingredient used is melted butter. *Glaze* also means very concentrated meat stock to be used in glazing ragouts, casseroles, etc. It can also mean glazing the top of a fruit with melted-down jelly or jam.

Gnocchi. An Italian paste dish made with flour, corn meal (yellow or white), semolina or cream farina.

Gratin. The completed dish is browned.

Herbs. Fresh herbs are used more often than dried and the most common ones are parsley, chives, tarragon and chervil. Of dried herbs, the most commonly used are basil, thyme, marjoram and bay leaf.

Jus. A very strong meat, chicken or vegetable stock.

Marinade. A mixture made of wines, herbs, peppercorns, a few flavoring vegetables, oils, and used for soaking game, meat or fish.

Marmite. A French, covered, earthenware pot used for stock and sometimes for soups.

Mask. To cover evenly with sauce.

Mirepoix. Carrot, onion, celery, turnip and green beans cut into very small even dice and cooked together in the oven.

Mornay. A cheese sauce or cheese flavoring.

Mousseline. Indicating a smooth, light substance sometimes made with egg and always bubbly.

Noisette potato. Small potato balls cooked in hot butter and browned.

Oil. The best oil for general purposes is vegetable or soy bean oil, with the exception of some Italian dishes where olive oil is used. For salad dressings it is best to combine olive oil and a tasteless vegetable oil.

Pain grille. Thin slices of crustless bread, baked in a slow oven until golden brown.

Paupiette. Birds without heads and made with a thin slice of meat, game or fish, sometimes spread with a sauce; then rolled up and tied with a fine thread and braised.

Potato flour. Potato starch used to thicken clear gravies.

Pilau. Hungarian, Armenian or Greek rice dishes.

Plats. Dishes.

Poaching. Cooking in deep liquor and never allowing to boil.

Pot-au-feu. Stock made from flank and top round of beef, giblets, veal bones and flavoring vegetables and used as the foundation for clear soups and aspics.

Praline powder. Lump sugar and hazel nuts cooked together with a little water and glucose until a dark brown, then cooled on a lightly oiled tin and, when quite cold, ground. Can be kept in an air-tight tin.

Quenelles. Farce formed into small egg shapes and poached in hot water without boiling.

Reducing. Boiling stock or sauce down to reduce quantity and to make a stronger flavor.

Shallots. Small, white onions striped with reddish blue. Excellent when garlic is not used.

Salpicon. A mixture of meat, chicken, vegetables, etc., cooked and cut in small pieces and served as a foundation for some dishes.

Sauté. Slow cooking in butter, cooked on the top of the stove, covered and shaken.

Scallops or Escallop. Thin slices of meat, game, fish, etc.

Shredded. Cut in thin strips the size of matches.

Soubise. Flavoring of onion.

Suchet. Flavoring of carrot.

Tomato coulis. A mixture of strong tomato purée and sliced, whole, skinned tomatoes, cooked in butter, with a flavoring of garlic.

Tomato paste. Canned Italian tomato paste.

Veronique. Garnished with grapes.

Vin ordinaire. Cheapest red or white wine.

INDEX

INDEX

ALL RECIPES ARE FOR FOUR PERSONS

ALL RECIPES ARE FOR FOUR PERSONS

ALL RECIPES ARE FOR FOUR PERSONS

ALL RECIPES ARE FOR FOUR PERSONS

ALL RECIPES ARE FOR FOUR PERSONS

ALL RECIPES ARE FOR FOUR PERSONS

ALL RECIPES ARE FOR FOUR PERSONS

ALL RECIPES ARE FOR FOUR PERSONS

ALL RECIPES ARE FOR FOUR PERSONS

ALL RECIPES ARE FOR FOUR PERSONS

ALL RECIPES ARE FOR FOUR PERSONS

ALL RECIPES ARE FOR FOUR PERSONS

ALL RECIPES ARE FOR FOUR PERSONS

ALL RECIPES ARE FOR FOUR PERSONS

ALL RECIPES ARE FOR FOUR PERSONS

ALL RECIPES ARE FOR FOUR PERSONS

ALL RECIPES ARE FOR FOUR PERSONS